EVENTS AS A STRATEGIC MARKETING TOOL

CABI TOURISM TEXTS are an essential resource for students of academic tourism, leisure studies, hospitality, entertainment and events management. The series reflects the growth of tourism-related studies at an academic level and responds to the changes and developments in these rapidly evolving industries, providing up-to-date practical guidance, discussion of the latest theories and concepts, and analysis by world experts. The series is intended to guide students through their academic programmes and remain an essential reference throughout their careers in the tourism sector.

Readers will find the books within the CABI TOURISM TEXTS series to have a uniquely wide scope, covering important elements in leisure and tourism, including management-led topics, practical subject matter and development of conceptual themes and debates. Useful textbook features such as case studies, bullet point summaries and helpful diagrams are employed throughout the series to aid study and encourage understanding of the subject.

Students at all levels of study, workers within tourism and leisure industries, researchers, academics, policy makers and others interested in the field of academic and practical tourism will find these books an invaluable and authoritative resource, useful for academic reference and real-world tourism applications.

Titles available

Ecotourism: Principles and Practices
Ralf Buckley

Contemporary Tourist Behaviour: Yourself and Others as Tourists
David Bowen and Jackie Clarke

The Entertainment Industry: An Introduction
Edited by Stuart Moss

Practical Tourism Research
Stephen L.J. Smith

Leisure, Sport and Tourism, Politics, Policy and Planning, 3rd Edition
A.J. Veal

Events Management
Edited by Peter Robinson, Debra Wale and Geoff Dickson

Food and Wine Tourism: Integrating Food, Travel and Territory
Erica Croce and Giovanni Perri

Strategic Management in Tourism, 2nd Edition
Edited by L. Moutinho

Research Methods for Leisure, Recreation and Tourism
Edited by Ercan Sirakaya-Turk, Muzaffer Usyal, William E. Hammitt and Jerry J. Vaske

Facilities Management and Development for Tourism, Hospitality and Events
Edited by Ahmed Hassanien and Crispin Dale

Events as a Strategic Marketing Tool
Dorothé Gerritsen and Ronald van Olderen

Entertainment Management: Towards Best Practice
Edited by Stuart Moss and Ben Walmsley

EVENTS AS A STRATEGIC MARKETING TOOL

Dorothé Gerritsen

and

Ronald van Olderen

With the cooperation of:

Moniek Hover
Jacco van Mierlo
Margo Rooijackers
Thomas van Velthoven

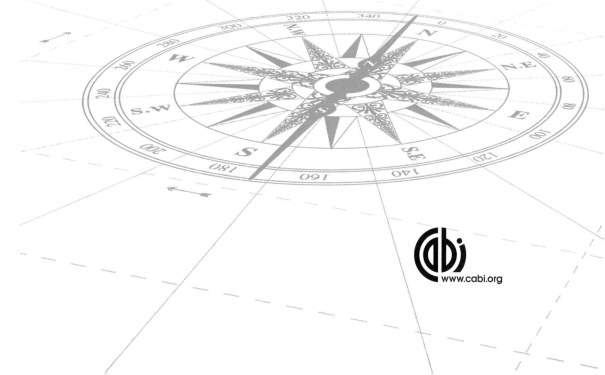

www.cabi.org

CABI is a trading name of CAB International

CABI	CABI
Nosworthy Way	38 Chauncey Street
Wallingford	Suite 1002
Oxfordshire OX10 8DE	Boston, MA 02111
UK	USA
Tel: +44 (0)1491 832111	Tel: +1 800 552 3083 (toll free)
Fax: +44 (0)1491 833508	Tel: +1 (0)617 395 4051
E-mail: info@cabi.org	E-mail: cabi-nao@cabi.org
Website: www.cabi.org	

Originally published in Dutch under the title *Het event als strategisch marketing instrument* by Dorothé Gerritsen and Ronald van Olderen. © Uitgeverij Coutinho b.v. 2011.

A catalogue record for this book is available from the British Library, London, UK.

Library of Congress Cataloging-in-Publication Data

Gerritsen, Dorothé.
  [Event als strategisch marketinginstrument. English]
  Events as a strategic marketing tool / Dorothé Gerritsen, Ronald van Olderen ; with the cooperation of Moniek Hover, Jacco van Mierlo, Margo Rooijackers, Thomas van Velthoven.
      pages cm. -- (CABI tourism texts)
  Translation of: Het event als strategisch marketinginstrument. Bussum : Coutinho, 2011.
  Includes bibliographical references and index.
  ISBN 978-1-78064-261-1 (pbk.)
 1. Strategic planning. 2. Marketing. 3. Special events--Management. I. Olderen, Ronald van. II. Title.

  HD30.28.G46813 2014
  658.8'02--dc23

                              2014000456

ISBN-13: 978 1 78064 261 1

Commissioning editor: Claire Parfitt
Editorial assistant: Emma McCann
Production editor: Simon Hill

Translators: Moniek Hover, Jacco van Mierlo, Margo Rooijackers and Thomas van Velthoven
Typeset by SPi, Pondicherry, India.
Printed and bound Gutenberg Press Ltd, Tarxien, Malta

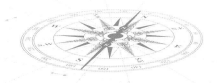

Contents

PART III: CHECK

About the Authors

ABOUT THE LEAD AUTHORS

Dorothé Gerritsen has been a Lecturer in Event Management, as well as the Coordinator of the Communication Centre at the Academy for Leisure of the NHTV Breda University of Applied Sciences, the Netherlands, since 1995. She studied communication science in Nijmegen. In one of the specialist areas open to students, event management, she initiates and supervises, together with Ronald van Olderen, research projects in the field of event marketing. Dorothé specializes in trade shows and conferences. In the past, she has also been a member of the Education Committee of the Centre for Live Communication, CLC-VECTA.

Ronald van Olderen is a Lecturer in Event Management and one of the coordinators in the specialist area of event management at the Academy for Leisure of the NHTV Breda University of Applied Sciences. He has been involved in the development of content for the specialist area of event management since 2001, focusing on corporate events in particular. Since 2004, he has been involved in initiating and supervising research in the field of event marketing, together with Dorothé Gerritsen. In this process, Ronald works closely with the Independent Dutch Event Association (IDEA) and the Dutch Association of Event Managers. In the past, he has held positions such as Marketing Manager at Sportief Holland Evenementen BV, and from 2005 to 2009 he was a member of the jury of the Gouden Giraffe Award, the award show for the business event industry in the Netherlands.

The establishment of the research programme into event marketing formed the seedbed for this book, of which Dorothé Gerritsen and Ronald van Olderen are the lead authors.

ABOUT THE CO-AUTHORS

Moniek Hover is a Special Associate Professor in Storytelling and Experience at the Academy for Leisure of the NHTV Breda University of Applied Sciences. She earned a doctoral degree in storytelling and experiences at Tilburg University. Her doctoral thesis was about a case study of the Efteling theme park, as a fairy-tale narrator. Together with Olaf Vugts (Director of Imagineering of Efteling), she is the driving force behind the Efteling Academy, an intensive talent development programme in the field of imagineering for NHTV students. Moniek frequently gives lectures and workshops on storytelling and experiences, both at home and abroad.

Jacco van Mierlo is a Lecturer in Event Management at the Academy for Leisure of the NHTV Breda University of Applied Sciences. After earning his degree from the Dutch Academy of Physical Education, he studied leisure science at Tilburg University. Since 1994, he has worked at NHTV, as a coordinator in the specialist area of event management and as project leader of the Experience Centre Events Management (ECEM). Jacco's specific area of expertise is public events. In the past, he has been a board member of the International Festivals and Events Association Europe (IFEA), a member of the jury of the Dutch National Events Awards and he was on the advisory board of *Festivak* magazine.

Margo Rooijackers studied cultural psychology at Radboud University Nijmegen. Since 1993, Margo has worked as a lecturer at the Academy for Leisure of the NHTV Breda University of Applied Sciences. Her areas of expertise are consumer behaviour, imagineering and research. Moreover, she works as a student coach at the Imagineering Academy. She is also coordinator of the Leisure, Health and Well-Being Project for the Academy for Leisure. From 2006 to 2010, Margo Rooijackers was employed by Tilburg University in the Master's programme in Leisure Studies. Margo is on the editorial committee of the NRIT Trend Report on Tourism, Recreation and Leisure, and she is also a member of the editorial network of *MMNieuws*. She has published numerous non-specialist articles, for instance in the area of leisure trends, imagineering and Leisure4Health.

After his studies in Development Geography and Social Sciences at the new secondary school Teacher Training Institute in Tilburg, **Thomas van Velthoven** developed several public campaigns for Africa and he was one of the founders of the brand-building process for Novib. He positioned Memisa as the leading provider of structural support to health-care organizations around the globe. Thomas reorganized marketing and communication practices for Red Cross Nederland and set up several innovative fund-raising initiatives in Europe for the International Federation of the Red Cross in Geneva. He switched from managing marketing departments within the charity market to consultancy work in the area of brand positioning for the commercial sector, for clients like Philips, Rabobank, Ben mobile telephony and BP. For 7 years now, he has been employed by the Academy for Leisure of the NHTV Breda University of Applied Sciences and Avans. In addition, he is still undertaking consultancy work.

Preface

The Olympic Games are a classic example of a major international event that is strategically utilized by several parties. Typical characteristics of the event include: grand scale, live, global, having a massive economic impact and having consequences for the local infrastructure, the image of a country, sports development and for the people who live there, also called the host community. By way of illustration, we will present some statistical details on the last Olympic Games, which were held in Beijing. Three new subway lines were constructed – extending the city's total length of track from 42 to 200 km, a new high-speed rail link from the airport to the city was launched and 31 new sports venues were built, including the National Aquatic Center, more commonly known as the 'Water Cube'. After the Olympic Games, the Water Cube attracted 2.7 million visitors from October 2008 to May 2009. An Internet survey conducted by the Chinese Tourism Bureau revealed that the Water Cube was on a par with the most popular attractions of the country: 170,000 votes went to the Great Wall of China, 136,000 to the Forbidden City and 137,000 to the Water Cube. A total of 4.7 billion people watched the Games on television, and the opening ceremony was an ambitious and spectacular show, watched by 2 billion people. A new image of China was born. Just the scale of it was huge. Dazzling numbers at the greatest event on Earth.

Events have impact; they are important and are ever more often utilized strategically, because they are perfectly suited to impressing people. Live meetings during an event are an effective way of engaging people on an emotional level, for instance by means of a brand or a city. This book is primarily about the way in which organizations utilize events as a marketing tool to reach out to and connect with their visitors. It provides an insight into the strategic use of events, by means of marketing theories, interlaced with practical examples. More and more literature on event management and project management has become available recently. Most of those books focus on the practical management perspective of events. The idea for this book was conceived a couple of years ago because of the increasing interest in event marketing among marketers. As it turned out, there was a need to study events as a means to achieving strategic marketing objectives. Over the years, the authors have gathered a wealth of material on this subject. Their knowledge has been brought together and organized in this book.

Many colleagues helped us during the writing of this book. We owe special thanks to those colleagues who wrote a chapter at our request because of their specific expertise: Margo Rooijackers (Chapter 2), Thomas van Velthoven (Chapter 6) and Jacco van Mierlo (Chapter 7).

Chapter 8 is based on a 2008 publication, *Imagine Your Event*, by our colleague, Moniek Hover. This chapter has been thoroughly edited and revised to conform with the rest of the book. We would like to thank her for making this possible.

Much of the knowledge and expertise presented in this book was gathered through students from the NHTV Breda University of Applied Sciences. We would like to thank them for their efforts and hard work. Furthermore, our own industry contacts have provided us with many practice-based examples. Their input has made the book more engaging and was indispensable in presenting a clear and realistic picture of the industry.

In conclusion, we would both like to thank our families for their support and patience throughout the process of writing this book.

Dorothé Gerritsen and Ronald van Olderen
Breda, September 2013

Information as well as illustrative and photographic material was kindly provided by:

- Robert Aarts, photographic design
- Esther de Beer, NHTV Breda University of Applied Sciences
- Wilco van Gool, NHTV Breda University of Applied Sciences
- Bart Haanen, Across Health
- Moniek Hover, NHTV Breda University of Applied Sciences
- Olga Kappel-Boekhorst, Deloitte
- Alec Lokhoff, Planet Event
- Jacco van Mierlo, NHTV Breda University of Applied Sciences
- Maarten Molenaar, Stichting Skyway
- Frank Ouwens, NHTV Breda University of Applied Sciences and f2o creative studio
- Margo Rooijackers, NHTV Breda University of Applied Sciences
- Albert van Schendel, NHTV Breda University of Applied Sciences
- Thesis authors and student project groups of the Academy for Leisure, Event Management specialization team
- Thomas van Velthoven, NHTV Breda University of Applied Sciences and Resultive

Plan

Part I is about the planning phase of the strategic use of events, which involves the left side of the EVENTS model (see Fig. 1.3).

After two introductory chapters, we will deal first with the subject of event marketing as a tool. After that, we will present four forms of marketing in which this tool is used.

1. Introduction: Using Events as a Strategic Marketing Tool
2. Trends and Developments: Consumers' Pursuit of Happiness
3. Event Marketing
4. Events and Customer Relationship Marketing
5. Events and Marketing Communication
6. Events and Branding
7. Events and City Marketing: The Role of Events in Cities

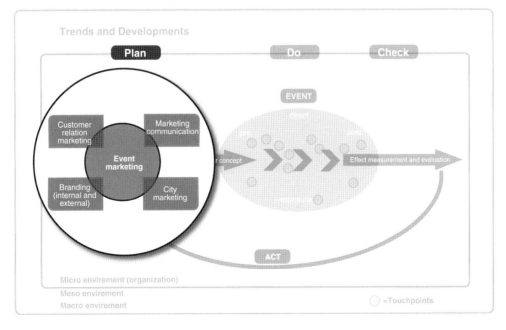

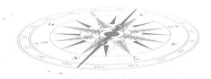

chapter 1

Introduction: Using Events as a Strategic Marketing Tool

In this chapter we will explain what events are and how organizations can use them strategically. Moreover, we will discuss several types of events and introduce the EVENTS model. Finally, the structure of this book is described, with a preview of Chapters 2 through 10.

LEARNING TARGETS

After studying this chapter, you will have learned:

- how events can be used strategically
- what a strategically used event is
- which types of events there are
- what the main differences between the various types of events are
- how the EVENTS model works.

THE STRATEGIC USE OF EVENTS

The sound of a roaring engine: a small plane skims past a gigantic, cone-shaped pylon, turning into the direction of a slender white bridge. When the pilot manoeuvres his plane under the bridge, the crowd holds its breath: will the daredevil survive this stunt?

Red Bull has created an international series of air races (also see Chapter 6) in which competitors have to navigate a challenging obstacle course. Pilots fly individually against the clock and have to complete tight turns through a slalom course consisting of pylons and bridges (http://en.wikipedia.org). Admission to the event is free, and it draws huge crowds. Red Bull manufactures the popular energy drink of the same name, and finds itself in the same league as Vrumona, Spa and Heineken. Its core business is producing, bottling and distributing energy drinks. Why would this company engage in organizing air races?

Red Bull has created the air race series for marketing purposes. The air races are part of a sophisticated strategy. The company organizes the races to give the Red Bull brand a sporty and adventurous image. This image is supposed to help Red Bull distinguish itself from its competitors, who sell more or less similar energy drinks. The adventurous image is supposed to tempt customers to single out Red Bull rather than, for instance, a can of Slammers.

To Red Bull, the air race is therefore not an end but a means: the drinks manufacturer organizes the races for strategic reasons – for brand strategy reasons, to be precise. The event is a tool to achieve the underlying objective of creating an adventurous and sporty image. This does not mean, however, that the specific nature of the event is irrelevant. Red Bull deliberately opted for air races and not poetry reading sessions.

This book is about the strategic use of events; about the ways in which organizations use events like air races to achieve underlying objectives. This is referred to as a strategic use of events because the event is part of a strategy – a carefully thought-out plan to achieve a certain goal. The event is the carrier of the message: in other words, it is a communication tool. Marketers and other communication professionals use events to get their message across to a specific target group or to increase customer loyalty. Messages range from 'Buy this product' to 'Nothing beats Groningen'.

THE EMERGENCE OF EVENTS AS A STRATEGIC MARKETING TOOL

Marketers and communication professionals use events as a strategic marketing tool more and more often. In 2010, the corporate community directed as much as 27% of their marketing budget to organizing events, according to a blogger on event marketing (evenementenmarketing.blogspot.com, June 2010). The authors of a recently published book on event marketing also report that event marketing is becoming an increasingly important component in the marketing communication mix (Wiegerink and Peelen, 2010).

Where does this increasing popularity come from? We believe there are three explanations:

1. Target groups are becoming increasingly intangible to marketers. Many traditional marketing communication tools have lost much of their ability to capture the target group's attention. Newspaper subscriptions have been declining for many years, for instance. This means that marketers today reach less people through newspaper advertising. The same holds true for radio and television: due to the steady growth in radio and television channels, viewer and listener attention becomes fragmented. All this has forced marketers to look for alternative means of communication. Strategic events are one of these alternative means.

2. Events are effective tools to ingrain your message in the audience's mind. They are perfectly suitable for adding a layer of emotional value to a product or service. Visitors of an event undergo the event and experience it, and the event gives them lasting memories to cherish. As a result, the message of the event will stick – provided that it is communicated in the right way, of course. In a time when products and services, and cities too, become more and more alike, this is a good way to distinguish yourself.

3. Events are excellent tools to contribute to the quality of life in a company or, for instance, in a city or part of a city. Events foster social cohesion, thanks to their interactive character.

EVENT MARKETING

The discipline that involves using events as a live means of communication is referred to as event marketing. Event marketing is marketing practices based on the use of events. In event marketing, events are part of, for instance, a communication campaign or a branding strategy. Sometimes the events are organized once (on a one-off basis), sometimes several times (on a regular basis). Chapter 3 addresses the subject of event marketing more extensively.

Event marketing is applied primarily in four types of marketing:

1. *Customer relationship marketing*: building, maintaining and intensifying relations with various parties.
2. *Marketing communication*: marketing products and services by influencing the visitor's knowledge, attitude and behaviour.
3. *Branding*: influencing, creating or changing valuable associations that a visitor has with a brand (external branding) and/or influencing, creating or changing valuable associations that an employee has in order to increase employee engagement and optimize the customer experience (internal branding).
4. *City marketing*: 'selling' a municipality or region to current and potential residents, visitors/tourists and businesses or organizations.

These four types of marketing will be covered in Part I of this book.

USING EVENTS AS A STRATEGIC MARKETING TOOL

Using events as a strategic marketing tool; now what does this mean precisely? In this book, we use the following definition:

> Using an event as a strategic marketing tool involves planning a unique event or series of events for one or more target groups where people come together, either physically or virtually, at the

invitation and initiation of a company/business, government body or non-profit organization. The client wishes to achieve an emotional added value by means of an experience, to support a predefined objective (communicative or otherwise) that has to be achieved among one or more of the target groups identified.

This type of event has a number of characteristics. The event:

- is a planned, unique, physical or virtual event or series of events for one or more target groups
- is held at the invitation of an organizing party; this invitation may also be public, so for everyone
- is aimed at achieving an emotional added value to support the communicative objective of the organizing party
- creates an emotional added value by means of an experience.

Several of these elements are reflected in our Red Bull example. After all, it involves:

- a planned event: the race and its spectators
- a target group: consumers who are interested in spectacular adventurous sports
- an invitation: Red Bull announces to the general public when and where the races will take place
- an emotional added value: the aim of the race is to create a distinct image for the brand
- an experience: spectators experience the excitement and sensation of the race.

EXPERIENCES

The definition in the section above shows that experiences are an important factor in the strategic use of events. But how does it work with these experiences? Why does Red Bull expect that the spectators of the air race will associate the brand with sports and adventure afterwards? In a nutshell, it works as follows – before, during and after the event. Visitors of an event are exposed continuously to sensory impressions. They see, hear and undergo all sorts of things. These impressions lead to an emotion; for instance, enthusiasm or aversion. As a result, the visitor experiences the event as either pleasant or terrible. After the event, the visitor takes stock (unconsciously). The event as a whole has then become an experience. It is precisely because events are sensory experiences that the visitor is especially open to any messages communicated during the event. The visitor of the race organized by Red Bull is part of the spectacle. He feels the excitement, is engaged emotionally and feels a connection with the values of Red Bull. From now on, spectators will associate Red Bull with adventure and spectacle, either consciously or unconsciously.

The explanation we have given here is a strong simplification and certainly not based on any academic sources. The psychological processes that are involved in acquiring experiences and associations are complex. There are numerous factors that play a part in the visitor's experience of an event: the visitor's mood, interests, previously acquired experiences, social environment and background. The better an event aligns with these personal factors, the more meaningful the event will be to the visitor concerned. Chapters 8 and 9 of this book will consider this in more detail. For an in-depth psychological study on experiences, you are referred to the work of psychologist, Nico Frijda (Frijda, 1986).

TOUCHPOINTS

The way in which an event is experienced is determined to a high degree by the visitor's experience of what are referred to as *touchpoints*. Touchpoints are interaction points between the organizer of the event and the visitors to the event; in other words, all communication and contacts between visitors and representatives of the organization. Sometimes, these points of contact are orchestrated carefully and deliberately by the organizer, and sometimes they occur accidentally. Touchpoints occur not only during the event but also before and afterwards. Take, for example, the Red Bull air races. In the pre-event phase, the organization announces the event to the target group, the general public. During the event itself, the energy drinks manufacturer is also unmistakably present, with its logos scattered around the site and its many representatives. And afterwards, the company posts photographs of the event on a freely accessible website, so as to allow visitors to enjoy the memory of the event.

When creating an emotional added value for a product or service, it is important for the organizer to pinpoint those points of contact that are crucial to the visitor. After all, bad experiences with the organization in either one of the three phases may have a negative impact on the experience as a whole. Fortunately, the opposite is equally true. The helpfulness of an organizer in rebooking a reservation or accommodating any special diet needs will give the visitor a positive first impression.

CORPORATE AND PUBLIC EVENTS

We can make a rough distinction between two types of events: corporate events and public events. Both types can be used in a strategic manner.

The points of departure in corporate events are the objective and the target group. The client or financier organizes corporate events to achieve something with a certain target audience (an exclusive event); for example, personnel events, company anniversaries, events for customers or the launch of a new car model.

Corporate events usually involve three categories of events, which we will explain briefly below.

- *Business-to-business events*: visitors are invited for business motives, and visitors go to the event for business reasons too. This does not mean that all leisure purposes are excluded. Examples are: trade shows, events for customers, anniversaries, conferences, or special events for customers as a part of major public sports events.

- *Business-to-consumer events*: visitors are invited for business reasons, but they visit the event for leisure motives. Examples are brand events, such as Lego Kids Fest in various cities in the USA (Detroit, Richmond, Denver and Cincinnati), the Red Bull Air Race in Rotterdam, the Netherlands, and public trade events like the national boat show in the Coca Cola Dome in Johannesburg, South Africa.
- *Business-to-employee events*: the target group are the employees of a company. The aim may be to create a sense of solidarity (through team building) or to reward and thank employees for their efforts. Examples of this are the staff party of Unilever or Shell; the team-building days of ICT company, EDS; a special event on the occasion of a merger for members of staff from both companies involved; or a staff outing to a major sports event.

Types of corporate events

Business events (business-to-business)

Events based on business interests and organized for corporate contacts:

- product presentations
- opening ceremonies
- dealer conventions
- kick-off meetings
- press presentations
- shareholders' meetings
- sports events
- small-scale business receptions
- large-scale business receptions
- national trade shows
- national conferences or symposiums.

Personnel events (business-to-employee)

Events organized by a company or organization for the employees of that company or organization:

- product presentations
- opening ceremonies
- company anniversaries
- kick-off meetings
- sports events
- open days
- incentives
- staff parties
- events for retired employees

- seasonal events
- corporate retreats, big meetings.

(Source: NIDAP, 2008; Verhaar, 2009.)

The point of departure in public events often centres around the contents. They are organized, for instance, for idealistic reasons, to entertain or elevate visitors or to satisfy a certain public need. Public events are public, organized for the sake of their contents and intended for consumers; for example, pop festivals, music festivals and cultural festivals, but also dance events, charity events and sports events.

According to Kuiper (2008), public events have four main objectives.

- *Aesthetic objective*: the organizer wants to show the public how attractive his product or type of product is; for instance, arts or cultural events.
- *Idealistic objective (educational/social)*: an event can be organized for political, religious or social purposes – a demonstration, for example.
- *Entertainment objective*: the event is centred around entertainment. These kinds of events are usually organized for commercial reasons; they are low threshold and attract large crowds. Examples are funfairs and dance events.
- *Commercial objective*: events can also be organized for pure economic considerations and without any specific entertainment objective, such as annual fairs or trade shows.

Public events often have several overlapping objectives. The main objectives described above are therefore not mutually exclusive. Many events with an aesthetic objective, for instance, also contain elements of entertainment. Entertainment is used increasingly to encourage people to buy something (commercial value) or to believe something (idealistic, persuasive value). And, as already mentioned, public events are used by the business-to-business branch as a platform for inviting business contacts.

Types of public events

Festivals

- Music festivals (e.g. dance, jazz and multicultural festivals)
- Film festivals (national and international festivals)
- Theatre festivals (e.g. street theatre and theatre on location)
- Arts festivals (a mix of theatre, dance, music, visual arts, film and new media)

Exhibitions/trade shows

Concerts/musical performances

Rallies

Sports events

Attractions, including funfairs

Markets

- Tourist markets
- Arts markets
- Pasar Malam (Indonesian word for evening market)
- Folkloristic annual markets, cheese and flea markets
- Village fairs

Commemorations and ceremonies

- Centennial events
- Public holidays and other commemorations of historical significance, such as liberation parties and official holidays related to the royal family
- Silent marches
- Speeches
- Unregulated street markets
- Concerts (including benefit concerts)
- Weddings
- Funerals and births/baptisms (members of the royal family or other celebrities)
- Day of the Queen's/King's speech

Parades

- Carnival parades and lantern parades
- Demonstrations
- Flower parades
- Dance parade, love parade and gay parade

Culinary events

(Source: Verhaar, 2009.)

FADING BOUNDARIES BETWEEN CORPORATE AND PUBLIC EVENTS

From the perspective of the strategic objective, the boundaries between corporate and public events are fading. The objectives of public events are moving increasingly in the direction of those of corporate events.

On the one hand, public events are used to an increasing extent by organizations to arrange business-to-business events in which the public event constitutes the central platform. An example of these kinds of events is the 'trade day' (day for professionals only) of the ITB (holiday trade show). One day of the ITB for consumers is reserved for industry professionals. Tourism professionals meet each other on that day at several symposiums, workshops and networking sessions.

This 'trade day' can be regarded as a business-to-business event in which a public event (the ITB) is the main event, the central platform. Other examples are: VIP lounges, networking sessions during the Olympic Games, World Football Championships and the Australian Open in Melbourne.

On the other hand, public events seem to be taking on corporate characteristics to an increasing extent. Commercial interests are getting bigger and bigger. Organizers of public events often have no alternative but to seek sponsor funds, because government subsidies are diminishing. This brings with it its share of obligations towards the sponsors concerned, such as setting up a special (separate) space for sponsors during the event. Public events with commercial interests can shift even further towards the corporate end of the spectrum, thus becoming a platform for the initiation of countless commercial activities. A good example in this respect is the Tour de France. Originally a cycling contest, the event has become a commercial public event with major sponsorship interests. Organizations use this platform to initiate their own events. For instance, local bank branches invited their own customers to a client event on the first day of the Tour de France.

Business-to-consumer events in particular, such as the ITB Berlin (the world's leading travel trade show) or the International Motor Show in Geneva, Switzerland, occur at the interface between corporate and public events. They have a business and/or commercial goal, but are open to everyone who is interested.

The fading boundaries between corporate and public events have been visualized in Fig. 1.1, which will be explained further below. The figure is about events that have overlapping objectives. What is important in this respect is the perspective of the target group, as well as that of the commissioner of the event.

Corporate events

1. Business-to-business events (BtoB):
   1a The trade show 'Event' or a dealers meeting.
   1b Events for clients during Roland Garros in Paris.

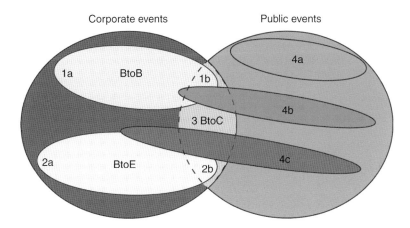

Fig. 1.1. Examples of overlapping between corporate and public events.

2. Business-to-employee events (BtoE):

    2a Shell or Unilever staff party or staff team-building day.

    2b Staff outing to a major sports event.

3. Business-to-consumer events (BtoC): Red Bull Air Race, World Championship in several cities like New York (USA, the Hudson River), Lisbon (Portugal, Tagus River), Abu Dhabi or ITB Berlin, or the introduction of a new car model to the public.

Public events

4. Public events:

    4a Opening ceremony of the Nike Brand Store in Basel, Switzerland or the arts festival 'The Fringe' in Edinburgh, Scotland.

    4b Castlebar International Four Days' Walks in Ireland, with sponsorship programme.

    4c Start of the Tour de France, with numerous side events organized by sponsors.

THE IMPORTANCE OF MANAGING EVENTS

Management is an important aspect in the strategic use of events. After all, the organizing party invests a great deal of money and effort in the event and consequently wants something in return. That is why the organizer will monitor the effects of the event (both during and afterwards) on visitors and, if necessary, make alterations to the project or parts of the project.

The management process consists of four steps:

- *Plan*: the organization decides to use an event to achieve one or more objectives within a certain period of time.
- *Do*: the actual organization of the event. In this process, it is very important for the event to be aligned with the objectives formulated previously, both in terms of category and set-up.
- *Check*: the assessment of objective attainment during and after the event. The organizer checks whether the objectives determined in the plan phase have been achieved. This phase involves effect measurement and evaluation.
- *Act*: the integration of the effect measurement results into the strategy. Depending on the outcome of the effect measurement, the organizer makes alterations to the strategy. Upon a successful outcome, for instance, it may be decided to organize the event again in the future (because it was successful) or, conversely, not to organize the event again in the future (because the goal was achieved).

And thus the circle is complete. The four steps together constitute what is referred to as the *Plan–Do–Check–Act* cycle (see Fig. 1.2).

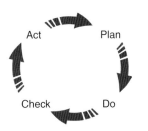

Fig. 1.2. The PDCA cycle or Deming cycle (source: Truscott, 2003).

In everyday practice, however, the cycle is not entirely completed. Effect measurement and evaluation are often overlooked, because some goals are difficult to measure or because all energy and attention is directed towards organizing the event. As a result, the party who commissioned the event will not have any information as to whether or not the efforts were actually productive and worthwhile.

THE EVENTS MODEL

This book has been written by means of what is referred to as the EVENTS model. 'EVENTS' is an acronym of 'Environment', 'Value', 'Effect', 'New', 'Touchpoint' and 'Strategy'. The model was developed at the NHTV Breda University of Applied Sciences as a tool to study systematically the strategic use of events (also see Box 1.1).

The idea behind the EVENTS model

Organizing events generally involves a lot of time and money. In order to engage the visitors to an event on an emotional level, it is important to realize that the events are not isolated happenings. They are strongly connected with their **E**nvironment and with the core **V**alues and the **S**trategy of the organizing party. The **N**ew concept and design for the event must be in alignment with these values and with the strategy. The visitor experience of the event starts as early as when the event is announced or invitations are sent out. During and after the event, visitors also come into contact (**T**ouchpoint) with the event. Finally, it is important to measure the **E**ffect of the event in order to be able to ascertain just how much it contributed towards achieving the strategic objectives formulated in advance.

The EVENTS model is an elaboration of the PDCA cycle. Just like this cycle, the model has four steps: plan, do, check, act. The model shows how these four steps are taken in the strategic use of events.

Box 1.1

Figure 1.3 illustrates the EVENTS model. It consists of a core and a layer around it. The layer represents the broader context in which event marketing is performed. The core represents the entire PDCA cycle: the 'plan' phase to the left (the axis with the four vanes), the 'do' phase in the middle (the oval) and the 'check' phase to the right (the arrow). The 'act' phase, in conclusion, is symbolized by the arrow to the bottom of the figure.

The outer layer of the model symbolizes the macro- and mesoenvironments that affect event marketing strategies. These environments exert influence on the organization. In these environments, there are quite a few parties that exert influence – either directly or indirectly – on the organization that seeks to engage in event marketing. The behaviour of

(Continued)

Box 1.1. Continued.

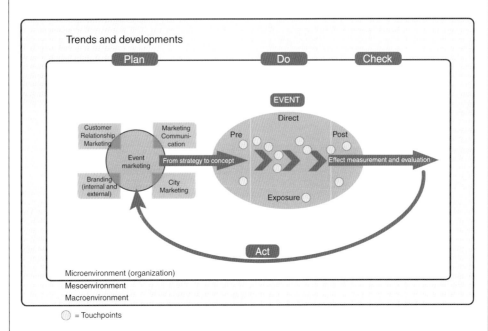

Fig. 1.3. The EVENTS model.

competitors or target groups may also necessitate organizations to change their practices. Economic trends and developments also affect the marketing strategies of organizations.

To the left of the model, we see an axis with four vanes. As already mentioned, this part of the figure represents the 'plan' phase. The axis represents event marketing. Each of the four vanes represents a marketing sub-area in which event marketing is used as a tool. As already mentioned, these sub-areas are customer relationship marketing, marketing communication, branding and city marketing. The arrow exiting from the axis illustrates the translation of the general strategy to the concept and design of a specific event.

To the right of the vanes, we see an oval on its side, which represents the 'do' phase. It displays the three stages of an event: pre-exposure, direct exposure and post-exposure. These are the stages before, during and after an event, which we discussed in the section on touchpoints. The touchpoints themselves are depicted by the dots in the oval.

Finally, to the right of the model, we have the 'check' phase. The large arrow to the right represents the phase of effect measurement. The fact that effect measurements are not only carried out afterwards but also during the event is shown by the small arrows in the oval.

The arrow at the bottom of the figure symbolizes the feedback of the effect measurements results. If necessary, alterations will be made to the strategy, which brings us back to the 'plan' phase.

THE STRUCTURE OF THIS BOOK

Chapters 2–10 inclusive, following this introductory chapter, are divided into three parts. The first part concerns the plan phase from the EVENTS model, the second part covers the do phase and the third part relates to the check phase.

In Part I, which is about the plan phase, we will deal first with a number of economic theories in which experiences and events play an important part. In this process, we will explain – basically by means of the experience and happiness economy – why events have become such a popular tool over the past couple of years (Chapter 2). We will also show why the contents and form of events are going to change over the years to come. Other themes dealt with in Part I are event marketing (Chapter 3) and the marketing sub-areas in which event marketing is applied. Customer relationship marketing, marketing communication, branding and city marketing will be dealt with successively (Chapters 4–7 inclusive).

Part II revolves around the do phase. We will describe how strategic objectives are translated to event concepts and designs. Chapter 8 presents answers to questions such as 'What is a good concept?' and 'What is the difference between an experience and perception?'. Moreover, we will go into detail about the methods to optimize the visitor experience (Chapter 9).

The final part of the book is about the check phase. In Chapter 10, we will explain how event organizers can measure the effects of their events and evaluate the research results. We will conclude the book with an overview of models for effect measurement and practical examples of effect measurement.

Event management, the elaboration of the concept and the organization of events in actual practice are themes that are not covered in this book.

chapter 2

Trends and Developments: Consumers' Pursuit of Happiness

Margo Rooijackers

In this chapter, we will focus on a number of economic and sociocultural developments that play a direct or indirect role in the strategic use of events. We will discuss what is termed the experience economy and the future happiness economy. In conclusion, we will explain how these developments present opportunities in terms of the strategic use of events.

LEARNING TARGETS

After studying this chapter, you will have learned:

- which macro-level influences there are on events
- what the consequences are (or have been) of the experience economy for the event sector
- how trends affect events
- what will happen after the experience economy
- when events can be meaningful to people
- how Rotterdam is making choices based on developments in its environment.

THE EXPERIENCE ECONOMY

If there were one economic development that accounts for the popularity of events, it would be the emergence of the experience economy. The experience economy is centred around the creation of experiences. In other words, this economy is not about products or services but about authentic experiences.

The experience economy is relatively new. Economists Pine and Gilmore distinguish three economic stages that precede the fourth stage, which is the experience economy (Pine and Gilmore, 2000). Each of the four stages is characterized by a specific way of value creation and a distinct 'consumer orientation', the criterion that determines whether or not the consumer makes a purchase. Below, you will find a brief description of the various stages (also see Table 2.1).

Agrarian economy: in this economy, emphasis is placed on extracting commodities from the natural world. At this stage, consumer sensitivity is connected with the availability of these commodities. Once they are available, a mutual exchange can take place.

Industrial economy: in this stage, the manufacturer concentrates on the production of goods. The focus shifts towards the cost factor. Price is a critical factor in the consumer's decision-making process.

Service economy: in the service economy, there is a shift from offering products to delivering services. Rather than price, quality is now the decisive purchase criterion for the consumer.

Experience economy: the current economic stage is labelled by the authors as the experience economy. The consumer wants to be engaged on an emotional level, and consumer sensitivity shifts from service quality to experience authenticity.

According to Pine and Gilmore (2000), the transformation economy will gradually take over in the future. In this stage, companies will take on the challenge of trying to achieve

Table 2.1. The progression of economic value in combination with the consumer's purchase criterion (Source: Pine and Gilmore, 2000).

Economic stage	Supplier's focus	Consumer's focus
Agrarian economy	Extracting commodities	Availability
Industrial economy	Manufacturing products	Price
Service economy	Delivering services	Quality
Experience economy	Staging experiences	Authenticity
Transformation economy (happiness economy)		

transformations or permanent changes in the lives of consumers. The decisive factor for the consumer's purchasing decisions is not specified by the experience gurus. We will come back to this matter later in this chapter. But first, we will take a closer look at the experience economy.

The aggregate experience

Traditionally, the event manager operates in the area of real-life experiences. Organizers make sizeable investments in the 'aggregate experience' and pull out all the stops to stimulate visitors' senses. It is not an exaggeration to say that the era of the experience economy has reached maturity. Suppliers are aware like never before of the fact that the product focus no longer suffices and that the consumer wants to be engaged on an emotional level. They try everything to turn their products or services into unique and distinctive experiences. They do so by means of sensory awareness, distinctive themes or developing compelling storylines, but preferably by blending every conceivable experience tool – in combination with each other – into their offerings (see Chapter 8 for an explanation of experience tools). For instance, angling is not particularly known as an exciting pastime. Still, every year in Ahoy (a venue in Rotterdam), a public angling exhibition is organized where every effort is made to create an optimal visitor experience (Box 2.1).

Box 2.1   Visma

Visma is Europe's biggest fishing show, which is held at the Ahoy venue in Rotterdam and where exhibitors in different categories – wholesale, retail, boats and fish tourism – present themselves to the public. Visma is positioned as *the* place where anglers come to meet other angling enthusiasts, to buy fishing equipment and to gather information. To satisfy the needs of the visitors, all sorts of activities are organized. There is a Visma theatre, where top anglers share their knowledge with visitors. At the 'Vaste Stokken Parade', visitors have the opportunity to try out 17-m fishing rods. And Landrover presents its Landrover Experience, a demonstration course where the vehicle's off-road capabilities are shown to entertain visitors. Moreover, a variety of demonstrations and workshops are held at a casting course designed especially for the show. Finally, Visma has set up its own online community (called sterkevisverhalen.nl) in order to target young people. This platform offers visitors the opportunity to meet each other online throughout the year. Young anglers are encouraged to share their 'cool fishing videos, angling photos and fish stories' on the site. (Source: www.visma.nl, accessed January 2011.)

More than just live meetings

The explosive growth of events-related online communities demonstrates that the sector is no longer just about live meetings alone. As for the future of the event sector, an intensified crossover between real-life and virtual experiences is to be expected. Technological innovations will contribute to this development even further.

In 2007, media company, DNB Media, already proved that the event sector was going to venture beyond mere live meetings. They organized a virtual concert of the Dutch band, Di-rect, which was simultaneously held in the TMF studios and Second Life: a pioneering initiative for that time.

Another illustration of the fading boundaries between the real and the artificial world is the remarkable alliance between the theatre and cinema branch. For a couple of years now, the Metropolitan Opera in New York has been featuring operas which are recorded live and shown simultaneously in a number of Pathé cinemas across Europe. For opera fans from Amsterdam, this means that they can enjoy Richard Wagner's *Das Rheingold* at the same time as their Swedish 'colleagues' in Lund, put on stage by Metropolitan in New York before a live audience. An interesting question here would be whether the different audiences have comparable opera experiences, or whether the experience of the cinema visitors in the European cities is of a different calibre than the live theatre experiences of the audience in New York. An initial exploration of visitor experiences produced reasons to believe the latter. Additional research will be required to confirm this finding. The outcomes of studies of this sort may serve as a basis in examining how artificial experiences in the future can gain in authenticity and visitor impact, and how live and non-live meetings can reinforce each other.

Co-creation

Another relevant trend is that of co-creation, which refers to the changing relationship between supply and demand. As a result of technological advancements and the emergence of new media, it has become easier for consumers and producers to enter into dialogue with each other. Consumers are becoming 'prosumers' (a combination of producer and consumer) and are starting to work together with suppliers. According to Boswijk *et al.* (2005), it is no longer just the service provider who creates the experience but the customer also can take the initiative and have more control over the production process. In this respect, it is the service provider's task to build a bond of trust with the customer. In their book, *The Experience Economy: A New Perspective*, Boswijk *et al.* present the following definition: 'Dialogue or interaction between organizations and consumers constitutes the basis for the co-creation of personalized value and/or experiences' (Boswijk *et al.*, 2007).

In the future, it may even be possible for the relationship between suppliers and customers to become so diffuse that consumers will know better and better where to find each other and, in the words of Jensen (presentation, November 2005), will become a serious threat – as 'ama-pros' (a combination of amateur and professional) – to the continued existence of commercial event agencies. As a corollary of this development, it is not hard to imagine that the professional sector will turn its focus primarily towards the business market and the market of large-scale public events in the long term, and that the ama-pros will direct their attention at niche markets of intimate and small-scale events for small groups of like-minded people drawn together for a common purpose.

Worth mentioning in this respect are 'secret events'. This concerns events which are accessible only to a select target group of fans, connoisseurs or close friends, who notify each other at the last minute via social media channels about the location and time of their event: a forbidden car race at a deserted industrial site, a dance party at a secret location or an illegal dog fight. Due to the secret and more or less closed character of this type of event, visitors tend to experience them as especially thrilling, and it also gives them the positive feeling of belonging to a select group of chosen ones. Commercial event organizers would do well to monitor closely the developments in this area and to see how they can add similar levels of excitement to their offerings. Secret events, of all sorts and sizes, are certainly expected to take an upturn in the future.

Devaluation of the experience concept

The above-mentioned trends and developments all hint to the fact that the concept of 'experiences' has become an inextricable part of the event sector. The other side of the success coin is that the experience concept is exploited excessively. When every local annual fair featuring traditional craft demonstrations is announced as an event which you must not miss, the credulous visitors of these events will stroll around hopefully, looking for something that, unfortunately, they are not going to find. The devaluation of the experience concept has been set in motion and the process is irreversible, meaning that inevitably the concept will become eroded and unusable at some point. At the same time, today's globally oriented communication society has resulted in consumers who are much better informed, as well as more articulate and demanding. A decrease in available leisure time is accompanied by an increase of disposable income and an increased propensity to consume. Today's event visitors want more in a smaller amount of time, and for this they are willing to open up their wallets. Add to the equation the strong growth in supply and it will be clear that an important challenge is awaiting the event manager of the future. After all, what will come after the 'Live Life to the Max' principle of modern consumers with the attendant adage of 'Seen it, done it, got the T-shirt'?

THE ADVANCE OF HAPPINESS: THE HAPPINESS ECONOMY

At the same time as the first cracks in the experience concept appear, the alternative is making a cautious advance. By now, countless names for this economic stage have popped up all around the world. In this chapter, we have already introduced the terms 'economy of meaning' and 'happiness economy' (Pine and Gilmore, 2000). Alternative terms are 'zineconomie' (an economy of meaningfulness, what you buy has to make sense) (Ter Borg, 2003), 'challenge economy' and 'economie van het geluk' (happiness economy) (Bakas, masterclass, October 2008). Characteristic of this new economic stage is that suppliers are taking on the challenge of bringing about permanent changes in the consumer and to help him give his life meaning (or more meaning). The key purchase criterion in this stage can be designated as 'happiness' (see Table 2.2). Event suppliers would do well to take a closer look at the happiness concept and make it their business.

Table 2.2. Happiness economy as an economic stage.

Economic stage	Supplier's focus	Consumer's focus
Happiness economy	Facilitating permanent changes	Happiness

Happiness is the ultimate goal that every individual pursues in his life. However, scientists, politicians or managers prefer not to burn their fingers on this subject. Why is it that scepticism sets in whenever the topic of the manipulability of happiness is raised?

Happiness cannot be programmed or organized, according to philosopher René ten Bos (presentation by ten Bos, November 2006). It is a subjective concept that is part of the realm of coincidence, selectivity and uncontrollability. His colleague, Cuypers (presentation by Cuypers, March 2009), also argues that humans are not capable of making their own happiness. You will find happiness when it is brought to you by fate. The possibility to manipulate your own individual psychological condition is a highly limited one. If you try too hard to become happy, you will overreach yourself, the hedonist paradox says. As Immanuel Kant put it, 'the essence cannot be found in how we may make ourselves happy, but in how we make ourselves worthy of happiness'.

Enabling happiness

In contemporary psychology, an opposing view is expressed as far as the manipulability of happiness is concerned. Traditionally, behavioural scientists concentrate on divergent behaviour or behaviour that can be classified as unhealthy, such as depression, anorexia and stress. According to the International Positive Psychology Association (IPPA), positive psychology is concerned with 'the scientific study of what enables individuals and communities to thrive'. What makes individuals feel happy, experience their existence as positive and useful, and believe that they matter? In positive psychology, the happiness concept is an explicit object of study. The focus is shifting to terms like quality of life, subjective well-being, optimism, positive emotions and flow. One of the representatives of positive psychology is Martin Seligman, known for his book, *Authentic Happiness* (Seligman, 2002). He distinguishes three components of happiness, which are: positive emotions (such as fun, surprise, gratitude); commitment (family, work, free time); and meaning and purpose (knowing and using your own talents for the purpose of something that is bigger than you). As it turns out, the two latter dimensions appear to be the most important to fulfilment in life. Other researchers have come up with similar findings. According to Diener and Biswas-Diener (2008), family and friends, sense of direction, and meaning and purpose in life are critical to quality of life. Veenhoven, a Dutch sociologist, asserts that what people thinks make them happy will not necessarily be that what actually makes them happy (presentation by Veenhoven, November 2006). His studies have shown that happiness bears a strong correlation to having a good marriage, participating in clubs and associations, and having a job but, remarkably enough, not to having children. Veenhoven also believes that a person's context is important. According to him, fulfilment in life depends on the fit between the liveability of the external environment on the one hand (for example, level of prosperity, legal system, freedom) and the life skills of the individual on the other hand (for example, the ability to take action, independence, forgivingness). As it happens, objective societal characteristics account for about three-quarters of the differences in happiness across nations.

Orchestrated happiness

How are people's life skills improved, how is social cohesion in communities strengthened and how can a well-oiled society be accomplished? The application of positive psychology is a key concern of the Centre for Applied Positive Psychology (CAPPP). Attention is directed towards talent development in schools; coaching; leadership development; and community development. The guiding principle is that every individual has (latent) authentic talents that give him energy and allow him to function optimally, if he is able to put them to use. The trick is to make these talents flourish, not only in the interest of the individual himself, but also in the interest of the community in which he resides.

The management and organization sector has also become aware of the happiness concept. The renowned firm of Schouten and Nelissen promoted the concept by means of the 'Geluk in uitvoering' ('Happiness in progress') conference in 2006. The central question was 'Could you enable happiness?' and, if so, 'How can professional organizations stimulate happiness in the workplace?'. Leading national and international scholars answer this crucial question with a wholehearted 'yes'. The happiness factor is a relevant dimension in achieving rational organizational goals in terms of efficiency and profit maximization.

The notion of the enabling of happiness should be an eye-opener for leisure managers. If it is worthwhile for organizations to make serious business of managing happiness in the workplace, there must certainly be opportunities in the leisure sphere. After all, the leisure context comes second to none where it concerns individuals making their own choices. In sectors like labour and health care, the perception of free choice is considerably lower, because of current concepts like performance, obligations and responsibility. Events in particular would be useful in 'happiness management', since it concerns staging live encounters between people, with the intention of giving these encounters a positive emotional dimension. The challenge for the future is for events to be not only memorable but also transformational. In other words, the visitor is changed in a positive sense because of the event. Moreover, this change should be permanent rather than temporary. For instance, the visitor may learn or experience something at the event which causes him to take a different perspective to a certain issue; for example, the Festival Mundial, a large-scale world music event in Tilburg (the Netherlands) with the aim of fostering an open and tolerant attitude towards other cultures. But it may also be about boosting ties with friends with whom one attends a music event or about discovering one's own passion or talent while participating in a sporting event.

If the feeling of happiness can be influenced, the leisure or event managers of the future should not be experience stagers but happiness managers, with expertise in the area of 'quality of life'. They should have knowledge of factors that promote the consumer's individual well-being and be able to put this knowledge to use in the context of events. In this way, event management creates the enabling conditions within which the consumer can express his personal identity and within which he can strengthen and expand his relationships with others. Moreover, the ultimate event allows its visitors to add meaning to their lives and encourages altruistic behaviour. And this is only a small selection from the range of determinants that are related to the concept of 'quality of life'.

Helping people to help themselves

There is, however, a certain ethical risk to happiness management. Modern education has gone a step too far by also wanting to colonize students' interior lives, by means of life coaching. The all-important point of departure is that the individual's autonomy must not be compromised by patronizing or manipulating his emotions. In this respect, a parallel can be drawn with the entertainment concept from the literature on recreation. The aim of entertainment is not so much to help people, but to help people help themselves. Give children on the beach toy buckets and shovels and they will entertain themselves and each other; all day long. This is also what facilitating happiness is all about. It is crucial to create possibilities to allow individuals to follow their own dreams.

The successful event manager of the future will enable visitors to discover their hidden passions and develop their latent talents. Ideally, he will succeed in challenging visitors to make a difference by means of a meaningful contribution to a greater whole. Attention for meaning and purpose in the design and programming of events will inspire a permanent change in the visitor that increases the quality of his life, as opposed to a temporary climax.

Meaningful leisure products

The first signs of the progression from experiences to meaning have already manifested themselves. For instance, since 2007, Center Parcs has been offering its guests 'a state of happiness', rather than a holiday experience. And what about the 'holiday package with added value' as offered by Club Med in cooperation with DUOjob. This holiday programme, especially designed for stress-sensitive managers, comprises a series of workshops to learn to restore the work–life balance. The focus of products and services has shifted from the temporary flow experience towards the lasting optimization of the leisure user's contentment with life. Beneficial effects, supposed to last until long after the holiday itself, are pursued. The growth of convent tourism can also be explained by people's growing need for spiritual healing and purpose in life. This development can even be seen in the fitness and beauty sector, which traditionally focused on the exterior (the body) only. Health and wellness centres have blended their traditional physical exercise and dietetic offerings with mental coaching and spiritual workshops. All this takes place, preferably, in a setting in which mutual interaction between like-minded people is stimulated and the sense of community is promoted.

Events with added value

The event sector has been directing its attention towards the concept of meaning and purpose for quite some time now. Everyone is well aware of national and international charity campaigns. The most famous charity event ever organized was undoubtedly Live Aid in 1985. With this benefit concert, organizers Bob Geldof and Midge Ure wanted to raise funds for relief in the ongoing Ethiopian famine. The concert lasted 16 h and featured simultaneous performances by famous musicians in several places across the world, and it was broadcast live across many countries.

Events of a somewhat smaller scale, but also clearly focusing on meaning, are the events of the SoccorsoClowns in Italy: the music show, *SoccorsoClowns in Concert*, and the *SoccorsoClowns Theatre Tour*. Both events take place at different times and different locations in Italy and they have been designed especially for children with an illness or disability, the idea being that by going to one of these shows, they can be children again, if only for a little while (www. cliniclownsinternational.org, accessed June 2013).

Comparable initiatives are seen in the sports sector. The Johan Cruyff Foundation, for example, is committed to getting young people moving. The foundation does so by means of events such as the Johan Cruyff Games. A similar initiative is the charity, the Rafael Nadal Foundation. This foundation offers educational programmes using sport as a tool for personal and social integration, passing on values such as effort, self-improvement and respect in order to encourage self-esteem and confidence (www.cruyff-foundation.org and www. tennisdailynews.net, accessed June 2013).

Corporate social responsibility

There are plenty of examples of companies that have made social responsibility part of their corporate philosophy. The starting principle in a strategy of this kind is to take the balance between people, planet and profit into consideration in all business decisions. Corporate and other events can be used as a tool in putting the corporate social responsibility principle into action. This too is a development that is part of the happiness economy.

An example in this respect is HEMA's annual 'Helping Hands' programme. HEMA is a famous Dutch department store, with shops in the Netherlands, Belgium and France. During this 2-day corporate event, employees of HEMA headquarters do volunteer work for a good cause: hosting a high tea in a nursing home in Amsterdam, Brussels and Paris, or fixing up a children's farm in a residential community.

Siemens has taken action on its social responsibility by means of the Siemens Helps donation fund. Through this fund, employees can nominate an event for a donation from Siemens. This donation involves a financial contribution or help in the form of Siemens volunteers. A range of appealing initiatives has already been accomplished. Nevertheless, the reality is probably a little more unmanageable. Too often, well-intended strategic organizational objectives get bogged down in the reality of every day, and factual activities cannot seem to escape the appearance of 'window dressing'.

Still, the examples mentioned in this section clearly illustrate that the attention to meaning and purpose is not a new phenomenon in the event sector. Strangely enough, commercial event businesses have hardly made use of this angle up to now. It is clear that this is where their challenge for the future lies.

INNOVATION OPPORTUNITIES

The progression from the experience economy to the happiness economy is characterized by a shift of focus from experiences to happiness and quality of life. The changing economic context creates opportunities for innovation. The time has come for stakeholders in the event sector to reflect on the question of how to define their core business: creating experiences for consumers or generating meaning for people or society? What is typical of the happiness economy is the pursuit to increase the quality of life on an individual, social and societal level. Consequently, the event manager's focus area is shifting from staging optimal experiences to facilitating happiness. The ultimate goal on an individual level is to achieve an increased sense of happiness in the visitor. On a social level, it concerns optimizing the quality of life of society in general, and in particular to strengthen social cohesion within and between the various groups and subgroups that make up society. In this new economy, it is highly conceivable that the consumer will make a deliberate choice to visit events that contribute to his contentment with life and/or that have a positive influence on the quality of life in the social, political–economic and/or ecological context in which he finds himself.

The challenge for the event manager of the future is to create innovative event concepts – consistent with the happiness perspective – and develop an accompanying set of management tools or toolbox to ensure a successful outcome.

ROTTERDAM FESTIVALS

An example of an organization in the event industry that is orientating itself on the transformation economy is Rotterdam Festivals. This is an umbrella organization that coordinates the event policy of 150 businesses operating in the event and festival sector in Rotterdam. Rotterdam Festivals constitutes the link between government and event organizers and its aim is to stimulate cohesion in the cultural sector and optimize the city's image.

Rotterdam Festivals ordered a scenario analysis to be carried out to obtain an answer to the question of 'What challenges will the future hold and what will be their impact on the strategic policy of Rotterdam Festivals?'.

The scenario analysis

To give more substance to the ambitions of Rotterdam Festivals, a scenario analysis was carried out in the autumn of 2008 by a project group consisting of International Leisure Management students from NHTV Breda. A scenario analysis is a method to analyse possible future events by considering alternative possible outcomes and it is used as a tool to formulate strategic management recommendations.

A scenario analysis consists of the following seven steps (based on Notten *et al.*, 2003):

Step 1. Formulating a project plan (objective, design and contents).
Step 2. Carrying out a general trend analysis.
Step 3. Reducing trends to a limited number of key trends.
Step 4. Describing key trends.
Step 5. Constructing alternative scenarios.
Step 6. Developing storyboards for each scenario.
Step 7. Formulating recommendations.

Step 1 is the step of formulating a project plan. In this stage, the objective of the analysis is formulated and choices are made with regard to the design and contents of the analysis.

During Step 2, a general trend analysis is carried out. This can be done by means of the DESTEP model, which addresses trends and developments in demographic, economic, socio-cultural, technological, ecological and political areas.

The next step, taking the client's problem as a point of departure, involves reducing the large number of trends to a limited number of key trends. The two selection criteria in determining these key trends are the degree of probability that the trend concerned will persist and the degree of impact that is attached to this trend. The result of Step 3 can be represented in what is called a probability impact diagram.

After determining the key trends, Step 4 focuses on an extensive description of each of these trends, in which a line is drawn from the past through the present to the future.

In Step 5, based on the information from this in-depth trend analysis, a number of possible future scenarios are drawn up. Usually, two to four scenarios are developed. Depending on the client's needs, this may result in a probable, possible and preferable alternative and/or a profit, non-profit or public sector scenario. The various intervention possibilities available to the players concerned may also serve as a basis to develop scenarios. The scenarios that were chosen in the analysis for Rotterdam Festivals were derived from two dominant trends that were determined and plotted against each other on two axes. As a result, four different scenarios were produced.

Steps 6 and 7, in conclusion, consist of designing storyboards for the various scenarios and formulating recommendations in the area of strategic management for the client.

Within the framework of the scenario analysis, two key trends were selected for the future of Rotterdam as an event and festival city:

- the transition from experiences to meaning
- globalization.

These trends were elaborated into four alternative scenarios (also see Fig. 2.1):

- collective enjoyment
- collective awareness
- identity refreshment
- identity development.

Collective enjoyment

In this scenario, the increasing emphasis on experiences is combined with an ongoing globalization trend. Boundaries are fading, people are becoming increasingly mobile and the regional and national identity of people is losing importance. In this scenario, the people of Rotterdam feel more and more like world citizens and the city is one of the 'places to be' in the world. The events that go with this scenario are large scale and international, and contribute to the feeling of 'one world'.

Identity refreshment

In this scenario, an opposite trend is expected: localization instead of globalization. It is assumed that in an ever more international world, people will develop a need to return to their roots and rediscover and refresh their own identity. The main theme of events and festivals will be to confirm the unique identity of a group and to emphasize the mutual relationships between the members of a group. At the same time, these types of events may also serve to

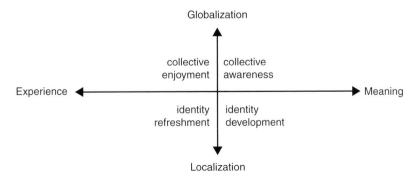

Fig. 2.1. Four alternative scenarios for the future of Rotterdam Festivals (source: Projectgroep Rotterdam Festivals, 2009, unpublished).

express one's cultural identity and celebrate the diversity with others. The key terms in this scenario are: back-to-one's-roots, authenticity and intimacy.

Both scenarios on the left side of the diagram have an ever stronger focus on experiences in common (see the section on the experience economy earlier in this chapter). Events and festivals in both scenarios will be parties centred around the 'Live Life to the Max' principle.

The choice for the collective enjoyment scenario ties in with the ambition of Rotterdam Festivals to turn Rotterdam into a major event city of international fame and allure. Attracting and promoting large-scale, compelling events, such as the International Film Festival Rotterdam and Jazz International Rotterdam, is also in keeping with this.

Collective awareness

'Making the world a better place' is the guiding principle in this scenario. The types of events that go with this principle are large-scale events with an international character, seeking attention for social/societal, political–economic and/or ecological problems occurring on a global scale.

Identity development

This scenario is much more about small-scale events with local themes which appeal to the individual's desire to make a difference, either for himself or for others in his environment, or for the community of which he is part. Whereas the identity refreshment scenario is about celebrating and confirming the identity of the individual and the groups to which he belongs, the identity development scenario places emphasis on further developing one's own identity based on the human need of wanting to make a meaningful contribution to something that transcends individual existence.

Both scenarios on the right side of the diagram are centred around meaning and purpose (see the text on the transformation economy earlier in this chapter). Events and festivals are more than parties or celebrations, and they are meaningful because they make a lasting and positive contribution to the quality of life of the individual, the group(s) to which he belongs and/or society as a whole.

The choice for the identity refreshment scenario would be more appropriate, considering the objective of Rotterdam Festivals of promoting participation in culture among the residents of Rotterdam. After all, in this scenario, mostly small-scale 'grass roots' events and festivals will flourish.

The scenario analysis has shown that Rotterdam Festivals has a choice to shift its current focus of creating experiences towards a focus of creating meaning for people and society in the future. This presents options for the development or promotion of innovative event and festival concepts and gives Rotterdam the opportunity to assume a pioneering role in the market (Projectgroep Rotterdam Festivals, 2009, unpublished, adapted by the authors).

SUMMARY

The experience economy no longer centres on products and services but on authentic emotions and experiences. Pine and Gilmore (2000) distinguish four economic stages, which are the agrarian economy, the industrial economy, the service economy and the experience economy. In the experience economy, aggregate experiences are pursued. Events in which the boundaries between the real and the virtual world are fading are consistent with this. All this is made possible by technological advancements. In this respect, co-creation is an interesting development too, with secret events as a distinctive component. The risk of a too great emphasis on experiences is that organizers sometimes raise too many expectations among potential critical visitors who want a true experience for their money.

In positive psychology, with Martin Seligman as the leading spokesman, happiness is regarded as being enabling. In the future, the happiness economy – which is all about inspiring permanent changes in the lives of consumers – will gain ground as a fifth economic stage.

The progression from experience economy to happiness economy presents opportunities for innovation. Events can be used, for instance, as a tool to promote social cohesion and personal well-being. The experience is no longer an isolated phenomenon, as it generates meaning and purpose. After a study of four possible scenarios for the future, this was also the challenge with which Rotterdam Festivals found itself confronted.

chapter 3

Event Marketing

Dorothé Gerritsen and Ronald van Olderen

We will start this chapter with an explanation of what event marketing means. Then, we will place this form of marketing in a broader context. After a description of the various types of event marketing, we will present the advantages and disadvantages of event marketing. We will finish this chapter with a number of tips relating to the application of event management.

LEARNING TARGETS

After studying this chapter, you will have learned:

- how event marketing emerged
- which approaches there are within event marketing
- what the strategic reasons may be for employing event marketing
- what the position of event marketing is within the marketing mix
- what types of event marketing we can distinguish
- what the strength is of events and event marketing
- when event marketing can be employed.

EVENT MARKETING

Event marketing is very much of current interest. Organizations are becoming increasingly alert to the strength of events as effective live means of communication. Events are used more and more often; for instance, by companies to bring their brands, products or services to the attention of current and potential customers, thus attempting to create a positive brand attitude. Since event marketing is only at the beginning of a glorious career, it is important at this point to define the concept.

© D. Gerritsen and R. van Olderen 2014. *Events as a Strategic Marketing Tool*
(D. Gerritsen and R. van Olderen)

The words 'event marketing' generate about three million hits on Google. All these websites exhibit a great diversity of definitions and descriptions: organizing events; creatively turning the message into a theme and a programme; the relationship of an event with other marketing and communication means; emotions and experiences; marketing of events; alignment of the event with the company's brand values, and so on. In the battle for the consumer's attention, brands, companies, countries, cities and even royal families are opting ever more often for non-traditional means of communication. Sponsoring, social media and event marketing are rapidly growing communication tools. The fact is that the event has secured an important position in the field of marketing.

Box 3.1   Nintendo Wii

For the purpose of the introduction of the Wii, a gaming console, Nintendo Nederland was looking for a strategy (PR plan) to introduce this gaming console to as wide an audience as possible. The budget was limited. The strategy had to obtain free publicity in all media. On the advice of an event organization agency, the management of Nintendo deliberately opted for the employment of a mediagenic event. The event comprised a press reception in the press room of the Olympic Stadium of Amsterdam. Journalists and other invitees were given a chance to try out various games: playing tennis, bowling, playing golf, baseball and boxing against famous top athletes. More than 50 journalists attended the event and wrote about it in the media. In this way, Nintendo succeeded in creating a veritable hype. The Wii was sold out even before its launch. (Source: Gouden Giraffe entry, 2008, unpublished, adapted by the authors.)

The above example (Box 3.1) shows that Nintendo achieved maximum results with limited resources by organizing an event. Traditional marketing and communication means, such as advertisements and printed media, are very expensive. Nintendo realized that the essence was the live experience of the Wii sports games. This would probably enthuse the primary target group much more than, for instance, an advertisement, with greater follow-up and media coverage as a result. In this example, Nintendo deliberately incorporated the event into its marketing and communication strategy. Additionally, the event generated an excellent platform for the account managers to get in touch with the media, with athletes and with consumers. All in all, this example shows how an event can be used strategically as a means to achieve certain goals: event marketing.

A DEFINITION

Event marketing involves marketing, events and communication. It is a concept that is attracting increasing attention from businesses, organizations and the media. By now, the term has become widely used, but it has not yet found a place in the *Oxford English Dictionary*. In the section on using events as a strategic marketing tool in Chapter 1, we have already presented a definition of the word 'event'. The word 'marketing' is a contraction of the words 'market' and 'getting'. Market getting became marketing.

> Marketing is the process of developing, pricing, promoting and distributing products, services or ideas that are tailored to the market; it includes all other activities that create value and systematically lead to increased sales or another desired response, establish a good reputation and ongoing relationships with customers, so that all stakeholders achieve their objectives.
>
> (Verhage, 2009)

Communication is an essential component in the definition of events as well, as that of marketing. As far as events are concerned, the communication objective is all-important; and as far as marketing is concerned, promotion is one of the tools to achieve the marketing objective. In Chapter 5 of this book, we will explore the relationship between events and communication more extensively.

MARKETING AND THE EMERGENCE OF EXPERIENCES

Over the past few decades, marketing has shifted its focus from an entirely product-oriented approach to a more communication-oriented approach. Some 30 years ago, companies that had a marketing plan had a definite lead on their competitors. Today, 90% of all companies in the industry apply the same marketing and research techniques, as well as means of communication. In other words, it is becoming increasingly difficult for a company to 'stand out from the crowd'. Figure 3.1 presents the evolution of business practices according to Rijkenberg.

Marketing originated from the economics discipline. Initially, businesses primarily had a product orientation: the product was the focus within 'marketing'. Product-oriented companies distinguished themselves by means of the quality of their products. In those early days, the quality of products was very high, which was all a business needed to set itself apart from its competitors. Starting from the 1920s, marketing was employed from a more sales-oriented perspective. The difference in quality between products was negligible at that time, and competition was based mainly on price differences. The era of Kotler, the marketing-oriented period, was characterized by an emphasis on distribution. 'How and where do I sell my products?' was a key question in this phase. The four Ps – product, price, place and promotion (communication) – were the ingredients for successful market operations. According to Rijkenberg (2005), this was logical, because as it turned out, there was a huge demand for all sorts of products that generally made life more comfortable.

As time went by, companies came to realize that there was only little scope left for product innovations, and what is more, they required substantial investments in promotion. Meanwhile, the consumer hardly cared about product innovations any more. The consumer was far

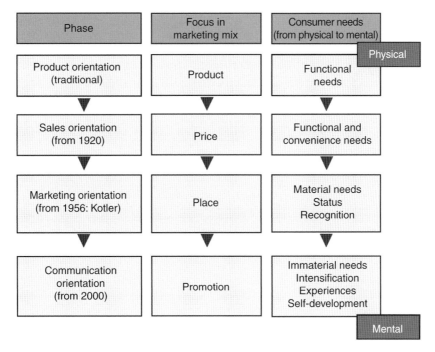

Fig. 3.1. The evolution of business practices (source: Rijkenberg, 2005).

more concerned with immaterial needs, intensification and experiences. Nowadays, businesses are acknowledging that – rather than the product – the crucial factor is customer retention, causing a shift to occur from transaction-oriented marketing to relationship marketing, the subject of Chapter 4. There is a need for 'added value' of the product, as a result of which society in the 21st century has developed a much more distinctive communication orientation. Brand values have become important in this phase. Consumers want to identify themselves by means of a brand.

EXPERIENCE MARKETING

In the past few years, a shift has occurred from traditional marketing practices to experience marketing. Experience marketing is an extra marketing tool and is, in fact, also a development in the field of marketing, which involves the creation of non-tangible and memorable experiences. It is about a subjective customer or consumer experience. Due to economic progress, products and services have become so easily available and mutually comparable that organizations are forced to look for new tools in order to protect their margins. According to Pine and Gilmore (1999), the solution can be found in adding theatricality and entertainment: buying and consuming must be turned into an experience. It is all about engaging the customer on an emotional level. Far from settling for the pure function of a product or service, consumers today want added value in the form of an experience. The experience is worth more to them than the mere fulfilment of a need. Furthermore, products and services in contemporary Western societies are only rarely designed to meet consumers' basic primary needs.

To be able to distinguish properly between products, services and experiences, the principle of value addition is crucial. In the case of an experience, the value addition can be found in the people themselves; the experience of the customer or visitor is the actual product. An experience is the result of the interaction between the event organized and the person concerned. A service, for instance, can become part of an experience when it is delivered in such a way that customers have an experience they will remember later, because it left an impression on them. The next example (Box 3.2) will show that the service of 'showing a film in a cinema' is turned into a unique experience through the application of event marketing. The cinema's marketing objective is to attract new crowds. This is done by offering event concepts with experiential elements to new target groups.

Box 3.2   Sing-along cinema

The sing-along cinema is one of the concepts by means of which cinema chains try to attract new crowds. Their websites are swarming with 'events' and 'specials': Turkish films and Bollywood films in major cities, senior afternoons and ladies' nights ('Enjoy a glass of prosecco, as well as delicious canapés and finger foods!'). Live satellite broadcasts from the Metropolitan Opera in New York invariably lead to a sold-out Metropolis in Antwerp. And the latest invention by Pathé International: girls' afternoon. Normally, vampire films have to grow on the audience over time, but *Twilight* was sold out straight away. Youry Bredewold, from Pathé International, reported a theatre full of screaming teenage girls. Cinemas are going through changes. Nowadays, events account for some 3–5% of Pathé International's turnover. They have capitalized on the wish of 'wanting to have an experience together with one's own kind of people'. The profit margin is attractive: a night out to the opera on the silver screen at Metropolis will set you back €32, a VIP ticket as much as €45. A bigger pond to fish from, that's the general idea. After all, cinemas are doing great. Most cinema visitors are aged between 16 and 31. It makes perfect sense to attract wealthy senior citizens to the cinema, too. And as it happens, events are an excellent way to do so. (Source: Van Zwol, 2010, adapted by the authors.)

DEVELOPMENTS IN MARKETING COMMUNICATION

Over the years, marketing communication has seen its share of important changes as a consequence of changes in production methods and market circumstances. Important developments in this respect are:

- big advertising budgets (starting from 1960)
- greater availability of marketing communication budgets

- one-to-one communication
- experience communication.

The most important development occurred around the 1960s, when consumer marketing made its entrance. Producers came to recognize the importance of products and services and directed their attention to mass communication. In the early 1980s, producers started engaging in advertising, promotion, sponsoring, direct marketing and public relations. Moreover, they acknowledged that there were two target groups to take into account: consumers and distributive trade.

Currently, one-to-one communication is becoming increasingly important. Messages are geared as much as possible to the values, wishes and characteristics of the consumer. The enormous communication volume makes it harder to reach the target group, forcing brands and organizations to look for alternatives. One of these alternatives is experience communication, or put differently, live communication (see Chapter 5).

The shift from traditional marketing to experience marketing has a clear link with event marketing. Within the field of communication, the emphasis has moved to the one-to-one relationship with the consumer. In this respect, events are a very appropriate medium: people can meet each other in person, all senses can be stimulated and an experience can be created. The event as a communication platform offers excellent opportunities to forge closer ties between suppliers on the one hand – brands, cities, products, services or regions – and consumers on the other hand. The consumer is allowed to experience personally what the organization is all about and what it stands for.

EVENT MARKETING: TWO PERSPECTIVES

Event marketing has its origin in the fields of marketing as well as communication. Event marketing can be regarded from two perspectives:

1. Marketing for events.
2. Marketing through events.

Marketing for events

The point of departure in marketing for events is that the event is the product to be marketed: events such as IMEX (the international trade fair for event organizations), Festival Mundial (a multicultural public event), Salone Internazionale del Mobile in Milan (the famous design furniture fair), New Orleans Jazz and Heritage Festival, International Motor Show Geneva and Sensation White in various cities in the world like Sao Paulo (Brazil) and Bucharest (Romania) and in Taiwan. The event is the core business, and in most cases, a brand name, too. Everything that the organizer does is for the purpose of the event. In other words, the event is the starting point of all business operations and can be marketed by means of various strategic approaches: branding, relationship marketing, marketing and communication and other disciplines. To put the product called 'event' on the market, a variety of resources and channels can be employed, such as the Internet, commercials, posters, social networks and advertisements. The ultimate goal is for the event:

- to be positioned effectively in relation to competing events
- to contribute to the organization's strategic goals
- to contribute to the organization's continuity and profits.

Marketing through events

Events can be used as an important part of the marketing and communication policy of, for instance, brands, products and services. The organization uses the event for strategic and/or tactical considerations. The ultimate strategic goal is the organization's continuity.

This book focuses on the event as a means to achieve a certain goal, which falls into the category of marketing through events. Based on empirical research among professional event marketers, we will apply the following definition:

> Event marketing focuses on developing, intensifying and expanding a relationship (or brand relationship) with one or more target groups, in which the event or the series of events is used as a marketing and communication tool and in which emotion and experience are brought together. A clearly defined objective, message and target group, consistent with the organizer's policy, is a precondition in this respect.

So, an organization may choose to engage in event marketing because it wants to communicate a certain message. It is important for this message to be conveyed effectively. That is why clear and measurable objectives must be formulated in advance. Getting the right message across to the target group seems easier than it really is. There is no point in doggedly pursuing event-marketing strategies, cost what it may. As it turns out, there are still a great many companies that use events in an ill-considered way.

REASONS TO OPT FOR EVENT MARKETING

The guiding principle of the various strategies dealt with in Chapters 4 through 7 is that the concept of event marketing is interpreted as broadly as possible. The goal of a strategy is to increase the sales of products or services and to ensure an organization's continuity or – for instance, in the case of a city – encourage economic activity.

There are various strategies based on which an event can be organized:

- *Relationship marketing strategy*: building, maintaining and intensifying relationships with various stakeholders;
- *Marketing communication strategy*: influencing the visitor's knowledge, attitude and behaviour;
- *External branding strategy*: influencing, creating or changing the visitor's valuable brand associations;

- *Internal branding strategy*: influencing, creating or changing the employee's valuable brand associations in order to increase employee involvement and optimize the customer experience;
- *City marketing strategy*: contributing to the objectives of a city.

We believe that achieving economic objectives by means of events is not the only concern. Events can also be used in the public sector (countries, regions or cities) to achieve strategic goals. In the end, these objectives will advance economic objectives. For instance, cities can use events to put their city on the map strategically. That is why it is interesting, for economic reasons, for a city like Rotterdam to win the bid to host the start of the Tour de France, but what may also play a role is that the city of Rotterdam wants to put itself on the map as one of the major sport cities of the Netherlands. Or the goal may be to generate more publicity, in order to attract more tourists (promotional motive). Another social reason may be to organize activities, relating to the Tour de France, for children from urban regeneration districts.

Below (Box 3.3), we give an example of a company that purposefully uses events to achieve strategic goals.

Box 3.3

Bogra is a producer and supplier of coffins, urns and other products which can be used before, during or after a funeral or cremation. Twenty per cent of its total production volume is exported to other countries, mostly to France and Belgium. Since 2005, Bogra has also been active on the German market. Bogra delivers directly to customers (business-to-consumer) or via regional wholesalers, including funeral transport companies (business-to-business). A few years ago, Bogra was planning to introduce a new line of coffins to its main client group, the funeral companies, with the aim of increasing sales. To this end, Bogra called in the services of a specialized event agency, which developed a communication track themed 'Choose your coffin', focusing on the fact that choosing a coffin is often an emotional moment; after all, it involves a choice for the final goodbye. People on the street were asked what kind of coffin they would like to be buried in, by means of a catalogue describing the three categories (product lines):

I – traditional/classic
II – modern/contemporary
III – deluxe/exclusive

The results from this survey were then used during a pre-trade show, to which the main clients of Bogra were invited. The pre-trade show for important clients was held in the basement of a fortress. Emphasis was placed on interaction and product information by means of the three product lines. Subsequently, the concept was translated into a trade show stand concept (a life-sized white coffin), with visitors literally undergoing a 'coffin experience'.

(Continued)

Box 3.3. Continued.

Recently, Bogra presented itself at the international funeral trade show in Düsseldorf with the theme of 'I love Holland'. On their stand there were mainly ecological coffins in a décor of red tulips and little lambs in a field. Woollen coffins, a green alternative for burials, were also on display. (Source: Gouden Giraffe entry, 2005, unpublished; and www.bogra.nl, www.your-event.nl, accessed September 2005, adapted by the authors.)

This example serves to show a number of things. Basically, Bogra wants to increase sales. The platforms to do so are a pre-trade show for top clients and a trade show for other client groups. At the international trade show, the company also concentrated on important potential clients. To Bogra, these platforms are excellent opportunities to have live contact with important clients. The events may not lead directly to increased sales, but indirectly they may strengthen the company's relationships with its clients or influence the mindset of current and potential clients with regard to the Bogra brand. So, it may be clear that the reasons for using the event (from a sales, customer relationship or branding perspective) should be formulated first of all.

Event marketing can be undertaken as an integrated part of a communication campaign or on a periodical basis. It is also possible that it concerns an event or a series of events as a part of an overall campaign. With its 'Choose your coffin' theme, Bogra initiated a campaign to introduce new product lines. Within this campaign, a survey of the clients' needs was carried out, a pre-trade show was organized and the company arranged representation at an international trade show. Bogra intentionally opted for these means. The overall campaign was supported by diverse media and means of communication.

Events that are used from a branding perspective may involve either internal or external branding. Internal branding may comprise not only internal events (employee training programmes) but also team-building events and events to increase employee involvement. Personnel is a valuable asset to an organization, it is a precondition to achieve its objectives, which is the subject of Chapter 6.

The Bogra example is an example of external branding: getting the Bogra brand to stick in the customer's mind. If customers (including potential customers) attend the presentation of the product and experience the coffin for themselves, then this will have an impact on the customer's brand associations, and it may even change his attitude towards the product.

EVENTS IN THE MARKETING MIX

Even though there are many different interpretations and applications, the marketing mix still constitutes the basis of the marketing policy of many companies. The four Ps (product, price, place and promotion) make up the foundation of the marketing mix, but other components can be added to the traditional marketing mix. A fifth P was added to the marketing mix at a later stage, the P for personnel, based on the idea that personnel contribute to marketing. The inclusion of event marketing in the marketing mix has produced the discipline matrix (see Fig. 3.2).

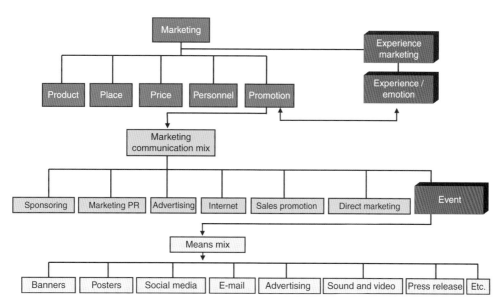

Fig. 3.2. Discipline matrix (source: Michels, 2006, adapted by the authors).

The discipline matrix is an expanded and updated version of the traditional marketing mix, with the addition of the fifth P for personnel. Furthermore, experience marketing and the attendant 'E' of emotion and experience are additional features. Experience marketing focuses on the subjective experiences and perceptions of consumers. The experience marketing parts are shown in shaded boxes, because they are tools that create live, three-dimensional (3-D) and all-senses experiences of the brand, the product or the service. As we have shown, event marketing is an appropriate tool to evoke sensations and emotions in consumers.

The event is shown in the marketing mix as one of the communication tools, apart from sponsoring, marketing PR, advertising, store communication, the Internet, direct marketing, sales promotion and personal sales. In event marketing, the event is the central point, which is supported by several means and channels of communication. The event can be regarded as a product. The purpose of the means and channels is to add strength to the event and also to extend the visitor experience. These means can be used in three phases:

- *The pre-exposure phase*: this is the phase that precedes the event, or series of events, in which visitors are encouraged to take part in or attend the event. The experience that is created during the event itself can also be spread out to the preliminary stage.
- *The direct exposure phase*: this phase involves the actual experience itself.
- *The post-exposure phase*: the phase after the event. What does the organization do to stay in touch with the visitor?

Figure 3.3 shows these phases in a diagram.

Fig. 3.3. Pre-, direct and post-exposure.

TYPES OF EVENT MARKETING

We distinguish different types of event marketing. The supplier may:

1. Conceive and organize the event himself (e.g. brand events, relationship events or brand venues).
2. Team up with an existing event.
3. Facilitate and/or finance the event: regional or national government bodies often host, facilitate and/or finance cultural or sporting events, by means of which they enter the arena of event marketing.

Conceiving and organizing an event of your own

Brand events

The 'Festival Anòlia Estrella Damm' (music festival from the beer brewery in Barcelona, Spain, in the old beer brewery) or the 'Audi Brand Event' are examples of brand events. At the Audi Brand Event, Audi organizes a dazzling show to launch its new A4 models, bringing to life the values of sportive, progressive and sophisticated. Due to the combination of audio-visual aspects, acts and entertainment, the overall concept exudes the core value of 'progression'. In this situation, Audi is the initiator, owner and main financier of the event.

So, brand events are events that revolve around a brand. Their organization may be in the hands of a professional event organizer. The sole purpose of the event is to create positive brand associations or reinforce existing brand associations. Through the event, closer ties must be forged with the target group, so that the brand becomes embedded even more strongly in their identity and lifestyle.

Brand events are organized to reach a specific target group, which is chosen on the basis of the brand values. The event provides for an experience in the target group, and its purpose is to increase brand familiarity and reinforce its image.

Brand venues

With its Heineken Music Hall and Holland Heineken House, Dutch beer brewer, Heineken, has created two powerful brand venues in its multi-channel strategy, which is a strategy aimed at communicating with the consumer through multiple channels. Heineken's objective is that the consumer comes into contact with the brand and experiences it. The associations that Heineken wishes to get across are conviviality and being together. A quick look at their website reveals that this involves, among other things, entertainment, music and sports.

Another interesting example is the Miele Inspirience Centres in Germany, MIC in short. As a manufacturer of high-end domestic appliances, Miele came to realize that customers were more inclined to purchase a product if they were given the opportunity of experiencing the product themselves. MIC is an inspiring showroom where cooking workshops and demonstrations are given and where conferences and seminars are organized on a regular basis.

In other words, brand venues are brand meeting places. They provide companies with the opportunity to establish a strong identity for their brand. Brand venues are also referred to with the term 'out-of-home marketing' and they fall within our definition of event marketing.

Relationship events

A good example of a relationship event which is centred around providing information to customers, as well as mobilizing customers, is the Pastrelli Relli: a car rally, driven in classic cars, organized especially for the main clients of Duyvis, a Dutch brand of salty snacks of PepsiCo International. Duyvis offered this rally to the contact persons of the headquarters of its main trading partners, to get them in the right mood and to get them to put Duyvis's new product, 'Pastrelli's', on their shelves. The event consisted of a teaser campaign in the preliminary stage and a rally with two pit stops. During the first pit stop, information was provided about the new product, and a second pit stop gave account managers the opportunity to have a chat with the contact persons (Gouden Giraffe entry, 2005, unpublished, adapted by the authors).

Relationship events are an excellent opportunity for the various parties involved to meet each other in a different setting, not only for a company's top clients, but also for future clients or stakeholders.

Internal branding (internal brand events)

The Italian fashion brand, Diesel, has set up its own internal branding programme, titled 'Diesel Love Power Experience', targeted at employees who handle customer contacts. The Diesel Love Power Experience was, in fact, an employee motivation training programme highlighting the relationship between employees and retailers – a relationship that is supposed to balance between Love (long-lasting and personal relationships) and Power (commercial success and free enterprise). The programme comprised several elements: an introduction training session, a personnel party, a team-building event, a performance interview and a goodbye party. The outcome was impressive: better relationship of the employees with Diesel; motivation to boost sales; open feedback culture, willingness towards personal growth; departure of employees who did not fit in with the company profile; more attention in the Customer Service Department to the relationship with retailers; and a wish to improve internal cooperation in the Sales Department.

To sum up, branding events are events to connect employees better with the brand, in order to improve business results in the long term, based on the idea that personnel are a critical factor in sales success.

Teaming up with an existing event

Sponsored events

An example of a sponsored event is the ABN AMRO World Tennis Tournament, which has been in existence for over 30 years. Sponsoring this event provides plenty of scope for the organization to foster relations with its target markets. ABN has developed special package deals to allow for live encounters with its target group. Other examples in this area include the Emirates Airline US Open Series (the famous tennis grand slam), Volvo Ocean Race and Red Bull Crashed Ice. What stands out is that these events are often sporting events; after all, sports is a pre-eminent platform for sharing and conveying emotions.

Sponsoring of events obviously presupposes interaction between the sponsor and the sponsored event. A sponsor provides money, goods, services and know-how. In exchange for this, the sponsored party commits itself to contributing to the achievement of the sponsor's communication objectives. Compared to other forms of marketing communication, this form has an indirect character. Sponsoring will only be effective if it is aligned properly with the other marketing communication tools of the organization. Events lend themselves well to sponsoring. Much the same as with brand events, a company can choose an event that evokes the right associations.

Box 3.4   Side events

The Nature Challenge, better known as 'Tiësto op de Maas', is a good example of a side event.

A couple of years ago, the Volvo Ocean Race had a stopover in Rotterdam, which gave rise to a series of side events to support the main event. Within this context, the city of Rotterdam commissioned a large-scale event, with the aim of bringing the Volvo Ocean Race and the Rotterdam stopover to the attention of a wider audience and to lift the programme during the Rotterdam stopover to a higher level. Moreover, the aim of this side event was to create a platform for companies, interested enough to invite clients and business partners, and which would offer them more than the sailing spectacle alone.

The result was the Nature Challenge: a multimedia spectacle featuring a 75-min concert by DJ Tiësto on a floating pontoon stage in the middle of the river Maas near the Cruise Terminal. The stage was a Volvo Ocean boat from a previous race, positioned on the pontoon. The port and skyline of Rotterdam played the leading part in this show. Tiësto played an exclusive DJ set, inspired by the stretches sailed by the boats participating in the Volvo Ocean Race; the atmosphere of the stretches was expressed in music, images, sounds and fragrances. Large screen projections on a couple of buildings by the river Maas supported the race images and the abstract atmosphere. Lighting, projections, fireworks and a laser show were all in synchrony with the music.

It was, in short, a very impressive spectacle, which generated substantial spin-off benefits for the city of Rotterdam. There were over 150,000 people on the quays. All in all, this event contributed positively to the image of Rotterdam as *the* event city of the Netherlands. (Source: Gouden Giraffe entry, 2007, unpublished, adapted by the authors.)

During events, a brand can also be present 'live', as a part of the main event. This can be done by using promotion teams. Chupa Chups promotion teams, for instance, hand out free lollipops at music events. Another example is the Glorix promotion team cleaning toilets – and making a grand display of it – at Mysteryland or other festivals.

A side event (Box 3.4) is a separate part of an existing bigger event. The supplier of the side event is not responsible for this bigger event, thus coasting along on the image that belongs to the main event, and the attendant target audience. Obviously, there has to be a clear link between the event visitor and the organization's target group.

Campaigns

Campaigns cause commotion. The intention is to generate a one-off lasting memorable experience that generates a lot of free publicity. The campaign may either be pushing the edge of what is acceptable or be entirely legal.

EDGE OF ACCEPTABILITY.   Ambush marketing refers to the practice of appearing to align a brand with an event for which that brand has not paid for the right to be a sponsor. Events that are very suitable for this purpose, in terms of the media attention they attract and their image, are the Olympic Games or the European or World Football Championships. An example in this respect is Bavaria, which was planning to hand out special 'Leeuwenhoses' to the audience attending a match of the Dutch football team in the run-up to the World Championships in Germany. The KNVB, however, already had a sponsorship agreement with Heineken, so that the special pairs of trousers did not make it past the stadium's entrance. Meanwhile, publicity for Bavaria was nevertheless created. Heineken had concocted a similar campaign 2 years earlier, during the European Football Championships in Portugal. Heineken horns were handed out to the audience, something that official sponsor Carlsberg was not particularly pleased with. At the World Championships in South Africa, Bavaria captured the media's attention with its Bavaria Babes. These ladies had entered the stadium as supporters of Denmark. In the second half, they caught everyone's attention, singing and dancing, after having changed to orange Bavaria dresses.

At the moment, laws are being developed which are supposed to make this type of ambush marketing impossible.

LEGAL.   Finding ways to associate their brand with an event does not necessarily require businesses to be present at the event itself; they can also organize other events themselves, centred around the theme of the main event. For example, a supermarket chain had a campaign that allowed customers to save for tickets to a concert, and a newspaper gave away tickets to a concert by Adele at the Royal Albert Hall in London. The 'Beesies' (small teddy bears) of Albert Heijn (AH; Dutch supermarket chain) is another example. Although AH had nothing to do with the organization of the World Football Championships 2010, it managed to tie in with the 'football feeling' with its 'Beesies' campaign. In 2008, AH also started sponsoring premier league football. In this way, AH is connecting its name with sports and health, as a result of which a link is established between the brand name and the emotions associated with football matches and football in general. The alliance also offers new possibilities for customer campaigns.

Relationship events

BNP Paribas offers its most important clients a Roland Garros Tennis Tournament VIP package. Being a sponsor of Roland Garros, BNP Paribas had an excellent opportunity to organize a range of hospitality events for its clients. These relationship events all take place during the Roland Garros Tennis Tournament. In other words, Roland Garros is an existing event, which triggers all kinds of other smaller events.

Internal branding events

We have already discussed internal branding events earlier. Internal events can be part of an existing event. In the example of the Roland Garros Tennis Tournament, it is possible for BNP Paribas to develop a programme for its own staff members. Staff members may then visit tennis matches and listen to various lectures from the management of BNP Paribas. The aim of BNP Paribas in this example may be team building or employee loyalty and/or commitment.

Hosting, facilitating or financing an event

National, regional and local government bodies may decide to host not only large-scale sporting events, such as Giro d'Italia, the Vuelta a España or the Tour de France, but also cultural events, dance events or international conferences. If these events are employed purposefully and strategically and supported by a government, then this falls into our definition of event marketing.

Event marketing has several forms of manifestation, with underlying objectives. The ultimate goal is to ensure business continuity and generate profits. Events are not always organized because of an economic objective; they can also create enabling conditions. The right goals have to be pursued in a well-considered manner, and it also has to be determined which goals can be achieved by means of which type of event.

The classification we apply is obviously not the only classification possible. In practice, all kinds of combinations are possible.

THE POWER OF EVENTS AND EVENT MARKETING

The use of events is gaining in popularity in many different variations, as has been seen above. But how can one explain the fact that companies or cities purposefully use events as a strategic choice? To be able to answer this question, we need to look at the power of events and their advantages and disadvantages. Experiences, emotions and values are becoming increasingly important in society today. The emergence of event marketing is a logical phenomenon within this development. The event is a means that can evoke sensations and emotions, thanks to:

- the direct contact
- the possibility of interaction
- the emotions and sensations that are evoked, together with the impact the event has

- the possibility to increase customer loyalty and to engage in networking
- the possibility of conveying a message in a very targeted manner.

THE ADVANTAGES OF EVENT MARKETING

Due to the possibility of immediate interaction with the target group, the supplier of an event can also take immediate action when something is not in order – the music is too loud or the food is too cold.

The setting of an event takes people away from their everyday work environment. An informal get-together presents opportunities to get to know each other in a different way. This may lead to situations that would never occur in the everyday work environment.

Interaction is also connected with experiencing things. During the event, the customer takes part in communication, he participates in the event; this is referred to as experience communication. Thanks to the direct experience (sensation), the impact of communication will be greater. The visitors of an event participate and can learn from what they experience. Being in dialogue with other people is a part of interaction; the supplier, as a representative of the brand, and the customers (including potential customers) exchange opinions and ideas about the product. This is the biggest advantage of an event: direct, face-to-face communication. The participants have the opportunity for an encounter (due to efficient programming), they are interested in the programme of the event (or else they would not have come) and they are capable of understanding the message (which makes them easily influenced by the supplier).

Personalized approach

A company wants to get some kind of message across about its own brand. Successful communication of this message will have a positive influence on the knowledge, attitude and maybe even the behaviour of the target group. No immediate results are expected, but the event is a means to approach the consumer in a personal manner. The message can be communicated very clearly and the setting of an event allows for taking immediate action in the event of any obscurities. It is even possible to work on the relationship with the customer. Companies expect their events to leave a positive impression, as a result of which the relationship will improve (see Chapter 4).

Integrated communication

Events can be combined very adequately with other media and means of communication. Whereas in the past events used to focus on the 'fun' aspect, today much greater emphasis is placed on content, integrated communication (cross-media) and the application of new media. Furthermore, under the influence of new media, the importance of personal encounters – personal contacts with business partners, clients and prospects – is growing.

Apart from the preliminary and subsequent stages, the event offers plenty of other communication opportunities.

Being different

With event marketing, through the choice of a certain type of event, a message can be conveyed to one or several target groups in a very targeted manner. The characteristics of the event can be fully aligned with the target group(s). So, the client determines who is invited to the event and which target group the event will focus on, to avoid unwanted guests showing up and to make sure that all money is directed towards useful marketing efforts. Business-to-consumer events are an exception in this respect. Marketing campaigns focusing on a specific target group will yield much greater returns than an undirected campaign focusing on a vague target group. As opposed to printed media (such as advertisements or brochures), the event is a means to combine different target groups and different objectives.

Generating purposeful attention

If you want to get through to the consumer, regular means of communication hardly suffice any more. Too many messages are fired at consumers all the time, so they no longer take any notice. An attractive and original event can draw consumer attention. This is where event marketing is different from traditional, regular means of communication, which are often no longer fit for purpose. The event is a live and 3-D medium, with lots of possibilities for making a product or brand attractive. Senses play an important role in this respect. Scent machines, for instance, can be used to disperse the scent of grass, to evoke a spring feeling. The beat frequency in music can either create a thrill, a buzz or a quiet and harmonious ambiance. The event sector is also becoming increasingly aware of what coloured lights can do to create a certain mood.

Unleashing emotions

Interpersonal relations are based on emotions. During an event, emotions can be unleashed to make visitors more approachable. More often than not, there are 'unknown' aspects of a person's character to be discovered. It is also possible to evoke group effects deliberately for the purpose of intensifying the experience. The 'aaaaah' reaction from the crowd when the Red Bull stunt pilots flew right along the Statue of Liberty in New York is one example.

Building networking opportunities

The presence of other guests at an event may be reason enough for some people to come to the event, too. Despite the fact that people can get in touch at any time, seeing each other in person continues to be important. The informal aspect plays a role here, too. People who have good relations with a company may act as ambassadors in contexts of this sort.

Appealing to trade journalists

Events are perfectly suited to involving trade journals. An event that offers a product or brand experience will generate more press attention than, for instance, a new brochure or advertising of the product or brand. Moreover, it is possible to engage in two-way communication at events.

THE DISADVANTAGES OF EVENT MARKETING

One-offness

A major disadvantage of an event is that it usually involves just that one moment when everything that had been planned so carefully in advance comes together. The execution of the event is bound by a certain time limit. Will the concept be expressed well? Will guests experience the event as exuberantly as it was meant to be? Will the programme be effective? In other words, errors of judgement can be made at any point, which will have a huge impact on the message that was supposed to be communicated. In addition, influences from outside can interfere with the event. Consequently, there is a certain risk involved in the use of events. Experienced event organizers will try to eliminate risks as much as possible by means of their expertise, their ability to convert well-considered objectives into one all-embracing concept and a well-balanced programme. What is more, they will go about their projects in a systematic manner, making adjustments as and when necessary. Very accurate planning, especially in the case of an integrated approach, is an important prerequisite.

Costs

It is commonly known that the use of an event in the form of a project is a costly affair. Personnel have to be freed up in the preliminary stage, and as the event nears, the number of work-hours required increases dramatically. An event is a very labour-intensive matter and can have a great impact on an organization. Without a professional approach, the costs can get out of hand. Costs per contact are considerably higher compared to other means of communication, such as flyers, direct mailing, newsletters and banners on sites.

Complexity

Some events are not even possible without external expertise and support. Technological advancements have led to a higher degree of professionalism of events. Just a few years ago, using a website in the preliminary stage was not something that was normally done. Today, you are nobody if you do not have a website. This development has repercussions across a range of business sectors: security, communication, logistics, audio-visual aspects, and so on. It is almost impossible to be a specialist in all these areas. That is why events are increasingly contracted out to experienced professionals.

THE STRATEGIC USE OF EVENTS

Is it always possible to use events? When will event marketing actually help to achieve certain objectives? What are the dos and don'ts of event marketing? Theoretical and practical research has generated a number of key questions that need to be answered in advance.

1. What is the objective, originating from the organization's strategic policy?
2. What is the message that has to be conveyed?
3. Who is the target group?
4. Which tools, means and media are best suited to achieve the objective?

Objective

Formulating objectives is part of the process of developing a corporate strategic policy. The first question is, of course: what are these objectives? The objectives must be measurable. Objectives such as 'creating a memorable experience', 'customer retention', 'building and expanding relationships' or one of the goals mentioned in the earlier section on the reasons to opt for event marketing may lead to the decision to use events as a means.

Message

The second important question that an organization has to ask itself is: what is the message? The message has to be formulated very clearly, because it is the point of departure for many activities. The objective(s) and the message can be transformed into an event concept and design. In this process, the marketer has to be able to empathize with the visitor. Only then will it be possible to create meaningful experiences.

Target market

It is also important to analyse the interests, needs and values of your target market. What is important in the choice of an event is the specific target group that has to be reached. Is an event actually the best choice? To obtain an accurate insight into the choice of the target group(s), a customer pyramid is a useful tool (see Chapter 4). Successful event marketing involves a personal approach to the target market, interaction between the target market and the brand. The target group has to be able to relate to the values of the brand or the company.

Tools, means and media

If the use of an event turns out to be the best choice, then this involves a market-oriented approach. If the event is the means or one of the means from the marketing mix, then the organization will have to ask itself which marketing communication tools and means can be integrated in order to add strength to the message and the objective. In this case, event marketing is part of the marketing communication policy; the event can be integrated with, for instance, the Internet, sponsoring or printed media. We have already written that events are also a good tool for free publicity.

The choice for an event

The choice to use an event is dependent on several factors, some of which have already been dealt with:

- the objective
- the target group
- the event's expected contribution to the objective
- the available alternatives in the area of marketing communication tools, means and media
- the level of support within the organization
- the level of feasibility within the organization (for instance, know-how and sufficient support)
- the risks involved in organizing an event
- the time path
- the costs.

When every aspect has been considered, a budget allocation of the marketing means can be drawn up and an activation budget can be requested in time in the company.

Customization

An event must be custom-designed. If event marketing is used in the most optimal way, the objective and the message will be converted to an event concept and design in a creative and authentic manner. The event concept and design also comprise the organization's core values. They also ensure that as many senses as possible are appealed to, for the purpose of a multi-sensory experience. The event is easily accessible and either formal or informal, and apart from entertainment aspects, it offers depth and meaning. During the entire process, in the phases of pre-exposure, direct exposure and post-exposure, there must be a link with the values that have been elaborated to the smallest detail. The quality of the event and the integrated means mix (see Fig. 3.2) must be strictly monitored, and there must be regular feedback.

Follow-up

The effect of an event has to be measured in order to be able to determine its return on investment (ROI). Successful event management requires a long-term view, in addition to effective cooperation between client and contractor. This will allow for constant monitoring within a track in which all marketing communication tools have been integrated. The event will then be the biggest live marketing communication tool, creating a dynamic balance together with the other marketing communication tools. Effect measurement and event evaluation will be dealt with extensively in Chapter 10 and the Appendices.

EVENT MARKETING: DOS AND DON'TS

Event marketing is in a state of flux. Attention to the dos and don'ts is therefore essential (see Table 3.1).

Table 3.1. Dos and don'ts of event marketing.

Dos	Don'ts
Objectives	**Objectives**
Measurable	Absent or unclear
Creating memorable experiences; building customer loyalty; developing and expanding relationships	Zero priority in the budget
	Underestimating required time and means
	Not enough internal support or not enough appreciation by management
	Event manager operates separately from strategic level
	Not a means to achieve a higher end
Target group	**Target group**
Analysing the target group (know, serve and trust the customer)	No target group analysis or interest survey
Personal approach	Passive rather than active participation
Interaction between target group and brand	
Identification with values	
Creating experiences, room for development (changes in knowledge, attitude and behaviour)	
Message	**Message**
Live meaningful communication and entertainment, engaging and stimulating the target group	No stimulating message
Means	Means
Event marketing is an integrated element within the total set of marketing communication tools to add strength to the objective and the message	Choosing the 'safe' way of traditional means

(Continued)

Table 3.1. Continued.

Dos	Don'ts
Timely budget request	No dynamic integration with other marketing communication means, low impact factor
Event	**Event**
Zero measurement (possibly)	Ad hoc engagement of event organization agencies
Every event is custom-designed	Company's core values are not reflected
Creative and authentic translation of the concept	No connection with other means
Engaging professional event organization agency, if necessary	Event manager is placed too low in the organization or not on a strategic level
Core values are interwoven in the event and all senses are stimulated	
Easy access and informal, some degree of depth/meaning	Not enough appreciation by and involvement of the management as regards the execution of the event
Elaborating everything to the smallest detail	
Always a link between objective, message, values and event	
Follow-up	**Follow-up**
Carrying out effect measurement for ROI, monitoring	Too many people involved, too many needs/wishes
Long-term cooperation, evaluation, feedback and adjustment	Failure of the event has major consequences for the image

SUMMARY

Events are used more and more often as a live means of communication. Event marketing is the discipline where marketing, events and communication come together. In this respect, one can identify a development from product orientation towards communication orientation. Experience marketing provides for memorable experiences, an emotional added value which the customer is asking for. The event can be regarded as a communication platform within the developments in the area of marketing communication.

The event has a place of its own in the marketing mix as a communication tool, in addition to, for instance, sponsoring, the Internet and advertising. We distinguish three types of event marketing. An event can be an event in itself, it can be part of a bigger event or it can be facilitated by regional or national governments.

There are many advantages to event marketing, including the personal approach, integrated communication and the opportunity to interest trade journalists. Disadvantages may be: the one-offness, the costs involved and the complexity.

For a strategic use of events, it is obviously important to determine accurately the objective and the target group. An event must always involve customization.

chapter 4

Events and Customer Relationship Marketing

Dorothé Gerritsen and Ronald van Olderen

The central theme of this chapter is the role of events in relationship marketing. After a brief sketch of the history of this form of marketing, we will discuss the three Rs: reputation, relationships and reciprocity. Next, we will focus extensively on relationship events. We will finish the chapter with an analysis of the limits to customer relationship marketing.

LEARNING TARGETS

After studying this chapter, you will have learned:

- how relationship marketing emerged
- what relationship marketing is
- in what way events are used in relationship marketing
- why events are used for relationship marketing purposes
- what the limits are to using events in relationship marketing.

A quick browse of the Internet will tell you that social communities are gaining in popularity. Examples of communities can be found in diverse areas: the Mazda MX-5 Club; sector organizations; football supporters; experts in the field of marketing, communication, events, and so on and so forth. The number of LinkedIn members – a professional networking site – is growing. People feel a need to connect with like-minded people and to share experiences with each other. Within these communities, events are often used for the purpose of virtual as well as live meetings. The Mazda MX-5 Club often organizes tours for its members. Sector organizations such as MPI (Meeting Planners International) or IFEA (International Festivals and Events Organization) meet their members at New Year receptions and conferences. In this way, networks are maintained, updated or built through various virtual and live channels.

Organizations and companies too have become aware of the value of good customer relationships and of communities. More and more often, they incorporate systematic networking strategies into their policy frameworks; which is referred to as customer relationship management. Organizations have come to realize the necessity of regarding customers as partners, and thus of building new customer relationships as well as intensifying existing relationships. Existing customers require less attention and energy from an organization than customers yet to be acquired. Binding customers to your company, product or service plays a crucial role in this respect, aiming to increase the customer's loyalty to the company or organization. But, the question is: what role do events play in this process? The following example (Box 4.1) will show how SNS REAAL (a Dutch banking and insurance service provider) has designed an event to get in touch with an important partner group, the intermediaries, who are responsible for a crucial portion of the sales of REAAL products and services.

Box 4.1   Relationship marketing at SNS REAAL

SNS REAAL is an innovative service provider in the banking and insurance sector, with a prime focus on the Dutch retail market and on small and medium-sized enterprises. It has a balance sheet total of more than €124 billion and some 8000 staff members. SNS REAAL consists of SNS Bank, REAAL Verzekeringen (REAAL insurances) and Zwitserleven. REAAL offers a comprehensive range of flexible and reliable insurance products to both business and consumer markets. The company has a realistic view of insurances and operates exclusively via intermediaries. Product leadership is the company's main focus, with the aim of creating innovative products and ensuring excellent administrative handling and support. Most of REAAL Verzekeringen's communication is handled through intermediaries (REAAL's primary distribution channel). A study carried out by REAAL demonstrated that the intermediaries were losing a portion of their distribution to direct writers (including Internet suppliers) and banks, due to shifting channels and changing consumer behaviour. Furthermore, it turned out that the REAAL intermediaries were not entirely familiar with the support that REAAL offered in terms of marketing and that they had a need for support (customization), especially in the area of know-how. In order to be able to position themselves as the 'partner in business' for marketing consultants, REAAL organized a marketing event: an event game to increase the intermediaries' awareness of the changing environment and the opportunities that still existed in terms

(Continued)

Box 4.1. Continued.

of the employment of marketing tools. According to REAAL, an event offers interactive possibilities for its participants to experience for themselves what opportunities there are. *Awareness* and *experience* are supposed to give the intermediary the feeling that REAAL is *the* partner in business.

The intermediaries of REAAL (top potentials, core and potentials) were invited by means of a personal e-mail (in keeping with the marketing concept of 'know your customer' and 'use several communication channels to reach your customer'). The company made sure that the event was imbued with its core values and the event fulfilled the objectives formulated in advance in various ways. The game that was developed as a part of the event was especially consistent with the image of REAAL as a realistic insurer: REAAL is alert because it keeps a close eye on market conditions, as well as trends and developments in society. At the event, a marketing film was played, showing consumers' capricious buying behaviour, the distribution channels that consumers use, their 'zapping' behaviour and so on. A presentation was given to explain the importance of sound marketing. A marketing simulation game gave participants a live experience of which strategies might boost their contract portfolios. The execution of the event was consistent with REAAL's image and national campaign. The company deliberately opted for a non-everyday setting, the Gashouder in Amsterdam, and a specific marketing-oriented programme, interlaced with spectacular show elements.

The evaluation carried out afterwards revealed that the intermediaries appreciated the event and that they gained new ideas in the area of marketing – ideas which they said they were going to put into action. All in all, the event improved the capacity of REAAL's staff members to get in touch with this particular client group. (Source: Gouden Giraffe entry, 2004, unpublished; and www.snsbank.nl, accessed November 2010, adapted by the authors.)

THE EMERGENCE OF CUSTOMER RELATIONSHIP MARKETING

Within marketing, there has been a shift from transaction-oriented thinking towards an approach that focuses on building and maintaining relationships. In Chapter 3, we said that, traditionally, marketing was about a transaction with an anonymous target group, without any preceding or following action, with the emphasis on attracting new customers. Price was always the most important component (price competition). A price that came about in a competitive market comprised all the essential information for both parties in order to accomplish the exchange. So, marketing activities were centred around an ad hoc transaction and the ensuing exchange of a good or service against money. The customers were mostly anonymous. Marketing was, in other words, thinking up a good campaign for a target group. The four Ps – price, place, product and promotion – had a central place within transaction marketing. Nowadays, extra Ps have been added to the marketing mix, including personnel and politics.

Transaction marketing is about earning money as quickly as possible, here and now. There is no long-term view. What is lacking in this approach is attention for meaningful, lasting customer relationships.

Making profit from a transaction became increasingly difficult due to the increasing competition between suppliers, which at the same time made it more difficult to attract and retain customers. As a result, the nature of the relationship between suppliers and consumers changed: a shift occurred from the transaction focus – attracting customers and thinking in terms of market share – towards a focus on building and maintaining relationships, retaining customers and thinking in terms of customer share. When a company invests in customer loyalty, it will need fewer new customers. Whenever it has new products or services to offer, this company can focus on its existing customers. All in all, there have been a number of events and developments in both the internal and external environment that have led to a shift in focus from transactions towards relationships. What this also entails for companies is spending more time with their customers, and this is done largely through events. Sometimes, a company teams up with an existing event or sports event; the Sony Open in Hawaii or the Rolex 24 at Daytona (USA) are two examples. On the other hand, devising and developing events of your own, for customers and business partners, is also a possibility.

EXPLANATORY DEVELOPMENTS

In this section, we will present an overview of the developments that account for the importance of relationship marketing and the role of events. Events are a magnificent tool for maintaining relationships. Meeting customers and communicating with them face-to-face in a leisure or business setting provides an organization with plenty of starting points for setting up an efficient relationship marketing policy.

Growing competition

Relationship marketing is growing in importance because markets have become a lot more transparent and because it has become easier for consumers to compare prices. The world in which we live is getting smaller and smaller, so to speak. Distances are no longer of any significance. A trip to America or Asia used to be a major and time-consuming undertaking, but today you just take the plane, which will bring you to your destination in less than no time. Thanks to new media and the Internet, relevant information is available to almost everyone. European companies have started looking for cheaper manufacturing operations and markets outside Europe. The result is that the degree of competition is increasing.

Technological advancements

Freedom of choice has increased, due to technological advancements. It is becoming increasingly difficult for companies to set themselves and their products apart from the competition. Technology does not stand still and new technologies are easily available and transferable. That is why there is an overwhelming diversity of products and services that are often very much alike and are well matched in terms of quality. The necessity of the consumer remaining loyal to a particular company is getting smaller as a result. Unparalleled freedom of choice and less distinction between products are the reasons why consumers have less pronounced preferences for a certain product variety and move between suppliers more easily.

The necessity to be loyal and/or stay with the same company, after all, is not that great, unless the supplier is capable of building direct and structural relationships with its customers. Companies can do so, for instance, by means of event marketing, relationship marketing and a well thought-out branding strategy (for branding, see Chapter 6).

Technological developments in the area of communication

Developments in the area of information technology offer marketers more and more scope for conveying their message to the individual consumer. Using traditional as well as new media, marketers can bring about a higher degree of interaction with consumers. Consumers are exposed to a lot of impressions and information. This information overkill has made consumers weary, to the extent that they are beginning to tune out information they do not want. They have become more critical in selecting information that is relevant to them.

Technological developments have also lowered communication costs with customers for businesses and organizations. Presently, it is possible to buy databases at a very low cost and fill them with accurate and up-to-date information. The decreasing costs have made it easier for companies to anticipate individual needs and desires.

Individualization

As a result of the individualization of society, marketers are struggling to find ways to approach individuals, who can no longer be regarded as members of a homogeneous group. We all have our own specific preferences and we want to be spoken to about matters that interest us. It is therefore getting harder to segregate the market on the basis of the traditional segregation criteria, which fail to accommodate individual needs, while consumers today are expecting to be approached and treated in a personalized manner. The purchase of a product or service continues to be important, but the process that follows the purchase is increasing in importance, too. To minimize dissatisfaction after the purchase, companies have to stay in touch with their customers. One might even say that the actual marketing process does not start until after the purchase process.

The necessity of direct communication

Owing to the developments outlined above, the emphasis is shifting towards customer retention. It is not the power of mass communication that is important here, but direct communication with the consumer. The focus of marketing is therefore shifting from the product

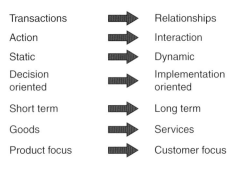

to the organization itself. Short-term thinking has made way for a strategic view, in which the company is a decisive factor for customers. The new generation of marketers no longer thinks in terms of customers, but in terms of relationships. Where the four Ps were centred primarily on promotion (transaction thinking), in the future, relationships will become pivotal (see Fig. 4.1). The ultimate goal will obviously still be the exchange or the transaction itself, but the exchange or transaction will be accomplished on the basis of good customer relationships.

Fig. 4.1. From transaction marketing to relationship marketing (source: van Kempen, 2005).

FROM THE 4 Ps TO THE 3 Rs

We have already shown that the four Ps are no longer adequate in terms of customer retention; they merely offer a tactical advantage. The three Rs stand for reputation, reciprocity and relationships. They constitute a strategic counterpart to facilitate real customer-centric operations.

Figure 4.2 shows a model based on the relationship between an organization and its customers, regardless of what type of organization. One example would be a company like AXA, a major global insurance company, which interacts with customers who have taken out an insurance policy with them, or a professional football organization like FC Barcelona, which maintains relations with sponsors.

Reputation

Reputation is based on the way people think and talk about the organization concerned, both inside and outside the organization. What do people say about the organization? The image of the organization in the eyes of others can be decisive to the organization's success. A good reputation will attract people, including potential customers. We will illustrate the importance of reputation by means of an example concerning a client and a contractor (an event agency).

Satis&Fy, one of the leading full-service production companies in Europe, is selling a concept for an event to Levi Strauss. When the exchange has taken place or, in other words, when Levi's has instructed the agency to elaborate and execute the concept, Levi's may decide to assign the agency another event project. In this way, a relationship arises between the client and the contractor. In this respect, it is crucial that the client's expectations, in this case the expectations of

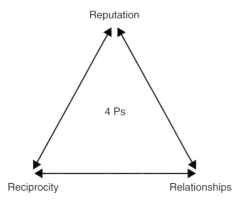

Fig. 4.2. Reputation, reciprocity and relationships (source: Storm, 1992).

Levi's, are exceeded every time. The relationship thus developed may confirm the event agency's reputation, which completes the circle.

A good relationship does not always need to begin with an organization's reputation, which is not what the model of the three Rs in Fig. 4.2 implies either. After all, it is also possible for a customer to have a positive experience with a supplier, giving his image of this supplier a positive influence, which may result in a lasting relationship. The three Rs are bound inextricably with each other and support each other.

Reputation does not come by accident. If an organization has opted for relationship marketing, this will require a certain line of approach: start thinking in terms of relationships instead of transactions. The people inside an organization must be fully aware of the fact that customer-centric operations are an absolute necessity and everyone must act accordingly. Computer systems are available for this purpose. A database, or customer relationship management system (CRM system) containing customer data, is a good place to start, but it is not the only possibility. It is the employees who will have to get things done, and to this end, their mode of action will have to change. An organization may have the most sophisticated computer systems in the world, containing every conceivable piece of information on its customers, but if it really wants to put this information to optimal use, its employees – especially those who have direct contact with customers – will have to act appropriately. Customer relationships cannot be imposed; they have to be invited from inside the organization. One way of putting it is that the personnel of a company has to fit like a glove with the company's DNA. This is the key ingredient for a good reputation. Moreover, reputation is something that is determined by customers. This does not mean that once a good relationship has been built, it will continue for all eternity. Companies will have to prove themselves over and over again. The customer's expectations will have to be fulfilled – and even exceeded. With the advent of the three Rs, the four Ps have not become superfluous; they make up the foundations on which the 3R model rests. If the visitors' needs are not satisfied, during or after an event, then the relationship will not be formed, let alone a good reputation.

Relationships

A customer is someone with whom an exchange is accomplished, based on a one-off activity. Diller's definition aptly describes the characteristics of a relationship:

> A relationship is an interactive process between a buyer and a seller, which involves the purchase and use of goods and/or services, which is driven by economic and non-economic goals, and which is direct, integrative and concerns more than one transaction.
>
> (Schijns, 2000)

Apparently, a relationship implies a person with whom a connection is established through an interactive process, and this connection is of a higher order than the transaction itself. A relationship does not even have to be driven by economic goals. Relationships occur in a wide variety of forms: potential customers, customers, local residents, government bodies, suppliers, stakeholders, employees. The interactive process is decisive, since relationships have a behavioural as well as an experiential dimension. The effects of the interactive process depend on the factual contacts, and on the subjective assessment of those contacts. This is the reason why a company can lose a pitch – in which a spectacular concept for an event is presented – despite a long-existing relationship with a client. The pitch was good, but the click just was not there.

The why of relationships

Relationships are based on mutual benefits. A relationship must bring benefits to both the company and the customer. Organizations would do well to focus on specific customers:

- customers that strengthen the organization's reputation
- customers who are appropriate to the organization's knowledge and skills.

Entering into a relationship produces three advantages: interaction, understanding and stability.

First, interaction is important. A customer can give feedback on the company's performance, in both a positive and a negative sense. Negative feedback produces input to do better the next time; for instance, to fine-tune certain processes or to maximize contact intensity. Positive feedback can be important in establishing whether or not the company has listened well to the customer's needs and whether or not all of the customer's objectives have been achieved. The most important thing is that contacts between customer and company are maintained and that both parties keep talking to each other without reproaching each other. What is worse than a client who says that everything is all right but who thinks the opposite?

Second, sustained contacts between a potential customer and a supplier will give both parties a better insight into the business operations. What does the company stand for; what are its core values; what kind of people does the company employ? There are numerous questions that are not given any thought whenever a new exchange takes place. The know-how of the company is taken into consideration. This will increase efficiency.

Third, and thanks to relationship marketing, customers will be less inclined to turn to competitors. Loyal customers are less sensitive to the advances of other parties or the possibility of a lower price.

Reciprocity

Reciprocity is what it is all about. The company's reputation and relationships may be excellent, but if there is no exchange, it will endanger its business continuity. The exchange not only must take place but also it must leave behind a positive feeling and confirm the company's reputation, especially so after the actual transaction. Just think of the evaluation of an event, after-sales care, effective complaints handling and quick and correct answering of questions.

EVENTS AND CUSTOMER RELATIONSHIP MARKETING

Through live encounters with, for instance, wonderful music, sensational theatre and strong catering concepts, it is possible to engage people emotionally. As a result, events are very suitable for use within a relationship marketing strategy.

Rather than making a profit on the transaction, relationship marketing is concerned primarily with making a profit on the relationship. This profit can be achieved only through exchanges with existing customers. In some cases, individual transactions will be loss making. But, the aim of relationship marketing is building a profitable relationship. Relationship marketing involves satisfying and retaining customers in order to maximize the customer's lifelong value to the company in terms of profit.

We apply the following definition of relationship marketing.

> An integrated effort of the organization in order to identify, maintain and build a network with individual consumers, and continuously reinforce that network, to the advantage of both parties, by means of interactive, individualized and value-adding contacts that relate to several, successive transactions.
>
> (Schijns, 2000)

Customer satisfaction and long-term relationships are generated through the interaction between marketing, quality and the provision of service to customers. High-quality services are a condition for attracting and retaining customers.

As well as being the result of marketing, quality and service, relationship marketing is also a tool to build customer loyalty.

There are many relationship marketing tools, but it is always difficult to capture precisely why a customer turns to the competition. Research has shown that decisions regarding business transactions are often made on emotional grounds. This means that tools to influence the feelings, experiences and opinions of customers are becoming increasingly important.

THE TARGET GROUP

Within a relationship marketing strategy, events are organized purposefully for a certain target group, which may be either an internal or an external target group. After all, organizations must not only develop relationships with existing and potential customers but also with suppliers, employees and influencers. If Levi Strauss, for instance, is planning to organize an event for its clients, then this not only involves its existing clients but also other interest groups on which Levi Strauss as a business depends. To offer added value to its customers, an organization also needs good relations with interest groups and external parties. Good relations with, for instance, a caterer may be decisive to the success of Levi Strauss's relationship event.

A concept will be more consistent if the organizations involved know each other and know how the other party operates. A shortage of drinks at a party, for example, can be solved by a telephone call to the company's own supplier, or another supplier with whom the company has good relations. It goes without saying that, as the relationship grows more intense, the parties involved will be willing to do more for each other. Even when an event has to be cancelled, good relations with one's suppliers can do wonders, such as an event planner charging only 50% of the cancellation costs instead of the full 100%. This is an example of the advantages that good relationship marketing can produce.

In relationship events, we distinguish the following target groups: prospects, customers, suppliers, competitors, influencers and employees. We will explain briefly each of these target groups in the following sections.

Prospects and customers

Establishing good relations with prospects and customers is priority number one. In the end, it is customers who make the company profitable. Furthermore, customers play a crucial role in spreading a business's reputation. When customers talk about your company in a positive way, they are an indirect source for potential new customers.

Suppliers

Organizations often work with subcontractors or suppliers. Good relations with one's suppliers often produce the greatest possible competitive advantages. Closer ties can be forged by, for instance, inviting these parties to the opening of a new office or a year-end closing party. Through events of this kind, the company shows its appreciation, which in turn may lead to greater synergy and closer collaboration.

Competitors

It is possible for competitors to work together. Take, for example, three companies pitching for an event. Rather than trying to edge each other out, they may choose to join forces based on each other's expertise, in order to design and organize the event together. It is not uncommon to invite competitors to informal gatherings.

Influencers

Government

Representatives of local or provincial government authorities are often invited to official functions, such as the opening of a new building or a first pile ceremony for a new construction project.

Financial institutions

It is very important to develop and maintain relations with financiers. The events to which financiers are invited will create a positive image for the company among the parties concerned. Members of financial interest groups, such as shareholders and members of the board, may also be invited to informal gatherings.

For instance, SNS Bank regularly organizes SNS Fundcoach evenings for its private investors. At these evenings, SNS Bank tells participants about the latest developments in portfolio management, strategies to be pursued and 'treasures' in the market. The primary goal of SNS Fundcoach evenings is to weave closer ties with private investors. The ultimate goal is for the parties involved to step up their investment activity (buying and selling investment products).

Press

The press play an important role in terms of event reporting. The news value that is generated by an event may help to achieve the event's objectives. So, it is important for a company to build good relations with the press and invite journalists to its events. A journalist will focus primarily on what is considered news value to the target group of the medium for which he works (see Chapter 5).

Box 4.2

A good example of a strategically used event for the purpose of generating maximum free publicity is the Grazia PC Catwalk in the upmarket PC Hooftstraat in Amsterdam. On an impressive 320-m catwalk, models showed outfits of top fashion labels. Thousands of spectators and hundreds of Dutch celebrities, *fashionistas* and other interested people came to the Netherlands' most famous shopping street to watch the special fashion show, organized by Mynth Events by order of Fashion & Museum District and *Grazia*, a weekly glossy magazine. Featuring clothes by Mulberry, D&G, Cosmic Cowboys, Oger, John and Vera Hartman and McGregor, the show was a feast for the eyes. Fashion labels for sale in the street's shops were presented on the catwalk in an original manner. Both existing and

(Continued)

Box 4.2. Continued.

potential customers were involved in the event. The innovative appearance attracted a young and trendy target audience. The show was covered by national radio and TV, as well as several Dutch newspapers.

This event was organized to increase name familiarity with PC Hooftstraat among the target group (including the potential target group) and to create a lower threshold image for PC Hooftstraat, with the emphasis on young people. Attendant objectives were generating national publicity, creating a buzz regarding the rejuvenation of PC Hooftstraat and attracting Dutch celebrities. Despite the limited means available, the organizers managed to present an innovative concept, and the objectives set were easily achieved. The facts and figures speak for themselves: front-page coverage in *Telegraaf*, the presence of 50 Dutch celebrities, €150,000 worth of free publicity, a satisfied client, PC Hooftstraat crowded with visitors, photographers and journalists. (Source: www.gouden-giraffe.nl, jury report 2009, accessed September 2010, adapted by the authors.)

Employees

Employees make up the foundation of every organization. Employees, and sometimes their partners and/or children, too, can be invited to the annual personnel party. In this way, a company can express its appreciation for the achievements of its employees over the past year.

An example of an event for employees is a gathering following a corporate takeover, an opportunity for employees of both sides to get to know each other and for synergy to be created.

CUSTOMER SEGMENTATION

Acquiring knowledge of one's customers is essential in relationship marketing. An event can be organized more efficiently when more information is available on the target group concerned. Nearly all organizations that are interested in developing and maintaining direct relations with their customers and stakeholders engage in customer relationship management (CRM). CRM is a corporate strategy that has taken a huge leap forward over the past few years. CRM involves gathering, storing and analysing – in a structural and continuous manner – information on individual customers in order to be able to develop and evaluate marketing activities specifically geared to these customers. IT applications and databases make up the basis for using this information. CRM processes affect the organization as a whole: marketing, IT, logistics, finances, production and development, human resources and management. That is why a CRM strategy must provide direction to every department or function within the company, taking the customer as a starting point.

These are the pillars of CRM:

1. Customer knowledge.
2. Customer relationship strategy.
3. Communication.
4. Individualized value proposition.

Customer knowledge

Knowledge of customers is indispensable in developing long-lasting relationships and delivering customized products and services. In this respect, it is important to record not only standard data but also emotional data on the customer.

Customer databases are generally very big and diversified. Organizing databases of this kind requires proper registration and segmentation.

Registration of standard data

What most customer databases contain are standard details, such as *individual data* – name, address, place of residence, additional details on the factual customer, sales, frequencies and times of purchase – and *demographic data* – the data required to identify certain groups.

Emotional data

What is often missing in databases are *emotional data*: information on the values, attitudes, motives and social environments of customers, and other matters that go beyond individual characteristics. These types of data are essential in organizing a relationship event.

Behaviour and experience are crucial elements in relationships. The effect of a live encounter determines whether or not the visitor is satisfied with the event. The subjective assessment of the event obviously plays a decisive role. Did the event meet the client's expectations? Did it appeal to the deeper motives of the person in question? In other words, it is about knowing what really moves people.

Suppose you are invited to a birthday party. You are not sure yet what to bring as a present and you are considering the regular gift range: a book, a DVD voucher, a bunch of flowers, a bottle of wine, perfume or aftershave. These are presents you might give to anyone. What if the person inviting you asks for an experience? This would change your decision process. What you need to know now is what this person is interested in, what he likes to do; in short, you will have to get through to the person's 'DNA' in order to find a suitable gift or activity.

Groups of customers are often invited to attend appreciation events, for instance a tennis tournament. The company assumes that everyone will enjoy this event, which – however – remains to be seen. This shows that having adequate emotional data in the customer database is conducive to a customer-centric approach.

Segmentation

Segmentation is indispensable to the registration of customer data. Jay Curry (1991) developed the customer pyramid to categorize customers, clarify customer behaviour and carry out analyses.

Picture 1 in Fig. 4.3 displays the ladder of customer loyalty; picture 2, Curry's pyramid; and picture 3, Hart's (1998) marketing costs. The customer pyramid is a tool to gain an insight into the customer database; based on this information, analyses are carried out of the efforts that are made in order to attract more customers. The pyramid shows which customers are important to the business and what their needs are. By handling these needs appropriately (relationship marketing), the business tries to get its customers to rise on the customer loyalty ladder (picture 1) and, as such, make them more important customers. Satisfied customers will stay loyal to the organization for longer periods of time, will be more willing to take part in events and, in the end, will become the 'ambassadors' of the organization.

According to Curry (1991), many organizations are striving to generate business from non-customers. In his eyes, this is a waste of time. Companies had better concentrate on their existing customers. Curry (1991) advises them 'not to spend too much time on small customers; after all, it is the big customers that generate most of the business, and – in all probability – the most profit too.'

Segmentation is often made on the basis of profitability. The term 'customer value' indicates the individual customer's contribution to the company's profit. The majority of the customers fall into the segment of 'small customers', according to Curry (1991). Only 1% of the customers belong to the 'top' segment, 4% to the 'big' segment and 15% to the 'medium' segment. Small customers represent 80% of the customer base. Each of the top customers accounts for a substantial portion of the profit. And although medium and small customers are important to a company as a group, they are relatively insignificant on the level of the individual relationship.

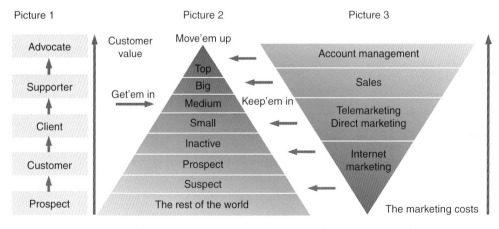

Fig. 4.3. Segmentation based on customer value (source: Curry, 1991; van Hart, 1998; Kneepkens, 2005; adapted by the authors).

An event to which top clients are invited is the example of Duyvis with its Pastrelli Relli, previously described in Chapter 3.

Inactive customers are those who have bought products or services in the past. This segment is one of the most important segments. After all, inactive customers are familiar with the company and can become active customers again relatively easily.

Prospects are persons who have not yet bought anything, but with whom a relationship has been built nevertheless. This relationship has been built through interest shown in the past. Prospects can become clients in a short space of time. Suspects, on the other hand, are persons with whom no relationship has yet been built, but to whom the company's products or services may be interesting. A suspect can become a prospect, and a prospect can become a customer.

The rest of the world has to be mapped out in order to identify which segments – persons or potential target groups – are not interesting to a company and which therefore do not require any marketing efforts.

It is possible, of course, to invite several customer groups to an event at the same time: potential customers, small customers or suspects. A precondition is that customers should have the potential to act as ambassadors and that small customers and suspects do not get lost in the crowd, because that is not what a relationship event is about.

Picture 3 in Fig. 4.3 shows that, in general, the marketing costs per customer at the top of the pyramid are the highest. The importance of customer retention grows as you move up the pyramid, and that is where a personal approach has more weight.

Customer relationship strategy

After gathering relevant customer knowledge comes developing a customer relationship strategy or loyalty strategy based on the corporate objectives. Depending on the nature of these objectives, a company can organize a relationship event, focusing on:

- achieving quick success
- building structural customer relationships.

With regard to relationship events focusing on structural customer relationships, we distinguish social strategies, psychological strategies and strategies of a temporal nature.

If the company is after quick success, the objective will be a tactical one and emphasis will be placed on the general or economic value. Price reductions or free services at events are examples of this. The company focuses on the value of the customer (in terms of money) in the short term. It goes without saying that this strategy may be detrimental to the company's profit margins.

If the company focuses on long-lasting, structural customer relationships, it has several strategies at its disposal: social, psychological or temporal strategies.

Social strategies may involve the role of the company's personnel during an event. How do the members of staff anticipate certain situations that will occur at the event? Empathic ability is crucial in this respect. When providing a service at an event, the personnel will have to judge each situation carefully and act accordingly. Creating a community around a brand or organization can also be a way to invest in a relationship. Social ties among the customers themselves are also likely to have an influence on customer loyalty towards the company. In conclusion, events can be an excellent tool for co-creation. Involving the customer in planning and designing the event is an example of this.

The strategies employed can also be of a psychological nature. After all, the purpose of events is to respond to the customer's needs, values and motives. With a comprehensive and accurate customer database, it is possible to employ a differentiated approach to reach customer segments. The customer's value to the company determines for whom the event is organized, how big it will be and in what form it will be offered (see also the customer pyramid). Another form of a customer relationship strategy concerns the creation of temporary values. Events can be used to generate process advantages to facilitate the availability of the product or service in order to save the consumer time. Companies give their customers certain privileges; for instance, by giving them the opportunity to check in earlier or order tickets earlier.

Evidently, the chosen strategy and approach, as well as the way in which the event is employed, are determined by the company's objectives. Recent studies have shown that the strategic embedment of events in customer relationship strategies is becoming increasingly common.

Communication

The best way to build dialogue with individual customers or customer segments has to be considered and determined on the basis of the company's objective and strategy. In other words: how can the objectives and strategy be transformed into communication? This involves the communication strategy, communication objectives, the message, the target groups, the media to be employed, the means of communication and so on. A network of communication channels will have to be developed by means of which the company can engage in communication anywhere, anytime, anyplace. Numerous communication channels and means can be applied in a relationship event in order to ensure the event's success, such as digital projectors, flyers, programme booklets and face-to-face communication. The event experience, however, can be extended by carefully considering – in the pre-event and post-event phases – forms of communication which will involve customers in the event (see Chapter 5).

Individualized value proposition

The product, the service and the price need to be adapted to the individual customer's circumstances. Companies need to develop competencies to deliver customized services to their customers. As described previously, customization involves the right alignment between the target group or customer, the company itself (and its reputation) and the organization of the event.

REASONS TO USE EVENTS IN CUSTOMER RELATIONSHIP MARKETING

Events are one of the tools or means that can be applied within the field of customer relationship marketing. The ultimate goal of relationship marketing is – either directly or indirectly – to retain profitable customers and increase spending per customer.

Reasons to use events as a relationship marketing tool include: showing the customer your appreciation, informing the customer, surprising the customer and motivating the customer.

Showing the customer your appreciation

Many events are meant to express appreciation for one's existing customers. Confirmation of the relationship plays an important role in this process. In principle, the company wants to thank its customers for their business in the past. Clients of AXA Insurance, for example, are offered opportunities to access various concerts, theatre shows and workshops. Customers and other key stakeholders are sent an invitation, and the setting is usually informal. It also happens that companies sponsor an event or a football club in exchange for free tickets or a VIP box. Subsequently, these sponsors invite their own customers. As a sponsor of the Roland Garros Tennis Tournament, BNP Paribas invites its own clients to this public event.

Informing the customer and confirming your reputation

Informing the customer is an objective that serves the fulfilment of the relationship (in which the relationship is connected with reputation). Events that are based on this objective are usually organized for customers and potential customers, and the programme generally has a more formal character. The event focuses on confirming the reputation that the company has built. REAAL Verzekeringen organized an event for all of REAAL's insurance agents. At the event, the insurance agents were informed about the latest developments and changes with regard to several products of the company. There were several top speakers who talked about regulations and market developments. Information on other topics was presented by REAAL itself. The presence of the top speakers contributed to the character of the event; a character that confirmed REAAL's reputation and expertise.

Surprising the customer

Surprising customers is one of the ways for a company to show its appreciation, basically say-ing that the customer is very special to the company. The setting is usually informal and the strength lies in the spontaneous, unexpected effect. This does not always have to be a large-scale event. Details are important too. Sending a postcard, a bunch of flowers or a cake for someone's birthday can be something that surprises the customer and has a positive effect on him or her. On the other hand, larger-scale activities are possible, too; for instance, organizing a party for a person with whom the company has cooperated for 25 years. In situations like this, it is also possible to combine the surprise with an existing event. To give an example, individuals who have made a structural contribution to the event industry are put in the limelight they deserve during the award ceremony of IFEA World in the category of 'the Hall of Fame Award'.

Motivating the customer

Although generating sales is not the primary goal of a relationship event, it will often be the underlying thought. This also holds true for relationship events aiming to motivate customers, in the process of which relationship fulfilment plays an important role. On the one hand, the event that is organized must be consistent with the company's reputation, and on the other hand, it must be consistent with the target group. This dual challenge must be considered carefully all the time. After all, it does happen quite a lot that an event does not address properly the target group's needs or is not organized on the basis of the company's core values. Events aiming to motivate customers are organized mostly for existing and potential customers, and the formal programme will also have certain informal aspects.

The pre-trade show organized by Bogra, for instance, which we have already mentioned in Chapter 3, had a clear entertaining and informal character, apart from comprising elements of 'providing information' and 'motivating the customer'. There was a performance by a singer and there was time to talk with each other informally. Obviously, the relationship experience (reciprocity connected with reputation) must be optimal in every relationship event. First of all, the event must be planned perfectly, it must be consistent with the target group's needs and aspirations and it must reflect the company's DNA.

After an exchange transaction, the customer will assess whether or not the transaction satisfied his expectations, or perhaps even exceeded them. This, in turn, will have an effect on the relationship and reciprocity (see Fig. 4.4).

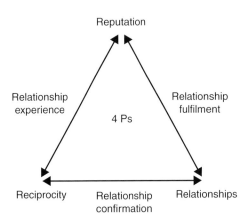

Fig. 4.4. Relationship experience, relationship fulfilment and relationship confirmation (source: Storm, 1992).

LIMITS TO CUSTOMER RELATIONSHIP MARKETING

Are there any limits that should be taken into consideration in the use of events within the framework of relationship marketing? And what is perhaps even more important: who imposes these limits? In general, there are few to no limits imposed, except within the pharmaceutical industry (see the next section).

Companies can communicate with their clients directly and determine for themselves what the limits are. It goes without saying that, normally speaking, the event matches the company's standards and values, and stays within the budget available. This suggests some sort of limitation or restriction. Companies can also have a code of conduct, specifying guidelines for relationship events for personnel, for instance, and for giving away promotional gifts. Moreover, the budget for an event can be bound by fiscal constraints.

Limits to customer relationship marketing in the pharmaceutical industry

A sector that is faced with legal boundaries in the organization of events for the purpose of relationship marketing is the pharmaceutical industry. This industry is unable to communicate directly with actual or potential end users, since the end user in this industry is the patient, and all direct communication between pharmaceutical companies and patients is prohibited. It is not the client (the patient) who opts for the product. That is why pharmaceutical companies have to focus on parties that determine (or partially determine) the patient's choice, such as medical consultants, pharmacists, GPs and, to an increasing extent, health insurance companies also. Once the choice for a certain product has been made, and the patient is using it, the industry is allowed to provide certain services to the patient, though to a limited degree. The code of conduct for the pharmaceutical industry in Europe is the EFPIA code (European Federation of Pharmaceutical Industries and Associations). This code is obligatory for all countries in Europe. In the Netherlands, the EFPIA code is complemented with the Code for the Advertising of Medicinal Products to the General Public. The general accepted practice is that the most stringent code will prevail.

Apart from legal standards, pharmaceutical companies impose limitations on themselves; for instance, with regard to contacts with medical practitioners. Any arrangements in this respect are laid down in a business code, by means of which the company covers itself against certain risks or distinguishes itself from the competition on ethical grounds. For current information on the conditions with which events in this industry have to comply (e.g. academic seminars, special events, giving and receiving hospitality, campaigns or get-togethers of another kind), you are referred to the efpia.org website, since the practices, rules and European guidelines in this area are changed on a regular basis.

SUMMARY

The increasing degree of competition and individualization, as well as technological developments, lead to a greater emphasis on relationships in the field of marketing. The three Rs – reputation, relationships, reciprocity – constitute the strategic counterpart to the four Ps.

The target group of events within relationship marketing can be either internal or external: clients, employees, suppliers, influencers (e.g. government bodies and the press). Customer knowledge is obviously very important in relationship marketing, including emotional data (which are often overlooked). Segmentation is essential to the registration of customer data.

Relationship marketing implies a relationship strategy, which may have a social, psychological and/or temporal character. A lasting relationship is the ultimate goal. Events are an effective means in relationship marketing, and they can be used for various reasons.

Apart from budget constraints, there are, in principle, no limits to relationship marketing. An exception in this respect is the pharmaceutical industry.

chapter 5

Events and Marketing Communication

Dorothé Gerritsen and Ronald van Olderen

We will start this chapter with a definition of communication. Next, we will deal with the communication model and the position of events in this model. We will demonstrate that events have news value, while addressing the relationship between new media and events. We will conclude the chapter with a section on the practice of communication and events.

LEARNING TARGETS

After studying this chapter, you will have learned:

- what is meant by communication
- what the communication model is and what the position of events is in this model
- what the function and effect of events is in marketing communication
- the ways in which events affect knowledge, attitude and behaviour
- how communication messages can be transformed into events.

A DEFINITION OF COMMUNICATION

Communication is a comprehensive term. It is used in various contexts and meanings: it may be about communication between two people, but also communication by way of a company's brochure. Events also fall into the category of communication.

The word 'communication' derives from the Latin word 'communio', which can be translated as 'community'. Consequently, communication can be taken to mean 'to make common', 'to share' or 'to understand each other'. The *Longman Dictionary of Contemporary English* describes communication as 'to exchange information', 'to tell people something' and 'to understand'.

Our definition of communication is as follows:

> Communication is the production and the exchange of information and meaning of verbal and/or non-verbal symbols which takes place between people, either wanted or unwanted. Information is conveyed, with a certain intention, after which this information is received and interpreted.

> (Michels, 2006)

THE COMMUNICATION MODEL

Communication is a process of interaction – either conscious or unconscious – between senders and recipients. Senders and recipients switch roles all the time. This process is often illustrated by means of a simple, elementary model, shown in Fig. 5.1, in which M stands for message.

S <-> M <-> R

Fig. 5.1. Simple communication model: S = senders; M = message; R = recipients (source: Michels, 2006).

This model is far from complete; in this chapter we will be working towards a more complete model. Communication connects people. For example, direct or virtual communication (the Internet, the telephone), in which a message is transmitted immediately, but also communication in a more figurative sense: coming closer together, learning to understand each other by sharing thoughts, opinions, values and arguments. Apart from the message itself, the communication process also involves the channels or media through which the message is communicated.

An event can be considered as a communication tool in both these meanings; it is a platform where people can meet each other in person and where they can connect with each other as well, and it is the medium or the channel through which the message is conveyed. In order to elaborate the simple communication model further, we need to take a step back and first take a look at developments within the field of communication.

LIVE COMMUNICATION AND EVENTS

Over the past few years, the number of communication channels has increased, but the use of these channels has become less predictable. One-to-one communication has become important: messages are tailored as much as possible to the needs and characteristics of the individual consumer. As a result of the enormous communication volume, it has become more difficult to reach the target group and increasingly companies are looking for alternatives. Events are one of these alternatives.

In this respect, communication professionals also speak of experience communication. The event is an experience which is orchestrated in such a way that the message is communicated to the target group. It involves an active dialogue between sender (organization/client) and recipient (visitor of the event), which is made possible by technological advancements. Consumers are turning into prosumers: they want to produce as well as consume. It is only logical that the sending is done from diverse groups and not just from one sender.

Communication professionals consider events as an effective tool and often describe them as the strongest form of communication; after all, it involves direct communication, something that cannot be ignored. As a consumer, one can experience a brand, try out a product or talk with like-minded individuals. This is a very direct form of communication.

Van der Zande has formulated the following definition for live communication:

> The on-site sharing of information, in which sender and recipient communicate with each other in person and in a direct way. The message is supported by the sender's body language, emotions and charisma. In this process, the interaction possibility intensifies the recipient's involvement.
>
> (van der Zande, 2007)

Live communication is a very effective form of communication for, among other things:

- creating experience moments
- building outstanding PR
- promoting a product or service in a unique way
- generating attention for one's message
- establishing loyalty with the product, service or company.

The example of Vodafone (Box 5.1) demonstrates how a communication issue can be transformed into the use of an event or live communication. As TV and radio turned out to be inadequate media, Vodafone used an event to get a message across – live – to a target group selected in advance.

Box 5.1 Vodafone case – Remember you're not at home

Aaaaha! The Actor Factory

To bring Vodafone live! UMTS to the attention of the public, Aaaaha! The Actor Factory set up a campaign. They advertised through television and radio. Vodafone was still looking for an extra way to generate attention for its service. Together with Aaaaha! The Actor Factory, Vodafone devised a concept for this campaign.

Objective

Promotion of Vodafone live! UMTS, a service which allows users to view live television broadcasts on their mobile phones.

(Continued)

Box 5.1. Continued.

Desired behavioural change

- Selling the new service
- Capturing the visitor's profile on the Internet

Target group

YAF (Young Active Fun)

Theme

The theme was carried through in the style of a television campaign called 'Remember you're not at home'. Watching television is no longer something you can do only at home.

Concept

Vodafone trained two actors for the purpose of a promotion day, so that the actors would know all about Vodafone's services and what kind of people Vodafone was targeting. On the promotion day, there was a mobile living room set-up, complete with sofa, lamp, TV guide and so on, and the actors played out a scene in a shopping street.

In the shopping street, a woman is sitting on a red sofa and watching television on her mobile phone. A man is sitting next to her (also an actor). He draws the shopping public's attention by inviting them to join the lady on the sofa and watch television with her. Meanwhile, he explains what UMTS is.

Outside the store, the promotion girl hands out flyers with information about the Vodafone campaign and a code for a prize to be won. Unlike a previous campaign, the prizes cannot be won in the store (as this led to overcrowded stores). Gadget seekers do not stand a chance in this setting. Only those who are really interested are reached.

This live campaign supported the TV campaign by showing people that you can watch television any place, any time. People who only came for the free prizes were given a code that they had to type in on the Internet at home. To this end, they first had to fill in their personal details and give Vodafone permission to contact them with news or special offers. This produced a great many target group profiles. (Source: van der Zande, 2007, adapted by the authors.)

EVENTS IN THE COMMUNICATION MODEL

In the Vodafone example, the use of the medium of television alone did not suit the marketing communication objectives and the event turned out to be an adequate supplement: Vodafone effectively conveyed its message through live communication with the target audience.

We can now add events to the simple communication model from Fig. 5.1 to create the model as depicted in Fig. 5.2.

The sender, in this case the organizer or client of the event, wants to get a message across to one or more target groups. In this process, he can choose a number of means, one of which is the event. The advantage of using an event as a means is direct communication with the individual members of a target group, while at the same time stimulating their senses. Live communication is two-way communication. The recipient decodes the message and can provide feedback straight away. In other words, visitor reactions are out in the open, on the spot.

As a sender, you choose the words and/or images for your message with the intention of evoking a certain reaction in the recipient; it is all about encoding the message as effectively as possible. As a result, you stand a greater chance that the recipient interprets the message as you intended it to be interpreted. The recipient will decode the message. What you want to make clear as a sender can be made clear in many ways. And remember that it is not just about the contents that you communicate. Form and content go hand in hand.

The example of the anniversary celebrations of Yacht (Box 5.2), a secondment firm for interim professionals, shows how the right mix of communication means is used for the purpose of the event in order to convey a message to the target group, in all stages (preliminary, main and subsequent).

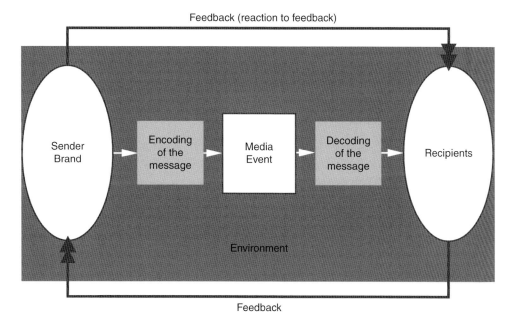

Fig. 5.2. Expanded communication model (source: Kneepkens, 2005; Michels, 2006; adapted by the authors).

Box 5.2   Yacht 2402

A major 'anniversary party' titled 'Yacht 2402' at a secret location (Passenger Terminal, Amsterdam) for all employees (without partners) was the result of the board's briefing. On 16 December 2006, Yacht marked its 2402-day anniversary (more than 6 years), and this was cause for a celebration. Yacht, part of the Randstad Groep Nederland, operates in the secondment of highly educated professionals in a large number of areas of expertise; professionals who are capable of achieving organizational goals together with clients. A sense of festivity and inspiration was what the event was supposed to convey to the 350 internal employees (Yacht office personnel), the 1950 interim professionals (personnel employed by Yacht) and 200 freelancers (who complete projects for Yacht with third parties). The idea that Yacht employees were a source of inspiration themselves was to be propagated by means of a stimulating, surprising message, imbued with the brand essence of Yacht: professional, result oriented, inspirational, and with a distinct focus on value for money.

A brief summary of Yacht's objectives:

- increase the sense of solidarity among all target groups
- improve customer loyalty, including interim professionals and freelancers
- foster a sense of pride.

The Yacht 2402 concept

In the realization of the concept, Yacht's brand essence constituted the point of departure. 'Being meaningful' is a key ingredient in this respect. Yacht's personnel can play a crucial role here, both internally and externally. This role was expressed in the composition and performance of the Yacht song *van betekenis* (including rap version). 'Being meaningful' was also carried through in the invitation phase, during which all Yacht employees were given the opportunity to contribute to the celebrations – and thus 'be meaningful' in an interactive way, via a website set up especially for the occasion. The four brand values were reflected in the styling and set-up of the party, by means of lounge areas scattered throughout the location, the colour setting in black and white (the Yacht colours); the dress code (black and white); HTML mails in black and white; the website; the catering (finger foods); and the entertainers and artists programmed.

The preliminary stage

An extensive interactive communication track was developed for the event, with the aim of involving the Yacht employees (a great deal of external parties!) in the party, reinforcing the 'we' feeling and the 'by Yacht, for Yacht' feeling, and making as many employees as possible enthusiastic about the party. Five months prior to the event, a 'mark the date' announcement was sent out by mail, accompanied by a fridge magnet with the date of Yacht 2402 on it. Three months prior to the event, the first HTML e-mail was sent

(Continued)

Box 5.2. Continued.

out, containing a click option to a special event website. The website featured the first information on the event and a questionnaire about numerous aspects of the party for guests to decide on (smoking/non-smoking, type of music, type of snacks/finger foods, etc.), and a clock that counted down the minutes to the date of the party. During the preliminary stage, pieces of information were added regularly to the website. Everyone was kept updated on the latest developments via HTML e-mail. The event website constituted the central communication medium for sharing information: dress code tips from stylists, photos uploaded by employees, possibility to vote for one's favourite cocktail and for the Yacht 2402 music top ten, a registration and cancellation procedure, and information on logistics matters.

The board, comprising 13 directors, wanted to connect with the employees in a recognizable, non-traditional manner. To this end, they put themselves in a somewhat vulnerable position. The board's interactive contribution consisted of a live variant of the television programme *Job Swap*, a reality programme in which a team of specialists train people for another job in a short period of time. At the event, the board members exerted themselves as cook, oyster shucker, cocktail shaker, camera operator, switch technician, sushi chef and even DJ. Their learning process in the preliminary stage was recorded on video.

The event

Yacht employees were transported by bus from the regional offices to a secret location. On the bus, Yacht 2402 water bottles and snacks were handed out, and a video message from the director was played. On arrival, members of the board welcomed every guest personally with a glass of champagne, with lounge music playing in the background. At 19:00 h, an opera singer opened the event, after which a voice-over narrator welcomed the guests again and declared the buffets officially open, which was followed by an unplugged performance by a semi-acoustic band featuring various soloists. At 19:58 h sharp, a countdown clock was displayed on video screens. The climax was nearing. The Yacht employees yelled out the last 10 s of the 2402 days along with the clock. At 20:00 h, the opening film started, featuring quotes from the board, regional directors and 'ordinary' Yacht employees. The film also revisited briefly the not-so-wonderful moments of Yacht, including the recruitment freeze in the past. The film ended with an image of the Yacht logo consisting of the photos uploaded and posted by the employees present. After that, and amid great interest, the short job swap videos were played, with bloopers of the board's learning process. The activities of the members of the board were shown on video screens live throughout the entire evening. The general director opened the dance floor, as a true DJ would, after which the party burst into full swing with a varied entertainment programme: a 'Yacht of the Proms' concert including a big live orchestra and soloists. A performance by Hans and Candy Dulfer, followed by a firework and confetti show, at

(Continued)

> **Box 5.2.** Continued.
>
> 24:00 h sharp, concluded the evening. On their way out, the guests were given a Yacht bag with a Christmas present. Before getting on the bus, they had the opportunity to eat some chips at the Yacht snack van. On the bus, everyone was given fleece blankets, bottles of water and midnight snacks.
>
> **Subsequent stage**
>
> On the Monday following the event, the visitors were sent a text message to inform them of the fact that the website was updated with photos, the opening film and the job swap footage. Yacht employees could submit comments to appear in the guestbook, as well as upload photographs they took. A special art print displaying the Yacht logo was put up 2 days later in all Yacht offices.
>
> The board members of Yacht were so enthusiastic about the party that they ordered a special video report to be made of the evening, which was also placed on the website later. (Source: Gouden Giraffe entry, 2007, unpublished, adapted by the authors.)

THE FOUR ASPECTS OF A MESSAGE

There are four aspects to a message (Schulz von Thun, 1982):

1. The business aspect.
2. The expressive aspect.
3. The relational aspect.
4. The appealing aspect.

We will explain these aspects by means of the Wimbledon Tennis Tournament in London. Through various tennis clubs in Great Britain which are associated with the British LTA (Lawn Tennis Association), tennis enthusiasts are informed of and invited to order tickets at a special group price. Information packs are sent to the management committees of the tennis clubs with a letter signed by the board of directors, presenting the dates of the matches, names of players who have committed to the event and the location. The information pack also contains a few posters of top-class tennis players, an answer form and a reference to the website.

Where do we find the four aspects in this message?

1. The business aspect. It involves objective information like data, times, location; in this example, these are the dates of the matches and the location.
2. The expressive aspect. When senders communicate, they always show something of themselves; in a conversation, this is expressed verbally as well as non-verbally. In this example, the expressive aspect can be found in the character of the information pack: professional set-up, posters that evoke a certain feeling.
3. The relational aspect. Not only do senders show something of themselves, but by addressing the other party, they also show how they see the recipient. Wimbledon and the tournament

managers demonstrate that they find the tennis clubs and their members important to the tournament's success. It is of major importance to have a sympathetic and enthusiastic audience.

4. The appealing aspect. The communication also has a clear goal. As a sender, one wants to get the recipients to do something; in this case, the goal is for the managing committees of the tennis clubs to put up the posters in their canteens and encourage members to visit the tournament by filling in the answer form.

There are many different ways to get in touch with each other. You can communicate in writing, orally and digitally. Communication seems simple enough at first glance, but in reality, it is rather complex. How do you choose the right communication resources in a certain situation, how do you strike the right tone, how do you select the right visual material, and so on. Choosing the right combination will ensure that you achieve the intended effect. The multitude of possibilities makes communication a fascinating, but at the same time difficult, subject.

THE COMMUNICATION MODALITIES

The field of communication is rooted in a number of disciplines, such as psychology, sociology and economics. Events are used as a means to convey a message for information purposes, for PR purposes and sometimes for advertising purposes. Although boundaries are fading due to technological advancements, it is useful to apply this distinction. It helps to formulate more targeted objectives. The boundaries between internal and external communication are fading too, especially because the Internet has made information accessible to everyone. Nevertheless, treating internal and external communication as distinctly separate processes will continue to be important in policy development. Events are very well suited to internal communication as well as external communication (also see the section on internal branding events in Chapter 6).

As an event organizer, you will be faced with the different modalities of communication, each with a different goal: the modality of information, education, public relations, advertising and propaganda. Sometimes, you and your project team will be tackling the question of how and when the event had best be promoted among the target group. And sometimes you will be in a meeting to establish which information is crucial in which phase and at which point in time. If you look at the extent to which the recipient is influenced, you can determine which modality of communication is involved; for example, announcements or information about opening hours: the 'information' modality. It is purely about providing information, without any further intentions. On the other end of the spectrum, you will find an extreme form of influencing in the modality of 'propaganda'.

So, each of the modalities comes with a certain goal. Michels (2006) has given the following descriptions:

- *Information*: sharing knowledge with the recipient without any intention to influence.
- *Education*: transferring information to influence the recipient's knowledge, attitude and/ or behaviour.

- *Public relations*: strengthening the sender's image and fostering mutual understanding between an organization and its target audiences.
- *Advertising*: influencing the target audience's knowledge, attitude and/or behaviour, and creating a distinct identity for a brand.
- *Propaganda*: communicating ideas with the aim of convincing others of an ideal (usually one-way communication).

EVENTS AS A MARKETING COMMUNICATION TOOL

It may be clear that events are an important platform for marketing communication and contact with the various target groups. The event itself is a tool amid an enormous range of possible communication tools, from which a responsible choice has to be made. Each choice (tool) has its own particular advantages and disadvantages (also see the section on events in the marketing mix in Chapter 3).

Good communication is characterized by efficient coordination between:

- goal
- message
- means/tool
- target group
- timing.

Despite the fact that countless physical and digital tools are available to us, there is no reason to doubt the event as one of the possible tools in which the marketing communication objective should obviously be directional. An important question in this respect is which role the event plays within the total field of marketing communication; it involves a strategic choice.

The choice for an event as a tool is a radical one: organizing an event costs a lot of time and energy, but this is counterbalanced by the enormous impact of the event. Once the choice has been made, all the stops must be pulled out to make the event a success. There are many parties involved in the organization of an event and the risks involved are relatively high. Apart from that, an event is usually a complex whole; it is a project within which and about which communication takes place. An event is an excellent opportunity to showcase your brand (or product, service, etc.) in the best possible light. That is why the management staff generally wants the organization of the event to be perfect. Nothing may go wrong: after all, the image is at stake. It is not for nothing that professional planners are often engaged in the organization of large-scale events. By now, there is a mature event management industry; there are event management study programmes, academic literature and sector organizations.

Energy drinks manufacturer, Red Bull, regularly organizes events to connect with its target group (also see Chapter 1). To attract greater publicity for their events, MSN was chosen as a strategic communication partner in the preliminary stage. Not only did this generate greater awareness of the Red Bull events, but also more clicks on the MSN sites. This clearly involves a win–win situation: there is efficient coordination between the goal, the message, the means and the target group (Box 5.3).

Box 5.3   Red Bull case

Energy drinks manufacturer, Red Bull, regularly organizes events. To generate more awareness for these events, Red Bull engaged the services of Calanza (www.calanza.com). With a view to the manufacturer's target group, the MSN portal seemed the most suitable place for building a website. This, however, was not all. Calanza created a tab in Messenger so that MSN users got to play an online game, which had been developed by Red Bull in cooperation with Calanza. By using multiple channels effectively, Red Bull attracted more visitors to its events and MSN received more page views. (Source: van Ooijen, 2009, adapted by the authors.)

EVENTS: MASS COMMUNICATION OR INTERPERSONAL COMMUNICATION?

The discipline of communication is commonly divided into two categories: mass communication and interpersonal communication. When an event is chosen as a means and when an event is communicated, the advantages and disadvantages of these two categories will have to be considered. Mass communication involves the sender communicating with a large group of people, whereas interpersonal communication is targeted at a limited number of persons, which allows for direct feedback. Each category has its pluses and minuses, and the choice obviously depends on the company's objectives. Events can reach a wide range of substantial target audiences. Their advantage – compared to the medium of television, for instance – is that the effects can be seen immediately and that people can meet up in person. Table 5.1 contrasts the differences between mass communication and interpersonal communication, as seen by Michels (2006).

EVENTS AND COMMUNICATION TARGETS: KNOWLEDGE > ATTITUDE > BEHAVIOUR (KAB)

In most situations, communication stimuli are used purposefully. Organizations have to think carefully about the levels at which they formulate their communication targets. It requires a vision and strategic thinking with regard to the use of communication (the message, the goal and the means). Traditionally, three levels are distinguished in this respect. In this section, we will explain how events may play a role on each of these three levels.

Table 5.1. Mass communication and interpersonal communication (source: Michels, 2006).

Mass communication	Interpersonal communication
One-way communication	**Two-way communication**
Sender has little idea of the effect	Sender has a good impression of the effect
Difficult to customize to individual recipient	Easy to customize to individual recipient
Low cost per person reached	Reaches few people at the same time
Recipient can turn away easily	Recipient cannot turn away easily
It is more difficult to create behavioural change	It is easier to create behavioural change
Examples: radio, television, national papers	Examples: personal talk, telephone call, conference

Marketing communication specialists agree unanimously on the answer to the question of when communication can be typified as successful: this is the case if it meets the KAB principle (Michels, 2006). This is an abbreviation of the three main targets in the area of communication: aiming at changes in knowledge, attitude and behaviour (not necessarily in this order). The ultimate goal of event marketing is to effect change in knowledge, attitude and/or behaviour. It implies that people know what to do (knowledge) and understand the reasons (attitude) of what they have to do (behaviour).

Knowledge

Many broadcast communication tools, such as television and radio commercials, but also newspaper advertisements, are aimed at publicizing a new product or campaign. If the tool is not used in a purposeful manner, the target group will not learn of its existence, which means that the product will not be sold. Determining the knowledge target is therefore crucial to the continuation of a business, and depending on the scope of the target group, certain channels will be opted for. A local shopkeeper will opt for his own show window for extra publicity; a multinational will decide on a prime-time television commercial. The strength of the tool depends on the question of whether the message reaches the target group in multiple places, at multiple moments and through multiple channels. As a result, people will talk about it with each other (through physical and virtual channels) and the objective of, for instance, 'publicizing a campaign' will be achieved. In other words, it is all about choosing the right channels, aimed at the right target group(s).

Attitude

To ensure that the target group is not only aware of the existence of the organization or a new product but also forms a positive image and considers contacting the organization or buying the product, it is important to think about the contents of the message. What is it that you wish to communicate as an organization? In most situations, you want the target group to think about the organization and the message, and to become enthusiastic. Tone and visualization are important in this process. The total package causes people to work out an interpretation for themselves. When you do this right, as an organization, and when you manage to achieve the desired attitude change, you will have achieved the second-level communication target.

Behaviour

Communication is also a means to induce certain behaviour in people, such as deciding to buy a product. It is wonderful if the majority of the target group is familiar with the company, and what is more, has a positive image of the company, but if nobody buys or joins anything, or whatever it is that is being pursued, then you have not achieved much. It is all about making sure that people actually do something. Apart from the choice for the right distribution channels (which is, of course, crucial in this respect), you also want people to actually buy your product or service. This can be achieved by rewarding certain behaviour, for instance, by organizing a competition (in every conceivable form), repeating the message and initiating promotion campaigns and customer card schemes. Entrance tickets to leading public events are often used as rewards. But it can also be the other way around: a range of campaigns is initiated to 'sell' an event, which will trigger people to actually buy tickets to the event.

EVENTS AND THE MULTI-CHANNEL STRATEGY

A multi-channel strategy is a strategy that is aimed at getting the communication message across to the target group through multiple channels at multiple points in time, in perfect congruence with each other. Strategies of this sort are very useful in marketing communication. A customer loyalty campaign can only be achieved with sky-high budgets. Still, the essence of it can also be applied very well on a smaller scale. It all begins with a good target group analysis: know your target group! If you know where people come from, what they like and how they tend to communicate, you can align your communication strategy with that and thus maximize the effect of your marketing campaigns. And what is more, you can try to influence the knowledge, attitude and behaviour of the members of your target group. The following example will make clear that it is important to formulate knowledge, attitude and behaviour objectives – based on your knowledge of the target group – after which, you opt for the right means.

Suppose you were commissioned to organize a new charity event for a charity in Scotland. The geographical boundaries for your target group have already been set. Later on, you can identify other, smaller target groups within the main target group. The event does not yet exist in Scotland, but people are aware of the concept, which has been marketed successfully in other regions. This means that there is zero name recognition in Scotland. So, you will have to work hard on your knowledge objective. At that point, you are thinking about the communication channels. It is important to know which channels the people in Scotland generally use: you will need to find out which regional papers, news channels, websites and free local papers are read and/or visited. To find out what is the best way to engage the people in Scotland, you will have to do an analysis. What will work and what will not work in this particular region? What images and what message will be the most likely to enthuse Scotland for the charity event?

Once you have made your choice for the channels, means and visualization, the question remains of how you are actually going to get people to visit the event and support the charity. You will have to look for ways to achieve this. This will be relatively easy for a certain part of the target group. If your programming is good, some people will come on their own volition. Just announcing the event will be enough. But, there will always be a group that is more difficult to persuade. Having detailed information on your target group and knowing when (in which phase) to target them actively will help you make a choice for a communication strategy.

EVENTS AS A MARKETING COMMUNICATION TOOL: GIVING SUBSTANCE TO THE MESSAGE

As you have already seen, events are an important means to achieve communication objectives. By opting for a certain concept and theme, the event already communicates part of its contents. By opting for a theme in connection with the organization of a conference by a sector organization, for instance, the organization already communicates what is currently considered an important topic in the industry. The programming and the choice for certain speakers also convey a certain impression of what is all the rage today within the industry or field of study. In this case, the conference is the tool to enter into dialogue with fellow professionals, to explain trends and developments, to identify consequences for the discipline, and so on. The conference is a meaningful tool which has the potential to lift the discipline to a higher plane. Before, during and after the conference, there will be reason for certain communities to communicate. The annual trade show, IMEX, for instance, recently decided on the theme of 'Still at the heart of the meeting business', which gave substance and meaning not only to the various seminars and workshops, but also to the layout and decor of the location. The IMEX vision delivers a packed education programme and initiatives committed to showcasing innovation in the meetings industry. It brings to IMEX 2013 a range of education sessions, streamed into eight *easy-to-find* topic tracks, a host of venues on the show floor to explore latest trends and exciting fun and new activities to the programme (www.imex-frankfurt.com, accessed May 2013).

EVENTS AS NEWS

In the previous sections, we have shown that events can influence knowledge, behaviour and attitude. Events often have such a great impact that they are reported on by various news media. This may involve news for internal as well as external media, depending on the size of the event, the public or private character of the event, the number of potential visitors, and so on. By organizing an event, a company creates something newsworthy by definition. The geographical scope of the newsworthiness of an event varies; the event may be local, regional, national or even international. It is good to be aware that events have newsworthiness. You can use this fact to your advantage by generating as much free publicity as possible. Free publicity is editorial attention in the press, such as print, radio and television. It involves a news item that is made by the editors of a media outlet. You do not have to pay anything for this, but the downside is that you have nothing to say about the way in which and the degree to which the item is covered. The great advantage of free publicity is that readers, viewers and listeners usually find the information more reliable and credible than communication messages that are spread via commercial channels.

What is news? What makes something news? There is no general answer to these questions. Nevertheless, a number of criteria can be given (Sterk and Kuppenveld, 2007, adapted by the authors). News is news if:

- it is different, unusual
- it comes from or relates to a celebrity
- it generates a high degree of involvement
- it has many consequences for many people.

An item that meets all these criteria is bigger news than an item that meets only one criterion, and as one criterion increases in applicability, the news is bigger, too. An example is when someone from a big city is living it up at a dance event on a Saturday night; this is not news. When a Member of Parliament (MP) is spotted partying at that same dance event, this is relatively big news with national coverage. After all, it is different, unexpected. The general image of an MP is that of a man or woman in a suit engaging in political debate. That is their national reputation. You do not expect someone like that to go to a dance party at the weekend. The second criterion also applies here: it concerns someone who has been elected democratically to represent the people. In other words, it is an important person, and in that sense, a celebrity.

Creating news value through events

The criteria for news value as mentioned above suggest that companies can also create news themselves. Events, to begin with, are news because something is about to happen that is out of the ordinary: something that is going to take place in a certain area or at a specific location, clearly visible to the people living in the surrounding area and attracting a lot of people. There will be signs in the city directing people to the event, perhaps even diversion routes: more than enough subject matter for news stories. The trick is to give events as much news value as possible by playing with the criteria. Launching new products at a trade show, for instance, is a common practice to increase the trade show's attractiveness for visitors. As a result, you will enhance involvement and your trade show will be different. You can also arrange a celebrity to open your event: this can be the general manager in the case of a personnel event or the Minister of Education in the case of a conference on educational innovation.

Personal interaction at events will ensure that people talk and write about the event, which is indicative of the significance of the event for society. A process of image and opinion formation will occur among people. Events can also be used to make a point; for example, demonstrations, silent marches and protest marches. When you manage to mobilize lots of people, you get to express your points of view and your organization will make an impression. Events are news by definition, which partially accounts for the great pressure that organizers are under and the importance that is attached to the event by its initiators, such as local government officials, board members, corporate executives and ministers.

NEW MEDIA

Developments in the field of new media have gained momentum and have a huge impact on the choice for media and tools, on the possibilities available to the sender to get his message across. Old or traditional media include print media (newspapers, journals, special interest magazines, trade show representation), television and radio. New media comprise the Internet (websites, blogs, Web 2.0), applications for mobile telephones, new audio-visual techniques (LED lights, holograms) and video gaming. Our definition of new media is 'interactive digital media or new developments in existing media' (see Fig. 5.3).

Radio, television and print media (newspapers, magazines) used to enjoy a relatively high degree of attention. The entire marketing and communication budget was allocated to these media. New media have given companies far greater choice in terms of reaching out to their target markets. Over the past few years, communication and advertising firms have extended their range of services to incorporate the entire spectrum of media, beyond traditional television commercials and newspaper advertisements. Budgets are being directed to more media

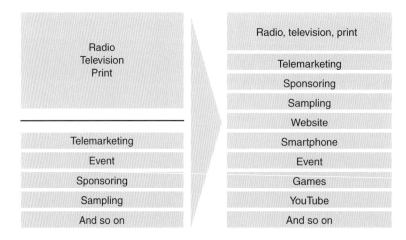

Fig. 5.3. Shift in media attention (source: presentation by Van der Poel, November 2008, unpublished, adapted by the authors).

outlets and tools. There are many reasons for this, but the main reason is that almost everyone has access to one communication channel or another, regardless of time and place. As an organization, you will have to employ a carefully balanced and integrated media mix.

- Media commissions have declined because advertisers buy and organize media space, thus pocketing the commissions themselves.
- The social media are on the rise, providing alternative advertising platforms.
- Today's consumers are capricious and non-committal, with unpredictable attitudes and behaviours.
- There is a tendency from target group thinking towards community thinking.
- It is becoming increasingly difficult to reach the recipients you want to reach, because of communication overload. The catchment range of traditional media alone is no longer sufficient.
- Radio, television and print media are less suited to modern experience communication.

Table 5.2 lists the differences between old and new media.

Below, we will provide a brief description of the four categories of new media.

Web 2.0

The progression of the Internet has been enabled by Web 2.0 technologies. The '2' refers to a second generation of web development: from a collection of websites to a platform for interactive web applications for end users on the Internet. Web 2.0 is characterized by the interaction and communication between users and by sharing information. It is personal and social, and also free of charge. Technically, it is an open source, which means that it provides free access to the source materials, it has open standards and it has data collection and programming possibilities. Examples are Wikipedia (knowledge), social networks (sharing contacts and information), weblogs, chatting, Flickr and YouTube. Webcasting is the live broadcasting of an event via the Internet. On-demand streaming means that pre-recorded material is broadcast via a portable device. Online ticketing involves buying and selling entrance tickets via the Internet.

Table 5.2. Old and new media (source: IDEA Project Group, 2007, unpublished, adapted by the authors).

Old media	New media
Closed	Open
Specific audience	Users
Supply driven	Demand driven
Mainly based on text	Mainly based on images

With the web, it is possible to make things – that are actually the same for everyone – seem personal; this is also referred to as mass individualization. Consumers can personalize products or services easily and cheaply by designing their own calendar or photo bag.

Mobile applications

Personalized and interactive messages can be sent to any target audience at any time via a mobile device (telephone, Blackberry, laptop with a mobile Internet modem). Mobile marketing is making its entrance, or put differently: marketing via the mobile channel. The well-known text messaging system (short message service) is part of this, but also mms (multi-messaging service as combinations of text, image, sound and video data), mobile Internet (thanks to a special format, websites can now also be accessed on mobile devices such as telephones), mobile television, Bluetooth (wireless communication), tweeting (exchanging quick and short messages with other users via the computer or mobile telephone) and mobile coupling (bar codes in a mobile telephone serve as entrance tickets). Developments have not yet come to an end; more possibilities will appear in the future. Apple, for instance, is planning to sell tickets to events. The company has applied for a patent; it involves a system that mainly adds digital bonus content to a digital ticket to concerts or sporting events on mobile devices (read: iPod or iPhone). The system is called Concert Ticket+ and it allows for ticket sales via iTunes. Apart from the ticket, the application will provide users with a floor plan, information about the concert venue and layout of the concert hall.

Audio-visual means

The various possibilities in terms of presentations are increased by developments in the area of new media. The impact of events, and also the communicative message, will increase accordingly; just think of laser shows, applications of light and sound effects. Projections of previously recorded 3-D material can be displayed by means of a digital projector or flat screen on a foil screen, to create a hologram.

Video gaming

Video gaming involves games via the Internet, for instance Nintendo's Wii. Through networks, the games can be played together by people all over the world.

New media and the role of events

New media can and have to be applied frequently within the events sector, which is what happens in actual practice. In order for these applications to be effective, they must comply with the following requirements:

1. The applications of new media must contain interactive and personal content.
2. The applications of new media must be based on cross-media approaches, throughout all stages of the event. This will strengthen the experience aspect. The message for

this purpose must be communicated via various new media platforms at various points in time.

3. The applications of new media must be consistent with the wishes and needs of the target group, as this will expand the catchment range.

It is also crucial for new media not to become a goal in itself; after all, they are subservient to the strategic objectives of the event itself and have a supporting function. The wonderful thing about new media is, of course, that they have brought countless new possibilities to get in touch with visitors before, during and after the event. In terms of content, as well as in terms of the various services, new media have become indispensable as tools to intensify the experience, the level of involvement and the provision of services to the visitor.

IN PRACTICE: TRANSLATING THE COMMUNICATION MESSAGE INTO THE EVENT

In order to attain the objectives of the marketing communication message, they have to be translated to practice in concrete terms. Below, you will find a couple of practical examples in a nutshell; they are by no means exhaustive.

In order to give real substance to communication, event organization agencies often work together with businesses which specialize in a certain discipline; in some cases, this involves 'full-service agencies'. Many organization agencies (including event organization agencies) team up with external businesses, which are called in because of a certain area of expertise, specific experience and know-how. A wide range of businesses offer support to event organizers in many different ways; for example, designing and building sets, developing promotional material, designing websites, arranging audio-visual equipment. When the partnership starts, it is crucial for the external businesses to have been informed accurately on the assignment concerned. Communication is a very important aspect throughout the completion of the assignment. There must be continuous communication between all persons and/or parties involved. Everyone must be well informed about the proceedings with regard to the event. Good communication will ensure that everything goes smoothly. The message which the event is supposed to convey should obviously be discussed extensively in advance. If the external business has not been informed well in advance, it may happen that the sets or props are out of character with the message.

Cooperation with external businesses is often necessary because few event organization agencies have set-building facilities of their own. Some agencies have their own designers, and subsequently have their sets created by specialist set-building companies or freelancers, or – in the case of participation in a trade show – by a standard design company.

The example of the World Expo in Shanghai (Box 5.4) shows how the stands for the World Expo were designed, based on the objectives of the various clients of the Dutch event agency, Hypsos.

Box 5.4   World Expo 2010

On 1 May, World Expo 2010 was officially opened: 'Better City, Better Life'. Hypsos, an agency that specialized in 3-D communication projects, was working on four pavilions at the World Expo in Shanghai for an audience of millions. Hypsos was responsible for the design and build of the pavilions of Urbanian, Hong Kong Connect, UITP and Johnson & Johnson.

Urbanian

For more than 2 years, Hypsos was one of the agencies that made up the design team of Urbanian, a pavilion which measured 14,000 m^2 in surface area. It was one of the most prestigious pavilions of the Shanghai World Expo.

Hong Kong Connect

Hypsos was project manager of the pavilion of Hong Kong in the 'Urban Best Practices Area'. The theme 'Hong Kong Connect – Smart Card, Smart City, Smart Life' demonstrated the leading role of Hong Kong in the development and application of technology aimed at making the lives of its inhabitants as pleasant and efficient as possible. This high-tech pavilion applied and illustrated smart-card technology on LED walls and big touch screens.

UITP

For the International Organization for Public Transport, Hypsos designed and built a very attractive pavilion. For this organization, which promotes public transport and sustainable forms of transport all over the world, Hypsos came up with an intriguing design that featured slopes, tracks and roads, hoping to spark visitors' interest. The main message of UITP in Shanghai was 'Public Transport: Solutions for our Future'.

Johnson & Johnson

Johnson & Johnson from New York was one of the sponsors of the USA pavilion and Hypsos was involved in setting up this pavilion. Johnson & Johnson propagated its corporate slogan 'Caring for the world, one person at a time'. The various aspects of Johnson & Johnson were displayed on 3-D monitors, and an interactive part of the presentation allowed visitors to ensure – via text messages – that Johnson & Johnson provided 'extra care' somewhere in China. All this could be followed via a special website. (Source: www. expovisie.nl, accessed January 2011, adapted by the authors.)

Printed matter

An event will only be successful if it attracts enough visitors. That is why it is very important to ensure potential visitors are enthused and informed prior to the event. It all starts with the invitation. An invitation is an important weapon in the competition for the recipient's attention. The invitation should arouse interest and spark the imagination but, above all, it should communicate the goals and intentions of the event.

Corporate identity

As a business, you may decide to have your corporate identity reflected in all printed communication relating to the event. You may also choose to design a separate logo especially for the event. When this happens, all stationery, envelopes, business cards and brochures will be adjusted accordingly. The general advice is to start your preparations at an early stage.

When you decide to outsource this component, you can engage a designer who will take charge of the entire process. The designer will request quotations from printing firms and will oversee the entire print production process, from design to distribution. Together with your designer, you can choose your own colours, style, typeface and type of paper. The designer will present his sketches and working drawings to you for review and modify (if necessary), after which he will format the final version.

Every piece of communication must reflect the same consistent identity. The colour scheme, the design and the overall look of all communication media must be the same, so that the connection with the event is clear at all times. In a time where visual messages are becoming increasingly important, a special event logo – as mentioned above – may fulfil a crucial role. Instant recognizability is not the only purpose of logos: they actually evoke certain feelings and emotions, such as memories of an experience or an event; the logo stirs something in people. This is an aspect of communication that certainly must not be underestimated.

Fig. 5.4. Olympic Games logo.

Turning strategy into action is a key component. The brand image, logo and typeface, as well as typographical standards, are all protected and registered with official bodies especially set up to this end. There is, of course, a very good reason for this. Research has shown, for instance, that the McDonald's logo enjoys 100% recognition among children in Western countries.

Almost everyone who sees the logo in Fig. 5.4 knows that it is the Olympic Games logo.

Location

The location has a considerable influence on the character and ambiance of the event. It affects the visitor experience of the event. Nowadays, it is no longer self-evident that events are held in party centres or theatres. The possibilities are endless: from old factory halls transformed into hip and trendy event locations to classy listed buildings that have had several uses. Whatever a company wishes to communicate through the event obviously affects the choice of location. The location in itself already communicates some of the experience (also see the experience tools in Chapter 8).

Catering

The culinary aspects of an event are often very important, if not critical. The variety and quality of catering has to be compatible with the target audience and the event objective, and gives the event a certain flavour. An important development in this respect is that caterers have discovered the market of events. They are focusing increasingly on all-in-one concepts for events, in which catering obviously plays a leading role. This should not come as a surprise, though; eating together has a strong experiential aspect and therefore has an impact on the overall experience (see Fig. 5.5).

Fig. 5.5. Catering concept of Maison van den Boer (source: www.maisonvandenboer.nl, accessed January 2011).

Box 5.5   Client: Boer en Croon Strategy and Management Group

Project: Help us organize a personnel party titled 'Go White, Go Wild'

'Go White, Go Wild' was going to be the theme. White and wild it was for sure, but surprising, too. We welcomed our guests at the deserted back entrance of the Angek Studio in the Amsterdam Houthavens. After a hilarious act – which took a rather serious view of networking – there was a countdown that led to the final revelation. As it turned out, there was a party area behind the stage and it was all decorated in white. This is where the guests were treated to a series of colourful surprises, until late in the evening.

SUMMARY

What is typical of communication is that sender and recipient switch roles all the time. Not only is the message itself important but also the communication channels. An event is a medium and a platform at the same time; it is the place where people meet, as well as the communication channel. Live communication is the key; it allows the recipient to decode and respond to the message immediately. As for the message itself, four aspects are important: the business aspect, the expressive aspect, the relational aspect and the appealing aspect. The four modalities of communication are information, public relations, advertising and propaganda – the latter modality usually involves one-way communication.

Good communication is characterized by efficient coordination between goal, message, means/tool, target group and timing. Events facilitate interpersonal communication and can be used to generate changes in knowledge, attitude and behaviour. Understanding the process of communication, the various means/tools and their advantages and disadvantages, and old and new media is important in this respect. Multi-channel strategies can be applied in this process as well, so as to get the communication message across to the target group via multiple channels at several points in time. Because an event often has news value in itself, free publicity is a welcome side effect.

chapter 6

Events and Branding

Thomas van Velthoven

This chapter describes the role of events in relation to branding. First, we will look at what a brand is and what the attributes of a brand are. Then, we will discuss the significance of brands for building a brand from the perspective of the producer as well as that of the consumer. This will be followed by a discussion of the building of brands. Finally, the phenomenon of *brand events* will be dealt with and attention will be drawn to the connection between strategies of brand building and the types of events dealt with earlier.

LEARNING TARGETS

After studying this chapter, you will have learned:

- what a brand is
- what the two meanings are of branding and events that can be distinguished
- how brands are built
- which brand strategies can be used at events
- how the principles of brand building and image transfer can be used at events
- what the role is of events within the framework of internal branding.

THE MAGIC OF BRANDS

Brands are an almost inescapable facet of our daily existence. Inner cities and shopping malls would present quite a different view if brands could not be displayed. It is virtually impossible to imagine the Internet, television and the print media without brand communication. Schoolyards and open-plan offices would be quite different scenes without the phenomenon of designer clothing, either admired or reviled, in which people dress to distinguish themselves from others.

It is true that a product can play a part in fulfilling a need, but a branded article goes beyond this; it fulfils the longing for certainty and alleviates the dilemma of choice. Perhaps a brand can best, and most powerfully, be defined as something that offers a promise – a promise of healthy relationships, of being seen, of feeling happy. Or that of a real party! After all, you do not uncork just a bottle of bubbly but a genuine Moët & Chandon. The creators of such a brand are like modern magicians in our society: they know how to enchant, they are the masters of the suggestive power to arouse emotions. Not through trickery or force, but by recognizing and using latent feelings and needs, and leading people to what they themselves find of importance. It is, after all, impossible to mislead people all the time. A company develops a brand in the long term by gaining the public's trust and never disappointing people.

With regard to events, the building of a brand must provide an answer to two questions:

1. Is it possible to turn recurring events into a real brand?
2. Can the event make a contribution to completing a brand proposition or creating closer ties with a particular brand?

Events as a product brand or a corporate brand

Although we come across brand names that are the names of companies in the world of events, names such as the Eurovision Song Contest and the Dance for Life, it is likely that on hearing those names the consumer thinks first of the event in question. So, this is about a product brand as a brand name, and what crosses the minds of buyers or consumers first is the products and/or services to which the event is linked, while they do not know the company behind it. There are plenty of examples to illustrate this: the North Sea Jazz Festival, the New York Marathon, the Roskilde Festival in Denmark or Rock Werchter in Belgium – well-known brand names, but the general public does not know by which company the event in question is organized.

In the case of corporate brands, buyers or consumers think primarily of the company. ID&T and Mojo Concerts, for example, are to some extent recognized names. But the number of people that can mention the products of these organizers spontaneously is certainly much smaller. Besides, not much is known in general about the so-called brand proposition, so that people do not know what the companies concerned stand for.

Events as brand or image transfer (brand event)

In relation to events and branding, we can distinguish two types. On the one hand, we distinguish events that are used to turn them into strong brand names. Events are then both the source and the objective. On the other hand, there are events as tools to reinforce brands, as mentioned earlier in this chapter. When an event is used as a tool for brand building, it will always involve the phenomenon of image transfer (see Fig. 6.1).

A concept like brand management suggests a certain expertise or strategy, but building a brand is much more than taking a series of premeditated steps. As a magician, you should be focused on particular rituals and incantations, be able to put yourself in the shoes of your audience, engage with your audience, manage your audience, but also detach yourself from it at the right time, and you should do it all with a passionate belief in what you are doing. This does not alter the fact that there are several practical principles that can be used in brand building. They provide no guarantees, but they do offer a better prospect of success. We will illustrate those principles by using the example of the Black Cross, a motocross event (Boxes 6.1 and 6.2).

Fig. 6.1. Events and branding.

Box 6.1   Black Cross – a 3-day stunt and music festival

Lichtenvoorde (the Netherlands) had a record number of visitors this year. The organization counted 148,000 paying visitors compared to 132,000 last year.

The festival at Lichtenvoorde ran into severe problems after heavy weather had destroyed a large number of tents in the grounds and an employee of one of the fairgrounds attractions had died on the Saturday. Still, the organization was content about how the festival had proceeded. The Sunday programme was sold out, with 65,000 people attending, and proceeded without serious incident. 'The atmosphere could only be described as excellent', according to the organizers.

Motor stunts

The 14th Black Cross started on a Friday without any problems. All of the 15,000 camping visitors reached the festival grounds without delays. On various stages, you could enjoy tens of bands and theatrical companies for 3 days. Moreover, motor stunts were performed each day, and there were motocrosses, sometimes with bizarrely dressed participants.

Whirlwind

Monday was a dark day for the Black Cross. On that day, a whirlwind caused damage to the tune of €1 million. Force 12 gusts blew down tents, barriers and platforms, and turned the festival grounds into a muddy mess. In spite of all that, it was decided, in consultation with the authorities, to open the grounds to the public. Fate struck again on Saturday when an employee of a fairground attraction from Breda lost his life.

The victim was testing the attraction when he got jammed in the mechanism. The local authorities and the organization decided to proceed with the festival and not shut it down.

(*Continued*)

Box 6.1. Continued.

As far as is known, the police arrested seven people in the grounds between Saturday and Sunday. The visitors were apprehended and fined for rowdy behaviour and causing bodily harm. They were expelled from the Black Cross Festival for 3 years. (Source: www.nu.nl/muziek, accessed January 2011.)

Box 6.2 An account by Antoine, one of the many visitors

What a fantastic scene, absolutely unbelievable. And so many people! That whirlwind may have caused some damage, but it generated lots of publicity. The programme was sold out today.

We've seen little of the motocross itself this year; we spent most of our time at the 3FM stage, the theatre meadow and the reggae meadow. Each had its own character, and so lively, amazing really. I wish it was like this in the whole country. My son had a massage on a motorcycle, quite an experience in itself. You would have had to be at the Black Cross to know what you would have missed. This is an absolute must for the whole family.

There was nothing that told you there was a crisis, because there was a lot of eating and even more drinking. Fortunately we'd come by train, so I could more or less drink as much beer as I wanted.

I suspect that next year I will come just to buy a few beers, and that my son and his friends will stay at the campsite and have a merry time for 2 or 3 days (…). We were soon completely worn out and went home feeling absolutely terrific. (Source: www.stichtingvlinders.nl, accessed January 2011.)

EVENTS AS BRANDS?

Motocross, stunts, music, theatre, quite a spectacle and a great atmosphere, all mixed together: that is the Black Cross Festival; a unique and bizarre combination that in 2013, its 17th year, drew even bigger crowds. The 3-day festival has now become the biggest and most spectacular motocross event in Western Europe, and is famous for the friendliness that is so characteristic of the region where it is held. The focal point of the festival is the spectacular motocross in which real world champions compete for the coveted Golden Helmet, but in addition, there are bizarre types of mopeds, self-made vehicles, heavy vehicles and sidecars, and for these it is the fun, not the speed, that counts. With more than 100 bands on 20 different stages, the entire festival grounds are throbbing with music. Besides, more than 300 theatre artists and many bloodcurdling and hilarious stunts make for an electrifying experience.

With 148,000 paying visitors and lasting for several days, the Black Cross is the biggest outdoor musical event in the Netherlands. But does that mean that it is a brand as well? Or, to phrase it differently: does the Black Cross also behave as a brand?

What is a brand?

This is a simple question, but simple questions often do not have ready-made answers. In popular terms, a brand stands for quality, for a particular aura, 'a good feeling', for the promise of a supposed quality or the perception of a particular product.

Chernatony and McDonald have come up with the following definition:

> A brand is a product, service, person or place to which, with the buyer or consumer in mind, relevant, unique, symbolic values have been added that are closely related to the needs of the consumer.
>
> (Chernatony and McDonald, 1992)

A brand is successful if it is able to uphold these added values in spite of the pressure exerted by the competition.

Brands are not tangible, but a construct: a network of associations that has found a place in our brains. This makes them subjective, but also dynamic. And although brands are the legal and economic property of the producer in modern economies, it is the consumer who really *owns* them. What a brand statement invokes in us is, in fact, 'our thing'. The power of branding lies in the strategic efforts of producers to create in the minds of many people a network of associations related to the brand with a large degree of similarity in its structure and elements.

Anyone who googles 'Black Cross' will be shown features of this event, such as merriment, lasting several days, camping, outdoors, music and beer. These are not very distinctive features and they may apply to the Roskilde Festival in Denmark and the Glastonbury Festival in the UK as well. But, there are also characterizations that are specific to the Black Cross: more or less unconventionally constructed vehicles take part in races at a motocross venue and the public is presented with displays, including many stunts; vehicles that have often taken clubs or groups of friends many months to build. Figure 6.2 shows the brand attributes of the Black Cross.

Fig. 6.2. Brand characteristics of Black Cross.

The Black Cross distinguishes itself clearly from other events. It has a certain aura, evokes a specific feeling and many people attribute more or less similar characteristics to it. So, Black Cross matches our most elementary definition of a brand: for many, the festival fulfils the promise of specific needs. That makes the Black

Cross indisputably a distinctive event and it also displays the characteristics of a brand. Does the festival behave like a brand as well: in other words, can you imagine that there is a magician who animates the brand?

Does the producer of the Black Cross, Feestfabriek Alles Komt Goed BV, handle its event as a brand? From a producer's perspective, it is essential to know what elements make up the construct, what the desired associations are, how to invoke them and which elements are preferably not seen or heard. The moment when this 'branding game' is performed consistently and successfully, Black Cross can be called a brand.

Brand thinking

Brand thinking is traditionally based on two principles:

- provide a competitive advantage
- create brand-added value.

The continual struggle of companies to distinguish themselves from their competitors shows that each product or service can be differentiated. This occurs in phases: from a generic to an expected to an augmented to a potential product (Levitt, 1980). Eggs are packed in batches of six or ten, in protective carton boxes. This means that the producer meets the consumer's minimum need of convenient transport. Further differentiation is then possible by producing a cholesterol-lowering egg by using special chicken feed. Such an adaptation goes beyond the minimum need of the consumer. To call something a potential product requires an addition that ties the consumer to the product. Through a code stamped on the egg, it will ultimately be possible to pay a virtual visit to the farm that has produced the egg. If we can believe Pine and Gilmore (1999), this will indeed be possible in the foreseeable future. They distinguish several phases in which economies are transmuted into ever new forms; in which companies make a new attempt to gain the favour of the consumer. A society in which the exchange of primary raw materials was the focal point was replaced by a product-oriented society in which, due to mechanization and economies-of-scale, the added value came under such pressure that the card of additional services had to be played. This phase was succeeded by the lifestyle phase, which was then followed by that of the experience market. The consumer does not merely buy a product with added services but a total and memorable experience. In this last, still utopian phase, they can see the emergence of a new commodity for the experience market: companies will become producers, or co-producers, of experiences that lead to a meaningful change in the consumer (see also Chapter 2).

The mutation of the Western exchange economy into an experience economy takes us straight to the heart of the leisure domain. The emergence of event producers, dating agencies or brokers in the creative industry is then a logical consequence. Marketing and branding have been linked to products for years, but it was not until recently that the service and experience industry started using the achievements of those fields of study. And the event and dating agencies in turn require differentiation to which brand thinking is one thing that can make a contribution. Building the brands of product and service providers and embracing a phenomenon like experiences, which is new to them, indeed places the leisure and event managers in the vanguard of strategic thinking in their original domain: theatres, museums, the worlds of sports and travel have been selling nothing but experiences for years. Therefore, it is an essential task for leisure and event managers to create a strong position for experience within the strategic brand policy of product and service providers, for example, through a live form of communication such as an event.

THE SIGNIFICANCE OF BRANDS

Meaning is attached to brands from two sides: the demand side is called brand-added value; the supply side is called brand equity.

The demand side: brand-added value

Brands have a so-called brand-added value. This concept, introduced by Riezebos (1995), has been further operationalized by Franzen (1996) as the added price a consumer is willing to pay on the basis of the difference in preference when a choice is made between the branded article *with* a brand name and the same article *without* a brand name. Using this concept, it is, for example, possible to find out how much more a student is willing to pay for a glass of Heineken or Bavaria beer than for an unbranded beer. A brand like Apple can offer its laptops at prices that are 30–65% higher than those of, for example, Acer or Dell.

It is a common misunderstanding that brand building and brand-added value are related to Maslow's theory of needs. Consumers were supposed to be prepared to pay much more to providers of products or services when pursuing the fulfilment of needs at higher levels; needs like appreciation, recognition and self-actualization. Even if this is indeed the case in times of plenty, it does not tell you anything about brand-added value, because this concerns the comparison of those who provide a brand and those who do not. The question of when consumers are willing to pay a premium in the form of brand-added value is then essential.

Over the past few years, an increasing number of researchers have come to share the point of view that brand-added values can be realized at all levels. Even in the case of a commodity like petrol (Shell Vpower), a brand can link symbolic, expressive and identity-affirming qualities. Whenever consumers find it hard to guess which expectations they are allowed to have with regard to the purchase of a product or service, and can derive a certain identity from a product category, building a brand is useful.

According to Chernatony and McDonald (1992), the functions of brands can affect consumers at different moments. The function of a brand can be that of identification, it can be related to assurance or it can be symbolic. During the orientation and purchasing stage, the identification or signalling function, as well as the assurance function, play a role. In the stage after the purchase, it is the symbolic function, that of owning something, that plays a role. These functions cannot be strictly separated. Moreover, the possessor function can affect the functions before or after the purchase.

Identification function

The identification function simplifies the process of choice for the consumer. How would we ever be able to make a quick choice from a shelf full of toothpastes if a brand name did not provide information to make identification possible? Without too much effort, the consumer recognizes the product, the product varieties, the intrinsic product attributes and the extrinsic product values. Colour, image, logo, design and holograms are cues that help recognition, so that, as a consumer, you know that you really have Signal toothpaste or an FC Barcelona shirt in your hands.

Assurance function

The assurance function offers a kind of guarantee of quality, but in addition it makes it possible for the consumer not to feel directly responsible in the case of failure. When one of the attractions at Disneyland is a disappointment, you do not have to think that it would have been better to take the children to another amusement park. In that case, you will look for emotional redress from the Disney brand, so that, as a parent, you do not cut a sorry figure. That makes the Disney brand risk averse.

Symbolic function

The symbolic function is an extra that comes with the brand after the purchase. Brands can add meaning to the lives of consumers. The symbolic function can be divided into an expressive function, a socio-adaptive function or an impressive function. The expressive function indicates that people show what they find important in life. Brands are an extension of someone's personality; they accentuate what a person stands for and what he finds important. The socio-adaptive function allows people to become part of a group. Brands give off the correct signals to subcultures and make it clear that someone wants to conform to the subculture concerned. In the case of the impressive function, it is not so much the environment that has an impact but the consumer's own feelings. If a visit to Sensation White makes someone feel great because of the special and paradisiacal decor of this dance event, the impressive function has been fulfilled. For a visitor who is focused on meeting the right people and being accepted by the group in question, the socio-adaptive function applies. This example shows that the efficacy of brands is dependent on the arguments of consumers.

The supply side: brand equity

Brand equity is the financial value that a brand represents for an organization or producer. Brand-added value offers the consumer added value due to the added value of the brand, but the producer can also look forward to a healthier balance sheet as a result of brand building. The financial value of a brand is often many times higher than that of the fixed assets on the balance sheet.

Brand equity is based on a series of certainties. A strong brand, for instance, has a group of purchasers and visitors who are loyal and who also propagate it to others. Nothing in this world is certain, but a brand offers some guarantee of potential buyers. Naturally, due to the preferential position taken by the consumer, a higher price can be asked for the products and services of a brand than for those that are unbranded. Besides, there is less price elasticity. From experiences in the retail sector, it is known that higher discounts can be obtained for strong brands when they are purchased. Even for the so-called A-brands, Spar (a strong brand with more than 12,000 shops in 30 countries) pays a lower purchasing price than the weaker Lidl. Such an effect can also be expected when strong event providers are involved, both on the purchasing side and in the process of acquiring sponsor contributions. To build a strong brand requires consumer insights, good marketing knowledge and excellent marketing and communication skills, but also the competence to carry out the strategic control of internal and external processes, consistently and over the years. This makes a strong brand an expression of high-level management as well; something that is much appreciated in the financial world.

BUILDING A BRAND

A brand contains the promise of an experience. A brand manager consciously determines how he would like to see his brand manifested in the minds of buyers.

Positioning is about creating a congruent relation between what the brand is, what is relevant to buyers and what distinguishes it from the brands of competitors. Sometimes, a brand builder is very free in building up brand identity; for example, when a completely new brand concept is being developed. Mostly, however, there already is an existing brand with features from its history or a strong link to the identity of the founder or founders. Positioning in the case of the Black Cross can be referred to as inside-out positioning. This means that the values and personality of the brand are a given, strongly linked to its founders. So, acquiring a better understanding of the internal aspect of a brand is an essential requirement for positioning. There are many methods of getting to the bottom of what a brand is. The methods that we will discuss in the following sections have been chosen for their orientation on values as well as their attention to external physical features. Accommodation, decor and multi-sensory stimulation can be utilized as distinguishing features with regard to events as brands as well as brand events.

Brand associations

In Fig. 6.2, we presented a number of brand attributes connected with the Black Cross Festival. They have been obtained from a survey among a small target group. It is relatively easy to organize such a survey. For example, people can be asked for their associations exclusively on the basis of the words 'Black Cross' or the logo. Naturally, a survey like this can only be conducted among people who have experience with the brand.

Biel (1999) has mapped out possible moments (see Fig. 6.3) when consumers come into contact with a brand (contacts) and on the basis of which they make associations (see Chapter 9 on touchpoints).

According to Lane (1993), building a strong brand image is dependent on three factors:

- the degree to which a consumer makes positive associations with the brand
- the intensity of the associations
- how unique those associations are.

Positive associations

Farquhar (1989) asserts that consumers assess a brand in three ways: from an emotional context, from observable characteristics and from intended behaviour. The degree to which consumers make positive associations with a brand is influenced strongly by the question whether they expect that the product or service will meet their needs. The quality of the product offered will be a key element of the consumers' assessment, besides the question of whether or not it is of added value to them. On delivery of the product or service, the company then has to prove that the association comes up to the expectations of the consumers. In their assessment, the consumers will, of course, take into account what the relevant features are in the context in which they will use the product or service. It is harder to make positive associations with product features that are relatively unimportant in the context concerned.

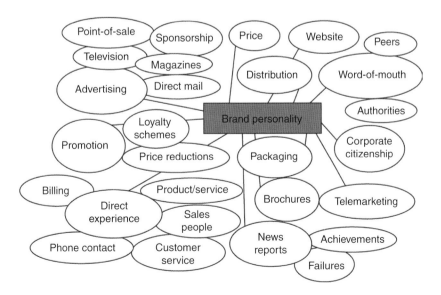

Fig. 6.3. Contacts (source: Biel, 1999).

Intensity of the associations

The intensity of brand associations depends on the way in which the information reaches the consumer and how that information supports the existing brand image. It is a function of both the quantity and the quality of the information. The more attention is paid to the contents of the information, the stronger will be the associations that ensue from it. There are two factors that will boost intensity: the personal relevance of the information to the consumer and the consistency of the information presented. The intensity of the brand association determines the speed and ease with which a consumer recalls the brand and the associations belonging to it. Another factor is the situation in which the consumer finds himself and the number of links to the brand in that situation. An attitude arising from behaviour-related experiences will be remembered more easily than an attitude based on indirect experiences that are not behaviour related. The degree to which the consumer is exposed to the information can also make it more likely that the information is remembered.

Unicity of the associations

The degree of uniqueness of brand associations is important because the brand must try to distinguish itself from other brands in the same product category. These unique associations should include superiority over other brands. This is an essential feature of the success of a brand. It is vital to focus consistently on this unique aspect, so that it is fixed in the mind of the consumer. Consistency in this context refers to the degree in which a particular association shows similarities to other associations of the same brand. Positioning of the brand is then used to obtain a sustainable competitive advantage or a unique sales proposition, so that the consumer has a convincing reason to buy the branded product. Unique brand associations can be based on features or advantages that are, or are not, product related. In many cases, the features that are not product related, like user type or user situation, will be the source of unique associations. Associations with a brand can also be shared with all brands in a product category. This usually concerns product-related features that are relevant to the consumer, and these features may also be a decisive factor in the response of consumers. Some of those features will be considered typical of or essential to all brands in a product category. In this way, shared associations make categorization possible, and the extent of the competition with other products and services can be determined. However, a disadvantage of shared associations is possible brand confusion.

Brand associative system

The aggregate of associatively linked brand attributes in a person's memory is called the brand associative system by Franzen and Bouwman (1999). This system is the residue of all brand observations and experiences that a consumer has absorbed in the course of time. Such brand observations and experiences in combination with the associations of the users of a brand (user image) can develop into a brand personality. People have a tendency, after all, to project human traits on to inanimate objects like a brand.

Separate brand attributes are mutually connected, but they can be ordered into a lower, higher or intermediary category. Building a structure requires an insight into the elements of an associations network. Reynolds and Gutman (1984) have come up with a means-end analysis, a method to determine how: (i) concrete attributes of a product or service can be abstracted to brand values; and (ii) how brand values in turn can be translated into concrete customer contacts.

The underlying model of the meaning structure analysis is the so-called means-end chain. Figure 6.4 shows the meaning structure of the means-end chain; a structure consisting of three levels, each with two sublevels.

1. Values or goals:
   Terminal values and fundamental values: the values that people find it important to pursue in their lives.
   Instrumental values: the way in which people try to realize terminal values in their lives.
2. Meanings/consequences:
   Psychosocial consequences: the way in which certain attributes of the product or service can be used by the consumer in a psychosocial context.
   Functional consquences: the consequences for the consumer of the use of a product or service.
3. Attributes of the product or service:
   Abstract attributes or benefits of the use of a product or service.
   Concrete attributes of a product or service.

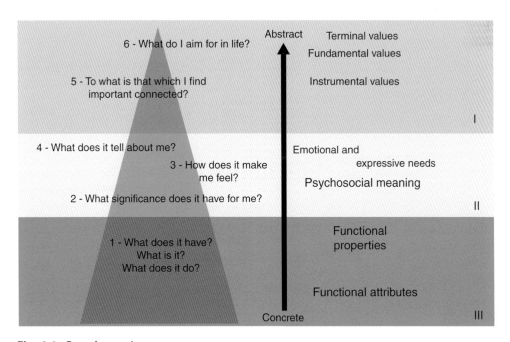

Fig. 6.4. Brand meanings.

In practice, it is certainly not always possible to distinguish three levels with regard to a product or service. The term 'meaning structure' refers to the fact that we lend meaning to everything that we see, hear and observe and that we, often unconsciously, place those meanings in a mental structure. We not only apply this to the people we meet (a form of stereotyping or pigeonholing) but also to products and brands as well.

Using the research technique referred to as laddering, Fig. 6.5 presents the means-end chain of the Black Cross (see also the section on quantitative measurement in Chapter 10). The 'cross' label is a concrete attribute. But, phrases like 'all is possible' and 'a fat lot I care' are connected with a terminal value, freedom.

So, the method of laddering is not only helpful in finding the connection between the various types of associations but also it presents us with the probable terminal values from which associations can be distilled. Events are generally experienced as entertainment products, and that is the reason why the more emotional attributes are also important when the client, the company, wants to develop a recurrent event into a strong brand.

The significance of the functional attributes of sensual brands should certainly not be overlooked. Indeed, they often affect the desired associations at other levels. The fact that the Gergiev Festival is organized in De Doelen in Rotterdam in a hall that is praised for its acoustics undoubtedly contributes to its popularity. And the enormous amount of attention that is traditionally paid to the decor of Sensation White in the USA is, in the eyes of the public, a distinguishing feature that will certainly contribute to how the festival is experienced and to the significance it has for individual visitors. Figure 6.5 shows that the elements of motocross, mopeds and stunts, are connected strongly with the terminal values of 'a fat lot I care' and 'everything is possible'.

Value patterns

Value patterns are very important in the positioning of brands and in giving them meaning. Since 'sensual brands' are sold on the basis of the need for happiness or identity that they

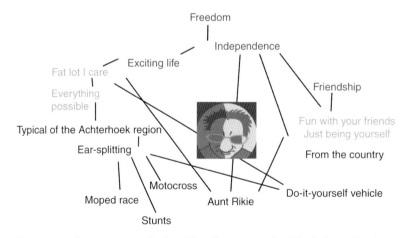

Fig. 6.5. Structure of meaning analysis with reference to the Black Cross Festival.

can fulfil, values are clearly essential in the development of brands in the fields of leisure and events. Vyncke (2002) refers to values as happiness criteria. The degree in which someone can realize their values determines their happiness. But, values are also the central element of the formation of a self-image. So, that makes values criteria of identity as well. People are searching for something new that is worth the trouble of identifying with. In clubs and, to a lesser extent, in churches, the role of brands is emerging as one that is of significance as a determinant of identity. Something that started as a joke with the magicians, Hendrik Jan Lovink and Gijs Jolink, and manager, Ronny Degen, when they first organized the Black Cross has turned out to be a very strong product, to say the least, with all the right ingredients for making it even stronger. The associations are related strongly to what the Achterhoek region stands for: an independent life, lived in your own way, living it up, a little rebellious expressed in words like 'nobody tells me what to do', averse to 'moaning and groaning'. Aunt Rikie, the queen of the festival, personifies those characteristics to perfection. But the other elements of the festival, such as stunts, cross and mopeds, are strong attributes that under the banner of 'everything is possible' and 'a fat lot I care' lead to an experience of freedom.

The Trendbox research agency has mapped out the value pattern of the Dutch people (see Fig. 6.6). The figure displays four value segments on the basis of the dimensions of collective versus individual and order versus freedom. These segments are a representation of

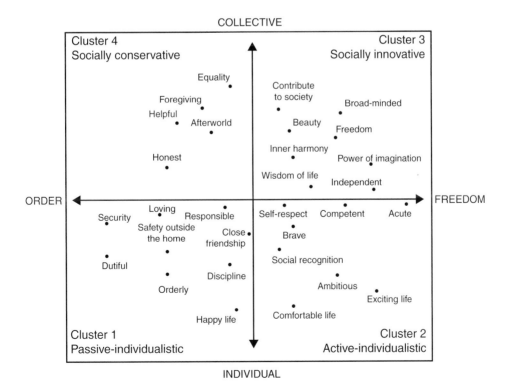

Fig. 6.6. Value pattern of the Dutch (source: Kralingen, 1999).

what people find important. The strong feeling of freedom is fed by instrumental values such as independence and broad-mindedness. In the eyes of its founders, the starting point of the Black Cross Festival was the idea for a nice party. It could be said that the Black Cross reflects the identity of its founders.

On the basis of the grouping of Fig. 6.6, Trendbox has come up with a refined grouping of eight segments (see Fig. 6.7) in which groups can be recognized with a more or less similar orientation on values, and thus on behaviour. The idea here is that a brand with an equivalent orientation will establish a natural relationship with groups of people in the segment in question.

The value of such groupings does not really lie in the absolute segments, because a population does not only change in its composition but also in its orientation. And although an environment-conscious event manager will now and then see new groupings drift across his desk, they are only presented here to show that as a brand builder you can reach more or less like-minded people in a society by using value patterns.

The relevance of features

Finally, besides the issues of grouping and hierarchy, a closer study of brand associations can also give rise to questions about the relevance of features. From the meaning structure analysis presented earlier, it appears that in contrast to the Achterhoek region, the element of 'countryside' has no link to other elements. Franzen and van den Berg (2002) distinguish brand associations, the key concept and mental assets. They claim that brand associations are relevant in so far as they lead to higher appreciation and/or persuade a consumer to buy

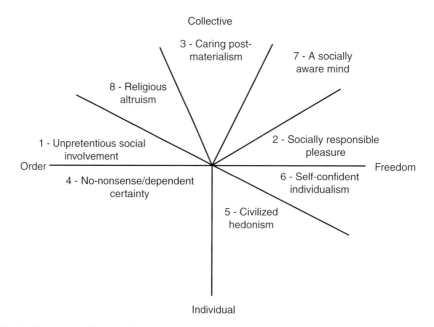

Fig. 6.7. Refinement of the value pattern (source: Kralingen, 1999).

something. Part of the brand associations of consumers is covered by the core concept. This concerns all associations that are relevant to the positioning of the brand in a person's memory (brain positioning). Finally, there are associations that are related to buying behaviour. They belong to mental assets. Those associations have a positive effect on the competitive position and the power of a brand. 'Stunts' and 'cross' are extremely relevant to the positioning of the Black Cross. As a consequence, these attributes merit the full attention of the brand builder.

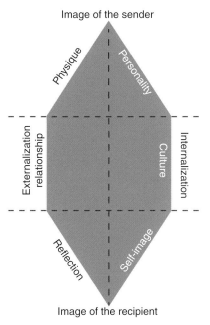

Fig. 6.8. Brand-identity prism (source: Kapferer, 1992).

Identity prism

Another method to discover what a brand stands for is the brand-identity prism developed by Kapferer (1992) and shown in Fig. 6.8.

The prism displays six aspects of brand identity: physical, personality, culture, relationship, reflection and self-image. Additionally, a distinction is made between the image of the sender and that of the receiver. What makes the prism such a powerful tool is that it makes it possible to analyse an existing brand carefully, but it can also be used to find out what the brand could or should be and what the brand or event manager must organize externally to convey the desired image.

The description of a strong brand should be like that of a person in terms of physical and personal characteristics, but it should also include elements of the stereotypical user denoted by the terms 'reflection' and 'self-image'. A brand has aspects that determine its inner side: personality, culture and self-image. But, on the basis of this inner side, it also displays an outer side that is in harmony with it through physical aspects, relationship and reflection.

What all strong brands share is that all those aspects are attuned to each other properly or logically. We will discuss the six aspects of brand identity next.

The physical aspect

The physical aspect concerns everything that a person links to a brand name in terms of physical aspects. How does the consumer recognize the brand? Is there a recognizable image or design style? What, in fact, does the brand look like? Although Kapferer does not include a multi-sensory function in his prism, questions could be asked, such as: what does the brand taste, smell or feel like? Aunt Rikie's logo is a recognizable expression of the Black Cross Festival. The importance of design as a physical signature reflecting personality is being accepted more and more widely with regard to brands.

Personality

Personality points to the character of a brand. By the way it is displayed or presented in the physical world, a brand shows that it has a distinct character. This can go to great lengths; for example, a brand that consciously uses a *personal endorser*: a person representing the brand. Aunt Rikie is the personification of the Black Cross. Aunt Rikie interprets this as just being yourself and an attitude of 'a fat lot I care'. Mark and Pearson (2001) have described archetypes that, in practice, can be recognized in brands as well (see Table 6.1).

Culture

Culture is the system of values and basic principles; it is what guides a brand. It is culture that provides a direct link between the brand and the organization. Fun in the way of the Achterhoek region: this is the culture, do not dress things up.

Relationship

The relationship shows how the brand is related to the buyer. In the case of the Black Cross, the relationship can be described as 'my best friend who is always in for a good party'.

Table 6.1. Archetypes and brands (source: Mark and Pearson, 2001).

Archetype	Helps people	Brand example
Creator	Craft something new	Williams-Sonora
Caregiver	Care for others	Zwitsal
Ruler	Exert control	American Express
Jester	Have a good time	Pepsi
Regular guy/gal	Be OK just as they are	Dirk van den Broek
Lover	Find and give love	Hallmark
Hero	Act courageously	Nike
Outlaw	Break the rules	Harley-Davidson
Magician	Affect transformation	Calgon
Innocent	Retain or renew faith	Oil of Olay
Explorer	Maintain independence	Levi's
Sage	Understand their world	Oprah's Book Club

Reflection

Reflection refers to the stereotypical user of the brand. Thus, the Black Cross Festival appeals to a young, non-urban person who wants to have a few days of uninterrupted fun. The actual target group of the Black Cross is much broader: from young families to the over-fifties, everyone who feels the appeal of the same set of values – fun, independence and freedom. The biggest mistake a company can make with respect to a brand is to present a portrait of a person in its communication who is an actual mirror of the target group. The trick is finding representatives of the value patterns in question.

Self-image

Self-image refers to the mirror that the target group holds up to itself. If the brand knows about the image that the target group likes to create of itself with the help of the brand, powerful information will be available for communication purposes. As the mother visiting the Black Cross with her son says, it is all about a setting in which he, as well as she, are free to do their own thing, letting their hair down: a carnival of the East. To obtain more information about self-image, researchers should be able to hear what is not actually said. After all, a male consumer will not say out loud that he buys Axe body spray to compensate for his inferiority complex toward women.

BRAND EVENTS: USING THE PRINCIPLES OF BRAND BUILDING

As said at the beginning of this chapter, there are events that are, or have become, a brand, or want to become one, and events that are used by companies to load their brands in the sense of giving it meaning. There are plenty of examples in the field of events of those that have developed into a brand, or have the potential of doing so, such as the Sziget Festival in Budapest, Hungary, the Rock in Rio in Lisbon, Portugal, and Tomorrowland in Boom, Belgium. Still, the number of providers consciously using a marketing strategy remains limited. But, in relation to events, the role of branding is more than merely helping an event to develop into a strong brand. The event as a brand has earlier been discussed extensively; here, we focus on the role of events connected with a strong brand.

Companies use events to explicate or accentuate their brand positioning. There are various strategies to do so. We compare those strategies with types of events and, with the help of concrete examples including that of Red Bull, the maker of energy drinks, we will show how an image transfer is created (an example of Red Bull is also provided in Chapter 1).

Red Bull, with its proposition of 'giving you wings', has several brand-specific and -sponsored events that the company uses to make its own brand positioning absolutely clear. This makes Red Bull a good example of a company that is willing to make a big investment in order to load its own brand positioning through the strategic use of events. Think of the Red Bull

Air Race World series and the Formula 1 teams, Red Bull Racing and Scuderia Toro Rosso. The firm became actively involved in Formula 1 by buying up Jaguar Racing and the Minardi team. Moreover, the company owns three soccer teams: Red Bull Salzburg, playing in Austria's top league, MetroStars, an American club whose name is now Red Bull New York, and SSV Markranstädt (Red Bull Leipzig), which plays in a minor league.

Box 6.3　Red Bull

The area between the Meuse tunnel and the Erasmus Bridge in Rotterdam will be the place to be this Saturday and Sunday for those who love a racing spectacle in the air. The Red Bull Air Race World Series is in the port of Rotterdam for an event that will be broadcast extensively by RTL GP on the RTL channel and the event it covers is described as follows.

The Red Bull Air Race World Series started at Abu Dhabi in the United Arab Emirates at the beginning of April and flew on to the American cities of San Diego and Detroit. In the Red Bull Air Race World Series, 12 pilots vie with each other to decide who is the best. Speed, precision and skills are crucial. After Rotterdam, the daredevils will go to London, Budapest, Porto and Perth, among other cities. As the races are about flying low at top-speed and extremely hard manoeuvres involving high G forces, only very experienced participants will perform in this spectacle. (Source: RTL 7, Saturday 19 July 2008, 12.00 noon.)

Figure 6.9 shows where brands use events as a branding and marketing tool. The objectives of brand building are given against a dark background. This concerns stand-alone brand building and has not been discussed so far. The light background covers brand building via the phenomenon of image transfer.

Image transfer

Image transfer is the transfer of valuable associations on the part of the consumer, or visitor, from one brand to another brand, product or activity. From all the impressions and experiences that people have with a brand, they create an image for themselves (Keller, 1993). People create an image of a phenomenon through chains, or networks, of associations. This produces a mosaic of impressions, the totality of which is the image (van Riel, 1996). At least two parties are required for an image transfer: a source and a target. The target, the public or a visitor or consumer, must have certain associations at a source, because otherwise there is nothing to transfer. There are three chief categories of associations: content, polarity and power.

The content says something about the *what* of the associations. Sensation White, for instance, can be associated with dance, paradisiacal, beautiful, out of this world. Polarity refers to the labelling of the content: positive or negative. 'Out of this world' may then be seen as the taking of 'pills'. Power, finally, is an indication of the intensity of the associations linked to a brand.

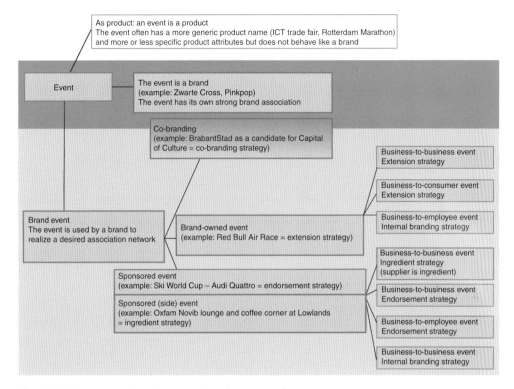

Fig. 6.9. Events as a branding and marketing tool.

Brand strategies

Brand image transfer is a part of several brand strategies: ingredient branding, extension strategy, co-branding strategy and endorsement strategy. Though internal branding as such is not a brand strategy, it is true to say that image transfer is indeed used in developing an internal brand. That is the reason why internal branding is incorporated in Fig. 6.10 and is discussed in detail in the section on internal branding events.

EVENTS BASED ON IMAGE TRANSFER

Below, we will deal with various events, each of which utilizes image transfer. In addition, a connection is made to the types of events (see also the section on types of event marketing in Chapter 3).

Brand-specific events

Brand-specific events are events totally controlled by the organizer, who is also the financier. At a brand-specific event, the aim is to convey as precisely as possible those associations that are valuable to and desired by the consumer. The source can invoke a very clear association

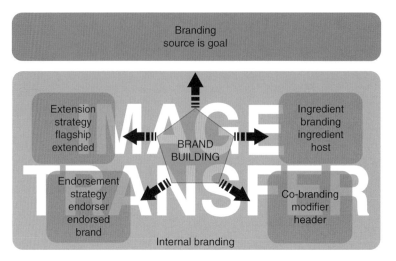

Fig. 6.10. Branding strategies connected with image transfer.

network that is channelled to a different setting and a different product form, and which can even grow into a cash cow on its own. Heineken beer uses the Heineken Music Hall in Amsterdam to try to channel associations and an experience to a new product form. The Music Hall could be seen as an extension, an extended product of Heineken, the flagship. Anyhow, this is about multi-channelling the Heineken experience.

Red Bull profits because the Red Bull Air Race enables the company to get across to a much wider public what is the meaning of 'giving wings to' and to boost the appreciation of the brand among potential buyers, generally young people. As a result, it is a successful example of a business-to-consumer event. When the air race is also a VIP event for stakeholders, distributors and retail chains, the moment has arrived that a business-to-business event has been linked to the brand-specific event. In that particular setting, the gives-you-wings experience can acquire an extra dimension with an appropriate decor and catering.

The wings can be regarded as a concrete attribute and the power of the bull as an abstract one. This is how Red Bull adds something extra to the idea of flying, in dizzying stunts, feats performed by stunt pilots flying between pylons and under bridges. The pilots are the embodiment of what is expressed by 'getting everything out of life'. And of course, they themselves need a boost from time to time to be able to sustain life on the edge (shown in Fig. 6.11).

Brand extension is a strategy that involves an extension of the brand to new markets, target groups and user moments, while preserving the brand name. The magazine of the same name as the Black Cross, for example, provides the possibility to entertain a relationship with the brand outside the actual event, in the pre- and post-exposure phases. This opens the door to other advertisers as well. The more value-oriented a brand is, the greater the potential for extending it, as is shown in Fig. 6.12.

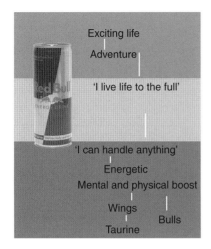

Fig. 6.11. Meaning structure analysis of Red Bull.

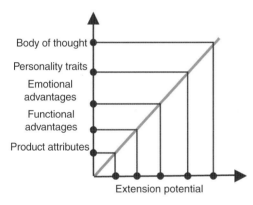

Fig. 6.12. Possibilities for brand extension.

Brand extensions are an attractive way to innovate. The brand has already been established among buyers, which makes it very likely that new logical products will be accepted. The marketing and communication costs involved in launching the new product do not have to be very high, and the risks are limited. Besides, the extension can clarifty the positioning of the brand. Thus, it is also a strategy to increase brand equity, a strategy that may be so attractive to brands that there is a danger of overstretching. The Harley-Davidson wine coolers and Bic underwear are examples of overstretching. The extensions failed because the products were too far removed from the core of the brand.

Sponsored events

An event is referred to as a sponsored event when a brand, the endorsed brand, attempts to link up to an already existing event: the endorser. The naming firm is a co-financier, but does not have complete control. Because the firm sees possibilities to reinforce its brand image, it joins an event organized by another party with its own brand. The World Cup ski races provided the Audi brand with an excellent chance to build a clearer image of the Quattro, a sub-brand in fact, in an original way. A sub-brand is one that shares features with the parent brand, but, in addition, it has its own association network that translates the brand value of 'independence' into 'control under all conditions'.

The meaning structure analysis in Fig. 6.13 displays the general build-up of Quattro. Originally, Quattro was the label of Audi's four-wheel-drive vehicles, but it developed more and more into a sub-brand. If ever there was an activity that could be used to bring out the performance element of grip, it is skiing on a knife edge: the World Cup is held in wintry conditions in the most famous ski resorts in the world. Besides its efforts aimed at the public, Audi can now organize hospitality events as part of the travelling circus of the World Cup that are aimed at suppliers and the bigger buyers of the brand, like fleet managers. Moreover, Audi has invested money in a facility of its own in Finland, where you can join the ice-drive experience for a week.

Audi also organizes one-day training events, skid courses, provided in the Netherlands by Gijs van Lennep, to gain the 'responsible' Quattro experience.

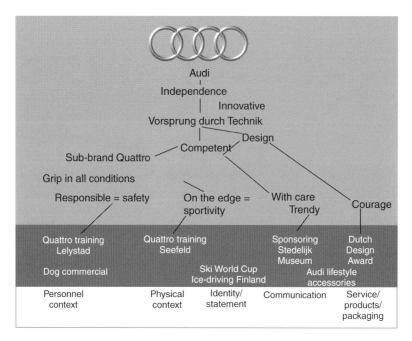

Fig. 6.13. Meaning structure analysis and the events within it.

Finally, a few words about the Dutch Design Awards. This is an event aimed primarily at the Dutch market and meant to highlight design coupled with boldness. The Dutch Design Awards have been organized for some time and have become famous for the presentation of the best that up-and-coming designers have to offer. Audi has sponsored the event for several years. In this way, Audi is reinforcing its position as a leading stimulator of design. Audi has a long-term sponsor contract to make the renovation of the Stedelijk Museum in Amsterdam possible, and also organizes events of a smaller scale at the museum. The collaboration with this leading museum in the field of modern art underlines the importance of design to Audi. The selected events have extra value because Audi uses innovative digital technology not only in the design of brochures, showrooms, commercials and its website but also in its cars.

In the case of Quattro, the strategy concerned is an endorsement strategy. Audi, the owner, feeds Quattro, the sub-brand. The upper value areas of the analysis are also valid for the Quattro brand. Quattro probably also adds something to the endorser, something like unbridled sporting achievements, but also responsibility. Thus, an almost perfect situation has come about in which both brands share and increase their power.

Sponsored side events are a subcategory of sponsored events. A brand does not lend its name to the entire event but to a specific part, because it is that part that conveys exactly what the brand wants to achieve. That is why Oxfam Novib, for instance, has set up an easily accessible coffee corner at festivals to reach young people with its not-only-aid-but-fair-trade message, and to acquire a young image.

Ingredient branding event

Sometimes, it is attractive to the host of an event to advertise prominently a partner (ingredient) who is part of the total event. The reason may be that the partner has a very high-quality profile among the target group, often due to patents. Thus, a musical event at which superior sound is important can obtain added value if a partner like Bose contributes to it. A mountain-biking event powered by Shimano can gain in strength. It is also possible that the chief host has a profile without much differentiation and needs the ingredients to convey particular clear signals. A relatively unknown women-only event, for example, can suddenly achieve a distinct profile by linking it to Moët & Chandon, Illy or Nespresso, and when powered by Omo, it will be a different kind of event altogether. Finally, an event may be new and unknown, and vague as well, because it belongs to a new category. A business event at which ingredients like Oxfam Novib, the International Red Cross, Yacht and Yer are displayed gives off a signal that it has something to do with recruitment in the charity market.

Co-branding

When two brands put a new product on the market under a shared name, this is referred to as co-branding. In the world of events, co-branding is common as a means of branding a destination, a city, region or country. Lafferty and Chalip (2006) have shown that the degree to which the combination of brands is suitable is related to the strength of the association between the two brands. With regard to the connection between the event and a place, city or region, the rule applies that the host should organize only those events that are linked to the associations of the destination in question. Another essential condition is that both brands are known to some extent.

The link between the 2010 Tour de France and the city of Rotterdam, where the start of the race took place, was all about the vitality of the city, sports, sustainability, the environment, healthy food and exercise. Everything under the banner of 'New Energy'. The positive attributes of the Tour de France as a dynamic sports event were linked to Rotterdam as a driven, innovative, dynamic city with great potential. The vitality of the city was communicated through club cycle races and a prologue as concrete attributes.

The idea behind the coupling of the Capital of Culture and BrabantStad 2018 is also based on the principles of co-branding. BrabantStad is the urban network of the five big cities in Brabant, Breda, Eindhoven, Helmond, 's-Hertogenbosch and Tilburg *and* the province of Noord-Brabant. BrabantStad is an enthusiastic and professional network with an investment programme of €1.4 billion and concrete projects that are carried out together. BrabantStad is the A-brand of this collaboration. The link to the brand of Capital of Culture opens up possibilities for stakeholders in the region for the self-examination of distinctive cultural attributes. It is then essential to create a faithful image on the basis of the attributes that link this region to mutual projects that can be undertaken to utilize those attributes better, and make them come across well. Just as in the world of co-branding of product brands – Philips and Douwe

Egberts with Senseo – this will lead ultimately to innovative insights, projects and attractions among certain target groups like international investors in employment. In Chapter 7, we will deal with the example of BrabantStad in more depth.

INTERNAL BRANDING EVENTS

When a company focuses an event on its own staff, this is referred to as internal branding. In her book, Barendse-Schijvens (2009) describes that a brand image is also formed by the employees, who act in accordance with the values of the brand. Ideally, the image of a company is built up from the inside, and not the other way round. Employees act in accordance with the brand values, either consciously or unconsciously. Each experience a customer has with the organization confirms the image of the service or product. Conveying the correct brand associations to the internal branding event will be most successful if it is controlled by the company itself. Another option is hiring a specialized event agency to make the link to the brand.

Some organizations have been value driven from the moment they were founded: the founder has a very clear picture of what the principles of the company are and what it wants to achieve. He makes a business model and selects staff on the basis of those principles, or moulds them to fit the desired profile. As has become clear in practice, it is not always simple in the longer term to make a company fit the original mould. As a result of the growth of the company, the absence of the original owner, or mergers and takeovers, the original principles may be watered down. Besides, changes in the market may require a reconsideration and reappraisal of the way in which the values have been worked out in the business model, the positioning of the brand and communication. When this moment has come, the organization can discover, or rediscover, its positioning, or confirm it and accentuate it again through the process of internal branding. Internal branding events can be a vital part of a campaign to attain that goal. Internal branding is a matter of aligning the external brand (marketing) with the employees (HRM) and the identity of the organization (internal communication). Examples of internal branding events are presented in Table 6.2.

Aim of internal branding

Internal branding has a dual purpose. The primary objective of internal branding is the optimization of the consumer or visitor experience. Marketers realize that a brand is reinforced externally when this brand is supported internally and is reflected in the conduct of the employees. The second objective concerns greater commitment on the part of the employees; employees feel more involved with the organization and the brand. Internal branding goes beyond internal communication. Internal communication is mainly a matter of getting a message across to the employees, knowledge. According to Ind (2007), there is a general misconception on the part of management that internal communication is something that always comes across. If it does not, it must simply be a matter of more communication. But, it should be realized that

Table 6.2. Examples of internal branding events (source: Liebregts, 2007).

Cause	Objective	Keywords programme	Communication
A merger event integrating two companies into one, official kick-off	After this meeting, employees of both organizations should be totally committed to the new organization and convey the correct message externally	Informative, pleased, proud, clear, collaboration, new, feeling at home in new organization	Prior exploratory year with new organization, recurring continually in communication. During event, explicit use should be made of values and feelings. Afterwards, at place of work, again form of communication by new organization
A kick-off leadership event, new identity, organization turned into separate company split into two different departments	Trust in management, understanding of corporate culture, challenge to think along, altering awareness, positive feeling, minimizing distance between management and employees	Surprising, understanding/ open trust, feedback, challenge, cooperation, confidence, respect, ambition	Prior involvement in event because of assigned task. Very direct communication during event via management, open! Afterwards, employees receive card with summary of the day
Improving and anchoring internal branding process, reinforcing attachment to brand. Generally applicable concept	Gaining insight by experience. The relationship among employees and the commitment they have to the original organization is becoming visible and palpable again	Transparency, trust, ambition, understanding, respect, together, warmth	During this event, communication is live to a large extent. This is continued afterwards, during a period in which focus is on communication of values for 3 months

(Continued)

Table 6.2. Continued.

Cause	Objective	Keywords programme	Communication
Staff meeting to express thanks and pride after year of reorganization	Personal commitment to company and employees reconfirmed by managing director. Employees experience moment of pride, for themselves and pride of the organization	Personal/open, gratitude, pride, surprising, social, 'me' feeling, together	Personal invitations mailed to home address because of target group: mechanics. Very direct communication on part of managing director during event. Afterwards, report by employee in house magazine
An annually recurring leadership event during which information is given about internal matters	Following internal branding process, informing and mobilizing managers with respect to organization now and in the future	Information, fun, networking, trust, ambition, together, open	E-mail with invitation sent by management itself. After event management will make tour of all outlets to create openness. This is also an annually recurring event
A short trip with integrated event together with entire organization, to live the brand	Reinforcing internal branding process, receiving and giving feedback, experiencing 'me' feeling within organization. Experiencing brand, working with brand	'Me' feeling, cooperating, breaking down walls, trust, personal, enterprising, self-willed	Teaser campaign followed by extra information on intranet. Task assigned beforehand. Dealt with during event and assigned new task on conclusion of event

besides top-down communication, it is vital to create facilities for bottom-up and horizontal communication. Culture and style are then more important than a set of procedures. To achieve identification with the principles of the organization, an activity is often much more important than communication.

When a brand involves direct contact with a customer, it is an essential requirement that the experience as propagated by the brand is in accordance with the experience at the moment of direct contact with the employees. But, internal branding is not limited to customer departments. It is a fact that its effect will be strongest if the entire organization and all its employees forge the brand, internally and externally, by the way they act, think and do things.

Corporate identity

If the original principles of the organization have been watered down, it will be necessary to polish up its identity. In addition to the methods that we mentioned of describing a brand, there is a model of the corporate identity of a brand. Groenendijk *et al.* (2000) have defined corporate identity as 'the strategically planned and operationally instituted self-presentation and conduct of an enterprise, internally and externally, on the basis of a prescribed entrepreneurial philosophy, a long-term business objective and a specific desired image, with the intention to make all functional elements of an enterprise operational as one entity, both internally and externally'.

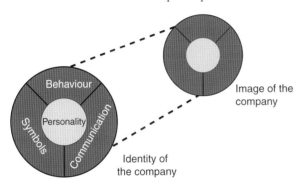

Fig. 6.14. Model of corporate identity (source: Groenendijk *et al.*, 2000).

The model presented in Fig. 6.14 is a tool to describe identity in practice. From the communication, symbolism and conduct of the enterprise, a personality crystallizes as a fourth dimension of corporate identity. The benefit of the model lies in the fact that it tells managers that practice-what-you-preach is relevant to their conduct, communication and applied symbolism. Moreover, the model offers something to go on when the three external manifestations of the identity of the organization and the desired aura of the event have to be brought into alignmment. The major weakness of the model is, however, its focus on the outer skin of identity. What determines the identity and what is found to be of vital importance within the organization gets no mention.

Bernstein's spiderweb method

Bernstein's spiderweb method has been described extensively by Cees van Riel in *Identiteit en imago* (*Identity and Image*) (van Riel, 1996). This method is not the only one that is used to map out the core values of an organization, but it is an effective method. People are invited in groups of a maximum of ten persons to define the core values of the organization. They are sometimes picked out randomly and sometimes they are selected. Subsequently, the participants indicate on a five- or ten-points scale the degree in which the organization propagates those values. By setting out those figures in a diagram, a spiderweb emerges that shows the core values and the degree of importance (see Fig. 6.15). Other stakeholders can be invited to do the same thing, which makes it possible to map out the differences in the internal and external experience of the brand.

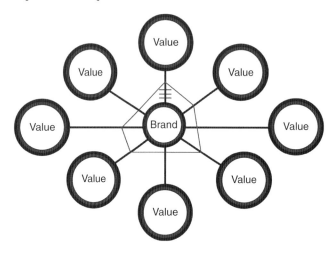

Fig. 6.15. Spiderweb method.

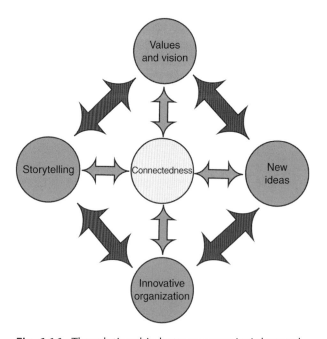

Fig. 6.16. The relationship between new insights and involvement in an organization.

On the basis of the information obtained internally, and possibly externally, a vision can be formulated. And from this, the brand promise that describes what the organization/the brand promises its customers can ultimately be distilled.

From the insights thus acquired, innovative ideas and new stories emerge within the brand created by the employees, and told on. The new ideas lead to a new way of organizing different processes and systems that are given shape by those involved, among others, and there is further encouragement for management and employees to continue on the path they have taken. The realization of the regenerating organization leads, internally and externally, to the first success stories, and they in turn will feed new storytelling (see Fig. 6.16).

Events are a unique way of loading brands and filling them with emotion. The following example of Deloitte Nederland (Box 6.4) clearly shows how an event conveys the essence of a brand and strategy with the help of emotions.

Box 6.4 Deloitte Nederland

Key data

Project management: Deloitte Nederland (Communication Department)

Creative concept and material and technical production: Otter creators BV

Location: de Efteling, the Netherlands

Date: 1 July 2010

Number of guests: 700

As a consequence of several developments, Deloitte has honed its services and branding. The world of its clients is getting increasingly complex in the field of tax advice. Standard solutions no longer suffice and clients want not only tailor-made advice but also advice in a broader context. Advice *and* implementation ensure maximum added value. The mission of Deloitte has been adapted to this changed requirement and is now 'We know how': deciding together with the client not only what should be done but also how it should be done. The driving values behind this are: think *and* do, passion, understanding what the client wants and a no-nonsense attitude.

Deloitte's strategy for the following years was adapted as well. The launch of the strategy was supported by a multimedia internal campaign. In addition to newsletters, a plenary webcast, decentralized team meetings and, at the end, a central live kick-off were organized to introduce the strategy. It was in particular the plenary closing event that was essential as the official starting point of the strategy. Deloitte asked event marketing specialists, de Otter creators, to develop the optimum creative and emotional programme. Their primary goals were: meaningfully communicating the renewed Deloitte and 'loading' motivation for the new strategy. An infotainment programme with various items was developed in a theatrical setting (the Efteling Theatre in the Netherlands), and after the programme, there was time for relaxation with a visit to the park and a concert to conclude the day. The choice of the theatre was a conscious one: a setting in which aids such as light, projection, music, cabaret, the presentation of formats and stage props were used to get the message across in an emotional way. Variation was the keyword that applied to everything. In spite of the relatively long official programme of 2.5 h, it turned out afterwards that the 700 guests had not felt it was very long at all! As a result of the different formats and the short attention spans required for various parts of the programme, a large amount of information was communicated to the audience in bite-sized, emotional chunks. Other features of the programme were interaction and a logical structure. For example, before the interval, various stakeholders and other participants were given the floor to explain why the new strategy was necessary. There were contributions from all over the world, to give substance to the 'as one' feeling. In addition, the strategy was

(Continued)

Box 6.4. Continued.

clarified by the optimum use of visual aids, and it assumed an identity because several of those responsible had been given a role in the programme. The use of voting equipment made interaction with the audience possible; the feedback thus obtained was in turn used as input for the programme.

After the interval, there was only one item on the programme, the concrete question of 'what's in it for me?' For individual staff in the audience, what are the implications of the Deloitte organization's new global strategy in the Netherlands? Three initiatives were dealt with in more detail, and by using humour, fascinating images and interaction, the consequences were made explicit to those present. Afterwards, the audience used keywords like 'proud', 'essential' and 'motivated' to characterize the meeting: absolute proof that an event can have an optimum effect as a tool to build and load a brand.

SUMMARY

A brand should be in alignment with the needs of the consumer. In this respect, brand attributes are of vital importance. On the demand side, brand functions include identification, assurance and symbolic functions. On the supply side, there is a role for brand building with the related brand associations and values. Some events have become brands themselves. The Black Cross is an example of this.

Companies use events to load their brands, to accentuate their positioning. Think of the air races organized by Red Bull. Among other things, the process of image transfer and co-branding is used in this context.

A company uses internal branding events to address its own employees, in which optimization of the customer or visitor experience is the main objective.

chapter 7

Events and City Marketing: The Role of Events in Cities

Jacco van Mierlo

City marketing is a form of marketing that utilizes events, among other things, to make a city pleasant to live in and attractive for inhabitants, companies and visitors, and to do this in a sustainable way. This chapter covers the emergence of city marketing and city branding, and the relevant developments in these fields.

LEARNING TARGETS

After studying this chapter, you will have learned:

- how city marketing has developed
- what is meant by city marketing and city branding
- the role events play in city marketing policy
- the role of events in how a city functions; what an events policy is
- what the impact is of city marketing and events on the major target groups of a city
- what an eventful city is
- how a city can utilize events successfully as a strategic tool.

This chapter is about the role of events in a city. Such events take place in a broad context; therefore, we have opted for a broad approach. Besides, an understanding of the real role of events within a city will be limited if we only look at it from the traditional way of city marketing.

Bear in mind, too, that existing publications already pay much attention to events and city marketing, but the role of events and how they can be exploited has been the subject of study to a much lesser extent.

After a discussion of the emergence of city marketing, we will describe the development of the role of the city and city marketing in the past century. We will also provide a definition of city marketing. Next, a link will be made to the core of this chapter; the role that events play or may play within the framework of how a city functions. We will deal with the role of events from various angles.

THE EMERGENCE OF CITY MARKETING

These days, it is hard to find any city that is not familiar with city marketing or is not yet consciously involved in it. Cities try to distinguish themselves from their competitors by positioning themselves as an attractive proposition. This has not come out of the blue. To understand contemporary city marketing, a bit of history is useful.

> Originally a city was a compact settlement usually enclosed by walls and canals and it had few rights and freedoms. Generally, it was not merely an administrative centre but also a trade and craft centre. What made a city attractive in those days was its autonomy with respect to feudal rules, the security it provided and the solidarity that was organised there. This was known through word-of-mouth.
>
> As a result of industrialization in the nineteenth century factories were set up in the cities and the workers settled near those factories in the cities. The attractiveness of the city was mainly determined by location factors from then on. The proximity of raw materials or a favourable site close to transport routes were decisive factors for a manufacturer who had to choose a city to set up a factory. Because of the money they could earn there workers were lured to the city. By then the administrative entity had become a municipality.
>
> The second half of the twentieth century saw the emergence of the service sector and factories were shut down. Increasing prosperity also enabled the employees to live outside the city where they worked. This gave rise to the building of dormitory towns outside the historic and industrial cities. This led to depopulation of the inner cities, because in the evenings and during the weekends the employees working in commercial or municipal jobs were watching TV in their dormitory towns. The inner cities turned into ghostly rows of houses from which all life seemed to have gone.
>
> (Noordman, 2004)

City promotion

City promotion was already being used in the 1940s in an attempt to retain the city for its inhabitants, or to get them to return to it. The following text is from a brochure issued in Amsterdam in 1939:

> Amsterdam is a city to live in. Amsterdam is not expensive! Live where you work! Cheap necessities of life! Fifteen museums, eight theatres, 34 cinemas!!

Each year thousands of families return! If you move outside the city, you will be poorer for hundreds of guilders due to expenditure on removal, furnishing, laying out a garden, and so on, but you will at least have one positive experience: Amsterdam is not expensive!!!

(Source: Buursink, 1991)

This is a clear example of promoting cities over the countryside, whereas these days, there is much competition between cities.

In those days, the municipal authorities saw that their duties went beyond the mere provision of information to the inhabitants; promoting their city was now part of the communication package. It was, however, not until the 1980s that this was referred to as city promotion. The aim of promotion was not only to attract residents to the city or to retain them (residential city promotion). Cities also aimed their promotion at tourists, and for that purpose the 'Verenigingen voor Vreemdelingenverkeer', tourist offices, were set up at the end of the 19th century (Buursink, 1991).

Although city officials made great efforts to retain residents in the city and to attract tourists by using city promotion, the period up to the beginning of the 1980s was dominated by discussions about urban decline and urban problems, in which the focus was on poverty, unemployment, criminality and poor housing. Cities had to contend with a bad image, well-to-do residents moved to the quieter and greener adjoining towns, and many cities were in financial trouble.

The emergence of city marketing

Although urban problems have not disappeared, the image of the city had taken a positive turn by the end of the 1980s. Opportunities and plans for development were now predominant, and at the same time a positive view of cities was emerging. Ashworth *et al.* (2004) claim that social and cultural causes are the reasons for the increasing competition among cities. They mention, for example, changes in society, such as the individual relationship with work, the structure of households, consumption patterns, the choice of where to live, and so on. Besides, major policy changes have occurred on the part of the government: central government allows cities more latitude and is stimulating and supportive. These changes have encouraged local governments to become players in the world of city marketing. As a result, cities work on a new future under their own steam, with a clear focus on strengthening the local economy. Later in this chapter, we will discuss the importance of the increased autonomy of cities and their task to provide other activities for the city's users, in addition to boosting the local economy. We will then also deal with the role of events.

CITY MARKETING

The developments that we described in the section above have, over the course of years, led to a situation in which cities have to compete with other cities in order to sustain the local economy. The city has to put together a profile of itself, to distinguish itself and to excel. After all, attracting inhabitants, firms and visitors, the primary target groups of city marketing, translates into tax revenues, employment and income for small businesses. This will also generate more and diverse cultural activities, of which events, as the bearers of culture, are a major component. The city should be sold as a place in which to live, work, go out and invest. City promotion by itself is no longer enough; city marketing is hailed as the new policy tool.

Market-oriented thinking

Cities increasingly regard themselves as a kind of company. It is true that cities distinguish themselves from their competitors on the urban market, but city marketing is different from marketing in commercial business. A market is a situation in which supply and demand are tuned to each other via the price mechanism. In that sense, a non-profit organization like a municipality is not a player in the market, and is less dependent on the market, too. Municipalities exert a more indirect influence on the market through their expenditure and investments. The point is rather that this involves a market-oriented way of thinking on the part of cities that is manifested by ties to business, the sense of competition and reflection on the ever changing environment. The market-oriented way of thinking alluded to here may make government policy much more effective. Attracting the right target groups to come and settle in a city or use what a city has to offer leads to a healthy financial organization that is strong enough to create a place where it is good to live, work and spend your free time, today and in the future. Properly speaking, it is not a profit in financial terms that is the starting point for cities but the aspiration to achieve an optimum level of well-being. This is not to deny the importance of a healthy balance sheet. Through the strategic use of events, and by facilitating and stimulating them, the level of well-being can be raised.

Fig. 7.1. Marketing mix for city marketing (the 7 Ps) (source: Kotler *et al.,* 1993, adapted by the authors).

The 7 Ps of city marketing

By taking a look at the traditional marketing mix, we can make it clear that there are similarities and differences when you compare the marketing of a product with that of a city (Kotler *et al.*, 1993). Figure 7.1 shows the marketing mix for city marketing (the 7 Ps).

It will be clear that, after what was said in the previous section, the city *product*, in contrast to the usual marketing products, is very complicated and diverse.

Place is all about getting the buyer (resident, visitor, firm) to the product; this means that the city should be accessible in a physical as well as a communicative sense. *Promotion* is often wrongly identified with city marketing in all respects, though it is only a part of it.

Another important point to make is that you cannot simply put a *price* tag on a city as a complete package. The price is generally determined by the various components of the package, but if there are too many components, the municipal authorities can only act as initiators and facilitators to make the city more attractive as a total package, or with respect to certain components. The P of *politics* refers to the fact that a municipal organization is set up differently from that of an enterprise that has to make a profit, and its objectives are also different. Well-being, not profit, is the starting point. City marketing is affected strongly by politics, and the political climate has an impact on the profile of a city. The *personnel* employed by the municipal organization must learn how to operate in a market-oriented and customer-friendly way. If a city wants to propagate a marketing strategy, it is essential that this strategy will first be ingrained in the minds of municipal staff. Besides, the inhabitants of a city function as its ambassadors, but they cannot be instructed in the way that an employee of a profit organization is. Aura and image are of vital importance to the *presentation* of a city and should be in alignment with the other Ps. The presentation of a city features things like infrastructure, setting, facilities, neatness, decor and security.

Consuming and producing

City marketing is not only a matter that concerns the municipal authorities but also something that involves all the parties that make up a city. Companies play a vital part because, as heavy users of the city, they benefit from a city that is attractive to both their employees and their customers. This affects their image in a positive way. The inhabitants are, as it were, the ambassadors of a city and make their satisfaction known by word of mouth. They largely determine to what extent a city comes across as a hospitable one. Visitors also determine a city's image, and they take that image home and tell people about it.

Companies, inhabitants and visitors can be regarded as both consumers and products. There is a relationship between city marketing and business, because firms, too, try to involve consumers as much as possible in the realization of their own products and bind them through an optimum experience (co-creation). There is an automatic involvement of consumers and interested parties within a city marketing policy; it is essential to confirm that involvement and, preferably, to reinforce it.

An attractive city

The American professor, Richard Florida, mentions 'the role of the creative class' in making a city attractive (Florida, 2002). According to him, the industrial economy is developing into a creative economy. Creative people are the engine of this new economy. Younger generations are mobile and increasingly opt for places that give them energy, where they are challenged. As a consequence of the increasing importance of this critical creative class, the members of which can find a place anywhere, cities are forced to devise strategies to lure creative talent. But, even though a city can do the best it can to be attractive, history shows that *the* attractive city does not exist. The development of cities has always been somewhat unpredictable, so that not everything can be planned, much to the regret of policy makers. In spite of this unpredictability, there are factors that can increase the chances of a city becoming attractive: enough interaction and a variety of things on offer.

Interaction

First, there should be enough interaction. It is the inhabitants of a city who create a situation that invites interaction, and the way a city is laid out may be helpful. The point here is not the number of persons, but rather the number of contacts, the density of the interaction. Meeting places such as parks, pubs, bars, restaurants and squares can have a stimulating effect, of course. In addition, events are temporary and flexible occasions where large numbers of people meet. Thus, they make a big contribution to creating meeting places in a city.

Diverse supply

In the development of a creative city, a vital role is played by a diverse supply of knowledge and technology, as well as the willingness of creative people to make use of this supply. Interesting new combinations arise from the communication between people of different backgrounds. A city with a diverse population mix can benefit from an equally varied knowledge and expertise. Diversity breaks through 'people like us' notions, makes room for creativity and attracts talented people from outside.

An attractive city is not only unpredictable but also densely populated, interactive, knowledge-intensive and diverse. Many cities, including those in the Netherlands, meet these criteria, but the attractiveness of a city should also be known to others. Its image is the decisive factor for a city to be regarded as attractive. Just like products, cities have a brand value and that is the reason why they invest in city branding.

CITY BRANDING

City branding is a trend in city marketing that focuses on putting a city on the map in a distinctive way. City branding can be used to build a clear city identity on the basis of well-defined core values, and is aimed at entering into relationships with target groups. According to Berci *et al.* (2002), the emergence of city branding is related to the increasing need for individuality in society. The public wants an ever increasing number of possibilities to choose from, diversity, distinctiveness and profundity to enhance its own individuality and to be able to connect emotionally with its natural habitat, while what is supplied is becoming more and more monotonous and predictable. In cities, too, uniformity is on the rise. Inner cities resemble each other more and more, with the same retail chains, but this is certainly also due to a tendency by the cities to copy each other for fear of missing something. The world is getting very close to a monoculture. The global village is arriving. It appears as if cities are losing the ability to distinguish themselves; they generate little or no emotion, attachment and involvement, and are in danger of becoming impersonal, anonymous and, ultimately, uninhabitable. Cities must do something to escape this vicious circle. It is no longer enough merely to adopt and transform successful ideas and formulas from elsewhere. Urban renewal is required to fulfil the desire for diversity. Increasing individualization and globalization are the starting points from which to shape urban development from a new tradition. Thanks to individualization, people have more freedom than ever to fulfil their own aspirations and enter into relationships all over the world.

Self-expression as a marketing tool

According to Berci *et al.* (2002), self-expression is the marketing tool of the future. This creates a new framework to shape the city from within, based on its culture and its character and the chemistry between its inhabitants. Therefore, a city will have to reflect on the factors that can reinforce the emotions and chemistry between people in a specific place. City renewal involves the creation of an identity with its own experiential value, profoundly original and non-reproducible, with the aim of enhancing the current market position of a city and making it more distinctive, as a result of which that unique position can be claimed even more convincingly in the future. Cities need a soul, and that soul emanates from its inhabitants. But, allowing something to arise spontaneously without interference from the top should certainly not be interpreted as laissez-faire. The renewal is realized in consultation with various parties, and policy is shaped by what is going on in society. Moreover, this policy offers scope for initiatives from society and facilitates these initiatives.

Urban development and creativity

People make a city; a city leadership that focuses on its citizens and is concerned with their happiness and well-being is doing all right. Contented inhabitants are, after all, the best spokespersons for a city. So, policy makers could do worse than putting out feelers in society. Ideas can be found anywhere. The trick is, starting from the simple insights of citizens, to find the correct key to urban development. A policy maker needs to have an open mind to be able to track down the hidden gems in a city. It is not only the creative class that plays a role in this context; each resident can be creative. What this is all about is creating the broadest support for an attractive city. Urban development is an art, not a formula. Compartmentalization is a feature of many cities and the distance between policy makers and everyday life in the city is too great. So, it should not come as a surprise that cities find it hard to be distinctive. The key to success is to ensure that renewal in a society is given shape by imaginative, daring and properly coordinated policy measures, investments and innovations. In this respect, it is more important to make good on promises than having an impressive campaign and a catchy slogan.

The digi-panel is a frequently used tool to enable the city leadership to keep in touch with what is going on in their city. It is a digital citizens' panel in which residents of 16 years and older can make their opinion known on a particular subject by filling out a questionnaire on the Internet.

Advantages of a city as a brand

The advantages of an attractive city are often connected with the economically driven desire to position cities more strongly in the midst of a scaled-up, mobile and abundant market of locations and destinations (Berci *et al.*, 2002). City marketing and city branding, used a strategies, can provide cities or districts within cities with an image, a cultural content, a soul, a brand. The brand can function as a source of symbolism and lead to added value in economic terms. A simple example is the historic market in the centre of the city, where a cup of coffee is more expensive than outside the centre. The urban brand is an indication of the status of cities as a tourist destination or as a residential or business location.

Within city branding, it is not only economic functionality that plays a role with respect to the attractiveness of a city. The sociocultural effects are relevant as well. Brands bring a certain degree of order or coherence to the pluriformity of contemporary society to make it possible to read each other and our surroundings better. The brand provides people, things and events with a sign and, as a result, they can be recognized as a part of the whole. This makes brands not merely a source of distinction but also of identification, recognition, continuity and a sense of community. Used in this way, brands can then also be economically successful. According to Berci *et al.* (2002), city brands appear to be more successful, as they are better able to penetrate the latent and tactical level of sentiments and affinities in or around a city. In this respect, the main question is to what extent they can provide direction and coherence to them. In other words: as a resident or a visitor, you do not love a city for its sights but because it fulfils your specific needs.

A DEFINITION OF CITY MARKETING

After the exploration of city marketing in the previous sections, we can define city marketing as follows.

Acquiring a distinctive relevant position to be able to attract the right enterprises, visitors and residents, and retain them, by establishing core values for the creation of a clear city identity from the inside out, and based on the culture and character of a city, utilizing the commitment of the parties involved and aligned to city policy, which leads to involvement with and a willingness to do something for a city in such a way that reality matches the image created.

City marketing has the following implicit assumptions as its starting point (Landuyt and Ummels, 2008):

- Attracting and retaining the right inhabitants, companies and visitors leads to more economic and sociocultural activity in a city.
- As a result of the increased mobility of residents and companies, the city enters into competition with other cities in the fields of economic and cultural activities to become more attractive. In other words: doing nothing about the image of a city results in a less positive image of it and a possible decline in comparison to other cities (a competitive disadvantage).

- The choice to live in a particular city, to set up a company there, or to visit it is determined by what a city has to offer and by subjective emotional considerations. These subjective emotional considerations come together in the word 'image': the image people have of a city.
- The image of a city can be created and, with the use of strategic interventions, can be intensified, enhanced or adjusted.
- A positive image is not sufficient; the image should also correspond to reality. A city should deliver what has been promised. That is the reason why organized activities to realize the image should be an integrated part of a good city marketing strategy and a good city marketing plan.

City brands are loaded by a wide diversity of resources. This is also clear from the definition at the beginning of this section. According to Kotler *et al.* (1993), four elements are involved in making a city more attractive. They are:

- *Urban design*: this refers to the design that reveals the character of a place and shows how it has been transformed in the course of time.
- *Infrastructural improvement*: infrastructure enables urban design.
- *Basic services*: good public services are a given in the competitive struggle between places, or cities. So, they should be readily available.
- *Attractions*: this concerns physical features and events in which residents, visitors, companies and investors play a part.

In this chapter, we will discuss this last element, attractions, in more detail. Events in a city have a strategic role in loading a city as a brand. This may involve not only public events but also business-to-consumer events (see the Red Bull Air Race in Chapter 6), (international) trade fairs and conferences.

EVENTS POLICY

With regard to events within the city limits, public or otherwise, municipalities are becoming more and more professionalized. Nearly all municipalities have now formulated an events policy, which is revised every few years. On the one hand, the municipal authorities want to have a good and clear picture of everything concerning an event; on the other hand, there is a growing understanding of the importance of events for the urban economy, the quality of life and the attractiveness of a city. It cannot come as a surprise, then, that an increasing number of cities put a lot of work into drawing up a clear and transparent events policy aligned to a city marketing policy.

The objectives for writing a memorandum of events, as the policy document is called, differ between municipalities. A municipality is free to formulate an events policy according to its own views. Still, there are many similarities. Here is a list of a number of aspects that often can be found in a memorandum of events in connection with an events policy.

An events policy:

- describes what is meant by an event, including a division into subcategories
- comprises a vision on the development of events in the municipality
- is aligned with the integrated city policy (also city marketing)
- discusses the desirability of events and the criteria used to assess them
- includes quality assurance with respect to events
- describes the conditions that an application should fulfil
- describes what to do if an event crosses the city limits
- comprises the process of applying for a licence and subsidy
- describes the organizational structure of the municipality that deals with events; for example, cooperation with an events organizer or an events coordinator or committee
- describes how events are facilitated
- describes the financial resources available for events
- comprises evaluation procedures.

Box 7.1 Example of a modern events policy: a summary of how the events policy of the Dutch city of Rotterdam was refined

Deeper into the city, farther into the world

Rotterdam is the ultimate events city of the Netherlands. That is the result of a consistent municipal policy. Our events reach almost all of Rotterdam's residents, and time and again it transpires that the people of Rotterdam are proud of 'their' events. We also celebrate our Rotterdam identity with our festivals.

An increasing number of people from out of town come to Rotterdam for our events. More than half of the visitors to the North Sea Jazz Festival, the World Port Days, the International Rotterdam Film Festival, Metropolis and the Summer Carnival are from outside the city. This benefits the economy and employment. But above all, the events are good for a positive image of the city. There is probably no other feature that gets Rotterdam on the front pages of newspapers in a positive sense so often.

Prospects are good. The need to celebrate our identity together remains great. The tourist market of visits to events is becoming more international and will continue to grow. People are willing to travel when they want to enjoy special and, above all, authentic experiences. Because of its character, the good infrastructure and the support of the people, Rotterdam can provide those experiences.

There are a few points of attention as well. The world is globalizing, and the international competition between cities is intensifying. Cities comparable to Rotterdam also invest in their own events now. Besides, it appears that in Rotterdam the upper limit of the number

(Continued)

Box 7.1. Continued.

of outdoor events has been reached, and the coordination model does not always point to new ways. More than ever before, events are organized outside the existing events structure. This fragmentation is causing problems of coordination and increases the risk of failure. Another consequence is that the clear Rotterdam profile is slowly but surely being diluted.

The time has come to tighten things up and provide more direction to the events policy. This should first ensure that visitors are offered the best possible Rotterdam experience, but it should also produce an effective strategy to raise Rotterdam's profile as a city where it is pleasant to live, work and stay.

Rotterdam has grandiose urban ambitions, as put into words in City Vision 2030, the inner city plan, the update of the economic vision, the cultural plan for 2009–2012 and the recently drawn up brand policy of the city. These are daring plans aimed at enhancing the quality of life in the city, but they are also intended to draw the attention of a national and international audience to its activities.

These policy papers show quite a few similarities.

- There is a strong will to put more emphasis on quality-of-life aspects and sustainability: quality over quantity.
- There is much emphasis on the importance of internationalization and acquiring a relevant international position. Rotterdam wants to position itself as an international city.
- The potential of the city is in the process of being rediscovered: show and strengthen that which is good and build on it.

These are the starting points for the creation of a tightened-up and inspiring framework for the events policy: a framework in which events will make a relevant and stimulating contribution to the development, the attractiveness and the image of the city. Starting from this vision and these ambitions, and anticipating opportunities and threats, will result in the following refinements of the events policy (see also Chapter 2).

- *A higher return from festivals for the city.* In the case of events with a big impact on the image of the city, we will invest more in the surrounding activities with entrepreneurs, schools and boroughs. Contacts with the international press will be intensified; the makeover of the city will be taken to a higher level.
- *Getting basic things straight, more focus.* We will re-establish order in the events model and create more focus. 'Better' goes before 'more' and 'bigger'. The issue is one of providing the visitor with attractive, meaningful experiences in relation to the city of Rotterdam. There will be stronger emphasis on the Rotterdam identity and prominence will be given to promising events that recur annually.

(Continued)

Box 7.1. Continued.

- *A stronger international profile.* To be able to make a significant contribution to bolster-ing the international profile of the city, the level of ambition will be raised and further action taken to acquire an international aura.

The result will be:

- *A permanent pioneering role.* Rotterdam can maintain its pioneering role in the field of events and develop it further. Through a better control of the process and public space, inconvenience will be limited and the support of all concerned will be sustained.
- *Deeper into the city.* The return from events for the city will be increased. The festi-vals will penetrate further into the city. More forms of cooperation with partners in the city will arise. The visibility, expressiveness and quality of events will be much enhanced and will also have a stronger Rotterdam flavour.
- *Farther into the world.* The international profile of the city will be raised. Rotterdam as a city that will be a topic in international news media all year long because of events that promote Rotterdam themes and belong to the top three of its kind in Europe.

(Source: Rotterdam Festivals Culture Plan 2009–2012, 2008.)

THE ROLE OF EVENTS IN THE CITY

Events play an increasingly important role in our society, and cities acknowledge this more and more. What was the role of events in a city in earlier days? And what is their real role in today's cities? These are the questions we will deal with in this section.

The role of events in the city in the past

Events have played an essential role in cities for thousands of years. Think, for instance, of the markets of pre-industrial society, like the Greek agora and the Roman forum, places that were brimming with life. Events were a vital diversion from the harshness of existence and were used by rulers to strengthen their position.

In the industrial city, too, events played a significant role in strengthening new urban tradi-tions. They were even becoming a threat to privileged religious and royal events. The church and the royal house came up with new events to keep in touch with the population. Examples are the building of royal concert halls and also the Dutch King's birthday, which was first celebrated in the Netherlands in 2013.

During the period of industrialization, when cities introduced more regulation, so-called Fringe festivals were organized as a kind of marginal phenomenon in an ordered society. There are still Fringe festivals today that test cultural boundaries, and in view of the sameness of various cities, this is no bad thing at all.

Festivals and events expanded into indispensable bearers of culture in the modern city and they were generally organized in or around the city centre. Events made money, contributed considerably to putting a destination on the map, advanced the commercialization of tourism, contributed heavily to the image of a city and were used to relieve the pressure on cities by spreading activities.

The contemporary role of events in a city

Even in times of economic crisis and declining industries, the authorities exploit the creation and marketization of cities as cultural centres in an attempt to create a new business climate. As culture and creativity had gained a position of central importance on the public agenda and entered the intercity competition, cultural events were assigned a new function, that of *generators of meaning*. There is a strong interaction between culture, economics and place in our cities. Events are used consciously as strategic, meaningful tools of experience to contribute to objectives formulated previously. In other words, events are powerful tools that make a vital contribution to the implementation of the objectives of city marketing. The role of self-expression in all this is an important one, and this applies to organizers, residents and visitors. Thanks to events, a suitable identity can be created and supported, and this is done from the inside out, from the culture and character of the city. This holds good both for events that have been organized in a city for decades and for new events that give voice to the character of the city, develop it and support it. In the way they promote character, events can be regarded as crucial counterparts of the monoculture of an increasingly globalized world.

Events contribute to the symbolic added value of cities and create a certain order and coherence in today's pluriform society. They also give people something to hold on to and enable them to understand better the world around them. But, events also provide a city with *points of identification that contribute to the emergence of a fresh identity of the city* that is outside the mainstream. Events reinforce subcultures and create togetherness. Thus, events have developed into important tools for urban development and the revitalization of the city; they add to the rhythm of a city. They bring out the various seasons: Christmas markets in winter, races in spring, outdoor performances and flower parades in summer and film festivals in autumn. Incidental mega-events are mixed in and create their own new rhythm, thus highlighting the non-cyclical special happenings in the city. There are, in fact, various urban rhythms that flow and blend together. They produce an atmosphere of excitement, a buzz, in the city. This sense of things starting to hum affects the way in which people look at a city; the image of a city improves and the inhabitants are (again) proud of their city.

'EVENTFUL CITIES'

Many contemporary cities have been transformed into festival and events cities. Richards and Palmer (2010) call them eventful cities. They refer to cities where cultural festivals are used in a harmonious way to achieve the following:

- improvement of the quality of life in the city
- creative activity

- an increase in public groups
- new forms of cooperation
- possibilities for recreation and education
- economic and social advantages
- improvement of image
- contribution to social objectives.

So, distinction is based not only on landmark buildings and imposing museums; it is often events that create a pleasant atmosphere and environment. Events give cities their appeal. Events have the following advantages over physical, infrastructural objects.

- Events are more flexible than physical infrastructural objects.
- Events can help physically flat surroundings to stand out.
- Events add something intangible to the physical culture of a city.
- Events can give meaning to place and time.
- Events are an element of the rhythm of a city.
- Events offer a better opportunity to create spectacle and atmosphere.
- Events generally create an atmosphere that draws people to the events; they want to be part of them.
- Events involve fewer expenses and can have a bigger impact in the short term.

Looking at the statements above, it is as if events are a universal remedy, but this is not what they will automatically turn out to be. In many cities, there is room for an improvement of the events programme, and it is hard to realize the desired situation in practice. Besides, cities should realize that there might be positive as well as negative effects. In the latter case, there will, of course, be negative consequences for the image of a city, and the impact will be bigger than that of positive effects; as a result, it takes more time to polish up a damaged image.

Box 7.2   Arnhem fashion city

Arnhem is a city that has been busy raising its profile lately, and city promotion has replaced city marketing. 'Green' and 'creative' will be the keywords of Arnhem's city marketing in the coming years. Arnhem has a powerful and enduring image as a green city, with a strongly developed creative and cultural climate. This is used as the starting point to look for ways to load core values.

The desire to be creative and innovative has led to a focus on fashion, a logical choice, because fashion is an obvious feature of the city, which has a fashion course and the Arnhem Mode Biennale, a large-scale fashion event.

Additional grounds for the focus on fashion are:

- huge growth potential
- unicity and distinctiveness
- good possibilities for raising the national and international profile, and for marketing.

(Continued)

Box 7.2. Continued.

Besides, the choice for fashion should contribute towards the following objectives:

- increase in employment and business activities
- more entrepreneurial starters
- better matches between designers and clients
- visibility of the city
- more tourists
- profiling 'Made in Arnhem' and 'Cool Region'.

Fashion was the key to developing the fashion district of Klarendal. Klarendal is a neglected working-class area without much perspective. Many dilapidated, badly maintained empty houses, or houses used for storage. This gave rise to social problems, and the municipality wanted Klarendal to be a nice place to live in again. Premises would have to have a display function and fashion was the obvious way to realize that.

A few driven people, creative residents and municipal authorities, who were not afraid to take a risk by investing in the area, have made it possible for new fashion designers to set up a business. A fashion chain has been set up, resulting in an area with a wide diversity of fashion disciplines. The mix of inhabitants (ethnic minorities, native people of Arnhem, entrepreneurs) and shops (a coffee shop next to a luxury fashion shop) makes for a nice and exciting atmosphere and ensures that the inhabitants recognize themselves in their borough, and are proud of it and of their city.

Extending and connecting the separate parts – ArtEZ higher professional courses, Klarendal fashion district, the fashion biennale and promotion campaigns such as 'Made in Arnhem' and 'Cool Region' – will assure Arnhem of a place as a fashion city on the international map. (Source: Wiebe Uithof, presentation at the 2009 Festivak trade fair; draft of core vision city marketing Arnhem 2010–2014; www.modekwartier.nl, accessed January 2011; adapted by the authors.)

THE ROLE OF EVENTS WITHIN THE MAIN TARGET GROUPS OF CITY MARKETING

Events contribute greatly to the realization of the desired situation as described in the broad definition of city marketing. Ultimately, it is really about a positive positioning of a city with respect to other cities, about a city where it is nice to live, work and play. What does this mean for the main target groups? This section will discuss residents, visitors and companies in the city.

Residents

Public events contribute to the quality of life and well-being of the inhabitants of a city or town. Events generate a merry and lively atmosphere and provide relaxation and recreation. Additionally, they contribute to social cohesion within a community. Thus, events in a certain area can put the residents in touch with each other and promote more understanding between various cultures.

The more successful public events are at accentuating the values of a community, the greater will be the contribution to social bonding. The better the event is able to appeal to the values of the community, the prouder the community will be of the event, making the contribution of the event to city marketing even greater. Moreover, this feeling of togetherness makes people more willing to participate in the event, so that the inhabitants make a positive contribution to the positioning of their city. In the end, this active participation will lead to more cultural diversity and sociocultural activities in a city. Besides, inhabitants who are content and proud are the best ambassadors: they care about their borough, are open and hospitable, speak in positive terms about their city and invite friends to visit events, public or not, in the city.

A good example of an event that brings the members of a community together is the Zundert Flower Parade in the Netherlands (Box 7.3).

Box 7.3   Zundert Flower Parade – Meeting the sun!

In Zundert (hometown of Vincent van Gogh), they are mad about their flower parade. Even their grannies and nannies were mad about it. The flower parade was organized for the first time in 1936. By the first Sunday of September, flower parade fever has taken hold of all the inhabitants of Zundert. Will the floats be finished in time? Are there enough dahlias? And who is going to win? Everybody should go to Zundert to experience it!

The Zundert Flower Parade is not just an event; it is an event that preoccupies the inhabitants of Zundert all year round. The parade bonds them together and is their cultural heritage. Young and old are involved, and several clubs even link their jubilees to the parade.

The four parade seasons

The day of the flower parade is New Year's Day in Zundert. Everything happens before or after the parade. When, on the Tuesday after the parade, the floats and construction tents have been dismantled and the builders, still tired of all the exertions, have stored away the undercarriages, the preparations for the next parade will start immediately. The next parade is in 363 days, after all!

Autumn

So, the new parade year starts right after the parade, and the first season of the new parade year is the parade autumn. This is a time of sadness, of retrospection, during which

(Continued)

Box 7.3. Continued.

Zundert looks back on the latest parade filled with feelings of melancholy. Did the right contestant win the first prize? And what way does the jury seem to lean? Dahlias intended for other parades are picked from the fields into the month of October. November is the start of the winter period, during which the dahlia bulbs are stored in holes or barns. Zundert concludes the autumn period by looking back at the latest parade by means of photographs and videos. This retrospective moment is the end of autumn and the beginning of winter.

Winter

The parade winter is the season in which it seems as if nothing much is happening in relation to the parade. But, appearances are deceptive; the parade winter is the period in which the executive committee and various subcommittees of the Zundert Flower Parade Foundation are fully engaged in making plans for the next parade. And the long, dark winter nights are the ideal moments for the designers to brood on new ideas. The parade winter is concluded by a special tradition: the presentation of the standard. The winning neighbourhood makes a standard of honour in the style of the winning design. The unveiling of the standard is part of a fascinating piece of drama that is attended by the entire parade community. The presentation of the standard is the close of winter and the start of the next parade season, spring.

Spring

The parade spring begins right after the presentation of the standard on the second Saturday of January. Neighbourhoods start preparing the construction site: designers make their models. The dahlia fields are waking up from their winter sleep, as well. In April, the dahlia bulbs are planted. And all of a sudden, parade fever strikes again. The parade spring is concluded by a model festival, a weekend in June, when models of the floats for the next parade are displayed to the public. The entire population of Zundert turns out and speculates vehemently on the likely winners. During the model festival, the chairman of the winning neighbourhood of the previous year hands in the challenge cup.

Summer

The model festival heralds the parade summer. Construction tents are put up, the undercarriage is wheeled in and the main frame is welded. As soon as the main frame is ready, it will be getting increasingly busy in the tents. There is work for more and more people, and parade fever is taking hold of the entire village.

Everything not related to the parade is postponed until after it. There is just one priority: the parade float. People work hard and feverishly during the warm summer nights. The colossal floats are slowly taking on their final appearance. The flower fields are busier too. The fields are harvested twice a week from the beginning of August.

(Continued)

Box 7.3. Continued.

The highlight of the parade summer is, of course, the parade itself. The greatest day, the day everyone has been working towards for four seasons. On the first Sunday of September, you can watch the fruits of a year's labour. Enjoy, because in 2 day's time, it is over.

The Zundert Flower Parade Foundation wants UNESCO to recognize its parade as a protected, intangible cultural heritage. This again underlines the position of the parade within the community of Zundert. The definition of intangible cultural heritage in the UNESCO convention is:

> This intangible cultural heritage, transmitted from generation to generation, is always recreated by communities and groups in response to their environment, their interaction with nature and their history, and gives them a sense of identity and continuity, thus promoting the respect for cultural diversity and human creativity.

The float builder from Zundert who manages to get through the somewhat woolly formulation will at once say: 'That's us.' Intangible cultural heritage is about tradition, passed on from generation to generation, but it is a tradition that is still alive and is one of the things that determine the identity of a community. The Zundert Flower Parade matches those criteria perfectly. (Source: www.Bloemencorsozundert.nl, accessed January 2011, adapted by the authors.)

Visitors

Attracting (large numbers of) visitors to an event generates much income for a municipality and thus contributes considerably to the local economy. Visitors not only spend their money on the event itself but also on additional activities like shopping, going to other attractions, a museum for example, and an overnight stay in a hotel, to mention only a few possibilities.

Public events are not only good for a local source of revenue but also they play an important role in transferring the desired identity and core values of the community in question. The profile of Rotterdam and Eindhoven, for example, is clearly that of sports cities as a result of organizing and landing major sports events.

Each public event has a particular content. If this content is aligned to how a municipality wants its profile to be, the event acts as a city marketing tool. And, of course, if an event attracts much attention from the media and many visitors, this will ensure great exposure.

Visitors to an event take their image and memory of everything that has happened home, into the world, which makes them in their own modest way ambassadors of the municipality, and they may return to a city for a repeat visit. Without realizing it, visitors play a vital role in enhancing the attractiveness of a city. Visitors from out of town bring new insights and different cultures to the city; thanks to events, an intercultural dialogue and exchange can have a good or better start.

Companies

Companies play an essential role in city marketing. As top users of a city, they benefit from an attractive city, with respect to both their employees and their customers. Moreover, an attractive city will boost the corporate image. Public events can also make a contribution to the customer relationship management of companies. Events are often used to pamper relations, presenting them with an unforgettable experience to underline the importance of business and personal relationships. Cities, in their turn, use events to tie companies to them. Companies in municipalities with the same core values will be willing to sponsor events. The result is a win–win situation that is good for the company, the city, its residents and its visitors.

CRITICAL SUCCESS FACTORS FOR THE EVENTS PROGRAMME

In their book, *Eventful Cities* (Richards and Palmer, 2010), the authors mention several domains that determine the success factors for event programmes (see Fig. 7.2). These domains are:

- culture (content)
- place (context)
- power (leadership, political support)
- relationships (involvement, forms of cooperation, independence/freedom)
- resources (financial and human resources)
- planning (long-term vision, clear objectives).

To these domains is added sustainability, as an umbrella principle.

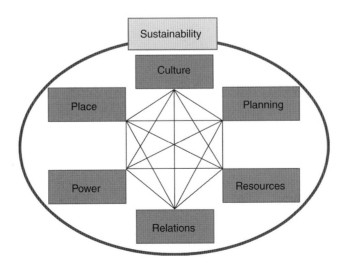

Fig. 7.2. Key areas with respect to an 'eventful city'.

The fact is that cities are also unique and have their own relationship with the supply of events. So, the various factors involved should always be seen in the light of a specific situation.

Culture

In an 'eventful city', culture in its broadest sense always comes first. There are events that are organized mainly to expose people to an experience, to bring about economic growth or to polish up a city. However, the primary goal of city marketing should be: ensuring a broad cultural base in relation to events, so that the cultural landscape of a city becomes part of the events programme. This means: recognizing the diversity of a city as well as attuning the event to a specific environment.

Due to the greater mobility of the past few decades, cultural diversity has grown. This provides new intercultural and transcultural opportunities for the substance of the cultural supply, which can mix the old with the new. All urban programmes and policies should be viewed through intercultural glasses. Intercultural cities provide new challenges for culture management and cultural festivals; they have the potential to stimulate intercultural dialogue and exchange. Cultural diversity in the events programme should not be allowed to result in different events for all groups. This would put the emphasis on differences instead of on the integration of groups. The focus should be on sharing and exchanging experiences. The events programme should also be innovative, a source of inspiration, provocation and critical reflection on the relationship between culture, including events, and a city. This will ensure that the cultural supply remains up to date, challenging and distinctive. To achieve this, unorthodox approaches to devising an events programme will often be required to give new initiatives a chance and to be able to anticipate with flexibility the ever changing needs of public groups. Attention should then be paid not only to highbrow elitist culture but also to popular expressions of culture in a city. This means that a creative director with the necessary knowledge and a good feeling for the situation can take on a guiding role when choices have to be made. It is more important to invest in quality than in quantity. This may lead to a reduction in the number of events, so that the focus will be on the desired outcomes with a well-balanced events programme. New events will then always be assessed critically to see if they are aligned to the values and objectives of a city, and the chief question in this context should be what they add to cultural life and what their meaning is to the inhabitants.

Place

Place refers to the local context in which cities can distinguish themselves. Each city has unique physical elements and must create spaces where people can meet and exchange ideas. Policy makers should pay careful attention to how those spaces should be laid out. This raises the problem of a city being required to be distinctive on the one hand and being recognizable on the other. Naturally, the atmosphere of the city is an essential factor as well. Events can play a big part in creating atmosphere, so that people feel at home and are proud of their city. Events utilize physical meeting places in a city and create their own meeting places that are transformed into places with their own magnetism as a result of special experiences and moods. This unique potential makes it possible to connect different meeting places in a city to an event and stimulate visitors to move from the familiar meeting places in the centre to new, unknown places on the periphery, which may give new meaning to those places in day-to-day life as well.

If events in different cities have a similar content or theme, embedding the event in a particular environment may be the key to distinction. As an event, the Edinburgh Tattoo in Scotland, for example, cannot be compared to other tattoos: it is a breathtaking experience against the backdrop of a brilliantly illuminated castle, giving you the feeling that Edinburgh is the one and only place for this event. This example shows that desperately shielding a place-bound event is completely unnecessary. Indeed, copies of place-bound events make the desire of the visitors for the only real event even stronger, because that is experienced as something authentic.

Besides place, time is an essential element of the event programme. Time refers here to the phase in which a city finds itself at a certain moment. Every city is in a particular developmental phase, historically, culturally, socially and economically. This context should be subject to assessment in an events policy.

Power

The public sector is the one that is responsible primarily for supporting the development of an event structure; it is ultimately answerable for the lasting effects of events. This must be organized within the municipal structure and aligned with the various policy areas. Though public participation in the decision process is necessary, it should be realized that many sustainable events could not take place without strong political leadership coupled to a long-term vision. This is where political power comes in. Politics must devise a framework for the residents and the event professionals. This is not the same as a totally laissez-faire approach; there must be some kind of structure. To give broad sections of the residents the opportunity to participate in the events programme, political leaders must draw up transparent evaluation and selection procedures, so that everyone can play his own role in the events programme, whether it is an existing programme or one that is being developed. In the end, choices will have to be made on the basis of programming qualities enhanced by intuition, experience and pragmatism. A professional, a creative director with autonomous powers of decision, can make such choices.

Business relationships and partnerships

The bond that an event manages to create between the various parties involved in an event that is going to be organized contributes to its total impact. Consider, for example, a situation in which the various cultural parties in a city think about the content of the event and involve visitors in the programming at an early stage. This is much like a partnership.

Trust is the basis of all relationships and partnerships, and should be supported by policy and responsibilities. This concerns not only the trust between, for example, the stakeholders of the event programme of a city but also the mutual trust between cities and regions. Against the background of global competition, successful cities realize that they are required to work together. In the long run, the advantages of cooperation outweigh the short-term advantages of a competitive approach of regional cities towards each other. In more and more regions, partnerships are established, especially where it concerns the positioning of cities, or regions, in an international context. The example below of BrabantStad (Box 7.4) shows that the cooperation between the five big cities of Brabant is a powerful force that gives them a good chance to become the European Capital of Culture. On its own, no city in Brabant could have achieved this.

Box 7.4   BrabantStad, cultural capital of Europe?

Each year, a Capital of Culture is presented in two European countries. In 2018, it will be the turn of Malta and the Netherlands. During that year, both countries will organize an extensive international cultural programme that is aimed at target groups from across the entire social spectrum, from amateurs, young people, lovers of popular culture to professionals, senior citizens and art connoisseurs. In 2013, a professional jury composed of Dutch and European members will choose the candidate with the best plan.

A European Capital of Culture is elected with the aim of accelerating the social development of cities. In short, culture as the driving force to take the lead, or extend that lead. Crucially, citizens have pride of place. It is a primary requirement that the local population is involved in the development of a city and that the participation of residents in cultural activities is fostered. Naturally, the jury also assesses the plans from a European perspective: attention to the cultural diversity in Europe and the connection between citizens, cities and regions.

Network

The aim mentioned above makes BrabantStad the ultimate Dutch candidate. At present, this is still a fragmented area and an administratively oriented partnership, but is also a network that can grow into a Mosaic Metropolis. The nomination and the title will be a boost to the network and enable it to work together on a promising and lasting cultural agenda. A few words about the term 'Mosaic Metropolis': in his design studio, Steven Slabbers, a landscape architect, developed in 2007 three scenarios under the name of Mosaic Metropolis. 'Mosaic' refers to the multi-coloured character of the five big cities of Brabant and their contrast with the countryside. 'Metropolis' stands for the development of those five into a metropolitan area with highly dynamic centres and high-quality urban provisions and attractions, cultural and otherwise. Thus, the Mosaic

(Continued)

Box 7.4. Continued.

Metropolis refers to the five big cities of Brabant, which are becoming increasingly urban while retaining their manageable size, and the surrounding villages, which are becoming more rural. And last, but not least, the Mosaic Metropolis will preserve its human scale and all the good things of life in Brabant during the transition to an innovative knowledge economy.

Europe

BrabantStad is also a perfect European example. While preserving their own identity, the various participants, in this case the five cities and surrounding areas, together weave a functional network that is bigger and stronger than its individual threads. Those threads extend across borders, for example to Flanders, with which we have had links of old. Brabant is also a candidate with its eyes on the future. In the course of the 21st century, the networks with which Brabant has been familiar for ages will gain in importance all across Europe. Moreover, the concept of Capital of Culture needs new impetus after 25 years on the European stage, and this will be an age that requires new administrative structures and has to deal with the weighty issues of cooperation and solidarity across sectors at all levels. Appreciating this, BrabantStad has chosen the motto 'The art of living together'.

This is a theme in which topicality and urgency find expression, and with which BrabantStad distinguishes itself noticeably from the other Dutch candidates who participate in the traditional way. Besides, nearly all rivals are single, existing cities. BrabantStad is not like that. We draw up our programme together with five cities and a province and, on behalf of this partnership, 's-Hertogenbosch can take care of the official entry. By nominating BrabantStad, we do not choose the easy way. However, we will make a convincing effort to set out a realistic course: a memorable course that can inspire Europe and with which the Netherlands can proudly position itself in an innovative way. We think that the course we have chosen is so essential that we will continue to work on achieving our ambitions, even if our nomination is not awarded.

Particle accelerator

From the experiences of other countries, we know that being awarded the title can be very profitable. In practice, this award and the celebration of being Capital of Culture of Europe work as a particle accelerator. Cultural provisions, social cohesion and economic power evidently develop at a much higher rate than during a normal period of policy making. It is not for nothing that so many Dutch candidates make a bid for the title. Only one can be the winner, and BrabantStad holds a strong hand. But even if the strong hand we hold does not result in the official title, the road to nomination can, by itself, produce many benefits. That, too, is a lesson that other cities have learned; a nomination is a strong stimulus for projects, identity, cooperation and planning. (Source: *Koers 2018 Brabant*, working document 1.1, July 2010, unpublished.)

Relationship with the media

The relationship with the media is of vital importance. To a large extent, the media determines the success of a city and its events programme. According to Rennen (2007), city events without extensive media coverage are not very likely to be successful (see also Box 7.5 below). An increasing number of organizers opt for setting up their own media networks. Thus, they try to reduce the dependence on independent, critical media and present themselves in a way that appears to be journalistic.

Due to the strong emergence of live news coverage, many events, while in progress, develop into historic events. The organization often plays the hand of good memories, because wonderful memories ensure that cities, media and companies can profit from the event for quite some time, even when it is over.

Box 7.5

Events have an impact on place image, mainly through media coverage. That is the statement tested empirically by Fatingan *et al.* (2009) and which has led to the following conclusion: by hosting events, places can attract positive media coverage. The Football World Champion Tournament in Germany is a good illustration.

Research has shown that by organizing that tournament in 2006, Germany managed to attract much media attention. The aim of the organization was to change the negative image of Germany, place image, into a positive one. Media analysis has shown that organizing the World Championship has, indeed, had a positive effect on Germany's image. After the championship, media coverage decreased quickly, but the tone was still more positive than prior to the championship. The conclusion is that organizing an event can generate positive media attention. (Source: Fatingan *et al.*, 2009, adapted by the authors.)

The impact of media attention on the visitors of events decreases as the media attention ebbs away. So, this forces cities to offer a variety of events with which the target groups in a city can be served. Besides, activities must be spread over the year and take place in sequence to hold the attention of the consumer and improve or preserve the image. It is true that events are not the only way to achieve this, but they can be important eye-catchers within the total policy concerned with the image building of a city.

The media can also encourage artists to come, because the aura of a city fits their own image or because they would like very much to perform in a particular city, which can keep the cost down to a considerable extent. Moreover, positive media attention will generate extra demand from local, national and international markets.

Positive media attention does not have to be very expensive, as is shown by the use of free publicity, among other things. Press bulletins are disseminated and journalists are invited, but awards can also help a city to distinguish itself. The best-known examples in the Dutch context are The Event City of the Netherlands Award and the City Marketing Award.

Resources

In order to realize good events programming, resources must be made available. This requires a good physical events structure. Think of indoor and outdoor locations in a city, provision of information, transport and visitor information. This requires funding. Financial resources are partly provided by the government, which sets the conditions and is responsible for the events infrastructure. But, businesses will have to make a contribution as well.

The organizers of events should wean themselves off subsidies as much as possible in the future and organize events like a business. This approach requires them to remain astute and discerning. Of course, the aim of the event and the role it plays in society determines the financial dependence on the government. In the case of an event that is focused strongly on social cohesion within a borough and is in alignment with the objectives of the city, that dependence will be greater. The discussion about resources for events is inseparable from the issue of quality versus quantity. A serious attempt should be made to find a good balance in events programming. Less will be more, if the quality of events is enhanced and the burden on the city is reduced to acceptable proportions. The discussion about resources is not limited to money; the commitment and involvement of people, human resources, play a vital part as well. Think of volunteers, for example, who complement the contribution of the professionals responsible for the events programme. Because of their large commitment, volunteers are willing to invest in a successful event. They are the links to the residents and foster involvement and support in the community. That does not alter the fact that briefing, training and supervising volunteers takes time and energy. Therefore, it is crucial, especially in the case of recurring events, that volunteers are inducted properly and that the organizer invests in their commitment to the event, so that trained volunteers with all their knowledge and specific skills are saved for the event as well as the city.

Planning

The events policy of a city requires the formulation of a clear vision containing the strategic starting points for individual events and a description of how events contribute to the collective objectives of the city. This policy must be laid down for at least 5 years, but a multiple of this period may be required in the case of large-scale infrastructural improvements and tactical changes in the environment. Planning should be integrated into other policy areas within the municipal organization, so that synergy is generated and events are made part of the entire cultural context of a city.

It is essential that planning includes procedures for monitoring and evaluation, both of the separate events and the events programme as a whole. The evaluation comprises various items and, ideally, deals with various aspects: economic, social, cultural and environmental. The results of the evaluation can be used for feedback and, if necessary, must lead to tightening up the current events policy.

SUSTAINABILITY

Sustainability used to be a neglected issue in the events sector, but that has changed in the past few years. The success factors discussed earlier, such as culture, place, power, relationships, resources and planning, must be placed in a sustainable framework.

In the past, it was usually only the economic effects of events that were detailed and not enough attention was paid to social and cultural values and the pollution of the environment. In the last few years, the 'green' production of events has been on the rise, even if it is a marketing objective in many cases and the event is not produced CO_2 neutral. Sustainability comprises more than just the environment and has various components. Approaches like *people*, *planet*, *profit* and 'socially responsible entrepreneurship' clearly show that sustainability, in its broadest sense, is the issue that will make a difference in the future. Organizations that are capable of sustainable production will be more profitable than those that are not. The people component refers chiefly to social equality and is thus linked directly to the cultural component. Think, for example, of fair working conditions and wages, intercultural respect, the participation of residents and other involved stakeholders in the decision-making process, and ensuring a broad cultural approach. The planet component comes down mainly to the CO_2 neutral production of events by using green energy, durable and/or easily degradable materials, reduction of waste production and separation of waste.

So, sustainability concerns a broad objective that includes sustainable growth, equal working conditions, taking responsibility for nature and the environment, and social well-being.

Getz (2009) sums up a number of points in connection with sustainability at events and relates them to the six domains of events programmes:

- minimizing negative effects with respect to economic, social, cultural and environmental aspects
- generating more economic benefits for local residents and fostering the well-being of communities
- improving working conditions and creating employment
- involving the local population and other stakeholders in the decision-making process
- striving for cultural diversity and contributing to the conservation of natural and cultural heritage
- creating valuable experiences by connecting visitors and residents in a meaningful way
- taking into account people with a handicap
- being culturally sensitive: fostering respect between visitors and residents, strengthening local pride and confidence.

To be able to attain results, the parties involved must collectively introduce sustainability in the events sector, and implement it. First, the provider and suppliers involved will have to search their own hearts. The first cautious steps are being taken. Support from politics, in the form of rules and regulations, is needed to develop sustainability to the full. Besides issuing new guidelines for production, the government can help make adjustments through the use of subsidies, and facilitate events that meet the guidelines.

On this issue, visitors are a powerful force. If visitors are convinced that events should be produced sustainably, the market will do the rest. But, taking the actual steps on the road to sustainability, as described in this chapter, is more easily said than done. It is a long-term matter. Still, the following steps can be taken in the short run:

- A (sustainable) network can be set up, the members of which inform each other, and that initiates actions.
- Local government can draw up guidelines for the sustainable production of events. This can be a model with stages spread over several years. On the basis of detailed cases at the local level, national politics can be involved at a later date.
- A study can be done of the (sustainable) effects of events, with a focus that shifts from economic to social, cultural and environmental effects. Educational institutes can play a vital role here. An additional advantage is that the new generation of event managers will gain an insight into the possibilities and impossibilities of sustainability and can then make the sector more professional in this field.
- Sector organizations can play an important role by informing individual companies of the potential of sustainability in the area in which they are active. This does not concern merely sector organizations linked to an event, but also the Chamber of Commerce, for example.
- Proceeding from the idea that sustainable events can be good for the corporate image, the sponsors of events should be more aware of the fact that they can make demands where sustainability is concerned. This can be done via networks or information sessions, for instance. Thus, sponsors will become more mindful of their new role.
- A quality mark for sustainability can be introduced for which companies can register on a voluntary basis. Getting awarded such a quality mark will deliver much positive publicity. If the quality mark is refused, the company concerned will have a clear picture of the areas where work still has to be done. The funding of this quality mark should come from all parties involved, government, sector organizations, business, schools and even the public.
- Events can be organized with a focus on sustainability as a strategically meaningful experience. This can be initiated by the various parties involved.

SUMMARY

All cities have by now become very much aware of city marketing. City promotion is not something new. Even the old Greeks and Romans did it. The traditional marketing mix of the original four Ps – product, price, place and promotion – is extended by presentation, politics and personnel in the field of city marketing.

City branding is a trend within city marketing. City branding involves a city working on a distinctive identity on the basis of core values. In this connection, self-expression is one of the marketing tools, and creativity, too, is an essential component of making a city attractive. City branding is about the city as a brand, and its starting point is the needs of residents, companies and (potential) visitors.

The events policy of a city should be in alignment with the city marketing policy, and must result in a well-balanced events programme. Culture, place, power, relationships, resources and planning are all success factors with regard to events programmes. Sustainability is something that affects everything and deserves a central place in urban events policies.

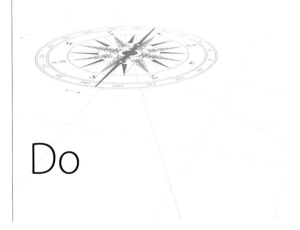

Do

In Part II, we discuss the 'do' phase of the strategic use of events, so the centre part of the EVENTS model.

We start with the translation of strategy into concept, and then we deal in more detail with touchpoints, the points of contact between the initiator of an event and the visitor.

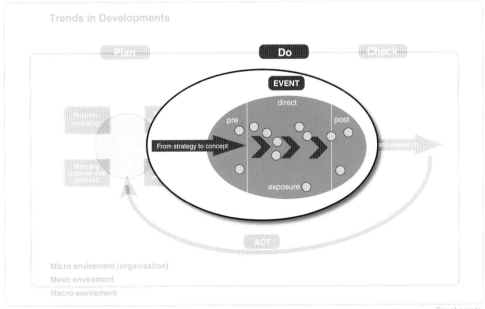

chapter 8

The Translation of Strategy into Concept

Moniek Hover, Dorothé Gerritsen and Ronald van Olderen

The concept and design of an event should be developed from the strategic objectives following from the four strategies of relationship marketing, marketing communication, branding and city marketing. The concept should be based on the values of visitor groups and on the values, vision and mission of the initiator of an event. This chapter is about how that can be achieved.

LEARNING TARGETS

After studying this chapter, you will have learned:

- how you translate strategic objectives into a concept and design for an event
- what values are in relation to an event
- how the experience model is made up
- what the concept of experience is
- how to develop a concept of experience based on strategic objectives
- how to make a concept of experience specific.

To be able to translate a strategy into a concept, you first need an analysis of demand and supply, the environment and the values of visitors, among other things. You must also know what requirements a good concept has to meet. A further important question is what happens to visitors when they attend an event. It is not until those questions have been answered that it is possible to stage the experience of an event by utilizing content, form and tools in such a way that they touch the visitor and the message comes across. This is perfectly illustrated by the events organized by the Skyway Foundation (Box 8.1).

Box 8.1   Skyway turns apparent impossibilities into possibilities

The Skyway Foundation stimulates, motivates and supports groups of people to participate in activities on their own that, to them, seem impossible to perform at first sight. It organizes groundbreaking events that inspire the participation of the target group in our society. The foundation's work is based on the values of purity, passion and open-mindedness.

Skyway is a player in the events business who stands out because the event is used to get a message across. That by itself is not unique: the Live Aid Concert is another example. But, Skyway specializes in events that seem impossible: music festivals for the deaf and photography projects for the blind.

Skyway sees what is regarded as impossible by a target group or an individual person as a source of inspiration, as a challenge to find out how something that is impossible can still be done. From this attitude, Skyway developed several innovative applications that stimulated the senses, so that deaf youngsters and those hard of hearing could still pick up the emotion of music.

Research has shown that emotions in music can be transformed into vibrations (through the specially designed sense floor and the feel-the-music suit), in scents (through the aroma jockey), in taste sensations (through the food jockey and/or ice jockey) and image (through video projection, text jockeys, sign dancers and sign interpreters who vividly translate the emotion on the stage).

These events, which go under the name of Sencity, enable deaf people and those hard of hearing to enjoy music. People who can hear also appreciate these events very much because of the innovative experience. For those who want to receive it, there is an underlying message as well: if you really go for something, you can do it, you can even make the impossible possible. This message is not actively communicated during the events in order to remove any barriers to attending it.

Skyway also takes up personal challenges in its own organization. All employees are asked what they consider impossible for themselves and would like to realize within Skyway. The organization works as a platform to support people to deal with their own challenges. What is required to access that platform is enormous ambition and the conviction that often people can do more than they think. Skyway's own policy plans are drawn up with a

(Continued)

Box 8.1. Continued.

challenge in mind as well. After the first event, the next step was setting up a musical event for deaf people in a local community on every continent. Skyway is now active all over the world. Events have been organized in São Paulo, Capetown, Johannesburg, Sydney, Miami, Mexico, Finland, London, Berlin and Madrid. In the Benelux countries, the concept has been extended by adding SENS11: musical events that provide sensory stimulations for people with and without a mental handicap. And with increasing frequency, Skyway is asked to apply its knowledge and skills to organizations facing a challenge.

Setting grand, seemingly impossible goals with an uncompromising ambition to attain those goals makes the talents in their employees come to the surface, enabling them to develop those things to which they want to apply themselves, whether this is graphic design, dancing, organizing or bookkeeping.

The energy thus generated in employees can be seen at the events, characterized as they are by an enthusiastic, open atmosphere with a high experience value. Visitors have an intense experience, a so-called transformational experience that will not be soon forgotten, and which may even change them permanently.

(Source: Molenaar, 2010; Skyway Foundation, adapted by the authors.)

VALUES OF THE TARGET GROUP

If event developers succeed in linking values to their events, the emotional involvement of the target group will be much greater. From that involvement with an event, it is possible for emotional ties to arise with an organization and/or brand, enabling the organization to distinguish itself from its competitors as well. A good translation of an objective into a concept or design of an event is then within easy reach.

The concept of value can refer to tangible items, such as a DVD, a signed photograph or a jewel, but it can also refer to intangible matters such as religion, health, happiness, relationships and entertainment. So, attending an event may also have an immaterial value, which also involves individual opinions of what is desirable or good. If you attribute value to something, you find it important. Emotional value is linked inextricably to material things. A ticket to a concert or a signed photograph of a pop star will then stand for the one and only time in your life that you have seen your idol. Through that ticket or photograph, you enjoy that moment again and relive that emotional event again.

The translation of strategy into concept

Values are an essential component of our cognitive system and they determine our expectations of people and things. Values affect how people think and act and handle information, and how they collect, store and use that information. In that sense, values are criteria that people use to test information, of whatever nature (Franzen and Holzhauer, 1987).

ANALYSIS OF SUPPLY AND DEMAND

It is not only the visitor to an event who has values. The initiator of an event has them as well: the city or brand wants to transfer certain values to the visitor. What are those values? What is the vision? To what extent do those values correspond to those of the visitors? The answers to these questions are essential to the successful exploitation of events. Through events, the values of an organization can converge with those of the visitors, on condition that the provider makes a proper analysis of the client or initiator of an event to arrive at a good event concept.

So, in order to bridge objectives and event, it is important to make a proper analysis of the demand and supply sides. A target group analysis focused on values and an analysis of the vision and mission of the initiator of the event provide the necessary basis for the next step of emotional bonding. To make this clear, we will first have a look at the effect of an event as a staged experience.

STAGED EXPERIENCE AND TRUE EXPERIENCE

Clearly, events are all about producing an effect on the visitors. How individual visitors experience an event is dependent on many factors. Here, we explain what the difference is between a staged experience and a true experience, and which factors affect the individual experience of an event.

The publication of *The Experience Economy* by Pine and Gilmore (1999) was certainly not the first to cover the economic value of experiences. But, as a result of their book, the idea that people wanted to be touched personally in the first place received widespread attention. Pine and Gilmore define experience as follows:

> An experience occurs when consumers get involved in something in such a way that they will gain a lasting impression. The event is memorable and very personal. The consumer is touched emotionally, physically, intellectually, indeed spiritually.
>
> (Pine and Gilmore, 1999)

In contrast to English, which has only the one word for 'experience', Germanic languages like Dutch and German distinguish between 'erleben' and 'erfahren'/'beleven' and 'ervaren'. 'Erfahren' and 'ervaren' refer to the placement of an experience in a mental framework. From the Dutch verb 'beleven', two nouns can be derived that mean 'staged experience' and 'true experience', respectively.

We define 'staged experience' and 'true experience' as follows:

> The staged experience is the (more or less delineated) event as it can be staged, put on, by a provider. It is the stimulus that can trigger a true experience on the part of a consumer.

> The true experience is the inner, personal, emotional response to a stimulus. The true experience can transcend the staged experience in time and space.

The staged experience is the event itself; it is about something that can be staged, a stimulus that should trigger something specific. The true experience is the result of the staged experience. Not every staged experience will lead to a true experience. Depending on the psychosocial frame of reference (see the section on the psychosocial framework), a true experience will, or will not, occur, or will be more or less intense. For example, when watching a football match, one person will have a strong experience, while the person next to him is not affected at all by the same stimulus.

LEVELS OF TRUE EXPERIENCE

Three levels of true experience can be distinguished when looking at the intensity of the emotion and the extent to which it is retained in the memory (van Gool and van Wijngaarden, 2005). With the help of the experience model in Fig. 8.1, we explain how you can arrive at a concept of an event starting from strategic objectives. We will refer to this model several times in the course of this chapter.

The staged experience in this model can be regarded as the event; the stimulus that you try to give its proper shape and staging to the best of your ability in order to attain certain objectives. It is impossible to predict exactly how that stimulus, the event, affects the individual person. There is a kind of black box, the psychosocial framework, containing a wide variety of factors that can have an effect on the way in which a visitor experiences the event. The outcome is a true experience that can vary from visitor to visitor. The three levels of true experience are:

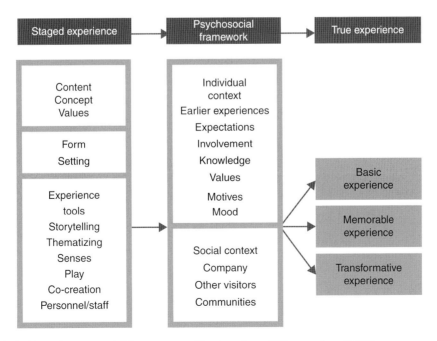

Fig. 8.1. Experience model (source: van Gool and van Wijngaarden, 2005).

1. The basic experience coincides with (exposure to) the stimulus. An emotional response occurs, but the experience has not enough impact to be retained in the memory for a longer period of time.

2. The memorable experience is at a higher level and results in memory value. This does not concern merely memory at a cognitive level but especially the ability to recall the emotion later.

3. The transforming experience causes a lasting change in the individual at the behavioural or attitudinal level.

Transformation is not an easy concept. And what is the meaning of 'lasting' in this context? When does transformation become manipulation?

Transformation is not the automatic result of every intense, memorable experience. In a study conducted in three war museums, the respondents described the experience of their visit in an experience report 2 weeks after their visit as emotionally charged: their experience was an intensely memorable one. However, their answer to the question whether their visit had changed their attitude towards the subject was negative. The attitude of the respondents remained the same as it was before their visit. Their involvement, and the underlying values, was perpetuated by their visit (van Buuren, 2006).

It is possible for an event to become a life-changing experience, provided that, thanks to the event, the person involved can express dormant values, as a result of which the experience has taken on a more profound meaning.

As has been said before that the level of experience attained can differ from person to person. Those differences can be explained with the help of the psychosocial framework. The same stimulus that triggers only a basic experience in one individual can trigger one that will remain in the memory of another for a longer time. In another person again, the experience may be the cause of a transformation. Figure 8.2 provides a visual display of the process from staged experience to true experience.

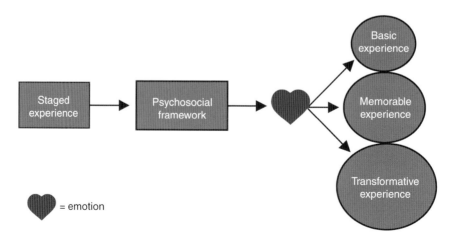

Fig. 8.2. Visualization of staged experienced and true experience (source: Moniek Hover).

THE PSYCHOSOCIAL FRAMEWORK

The psychosocial framework is, in fact, a black box: nobody can say with any degree of certainty what are the factors that are crucial to the realization of the experience. As a consequence, the effects of the event are uncertain as well. But, with the knowledge available to you, you can try to control the factors and design the event in such a way that the objectives with regard to the target group are attained. The following factors are involved: knowledge, expectations, motives, mood, involvement, social context, personality and competences, and values (see Fig. 8.1).

The first six factors are connected to the specific experience that the visitor to an event undergoes. We will explain them in order. After this, we will deal with the final two factors, those that transcend the experience: personality and competences, and values.

Knowledge

At first sight, knowledge and a true experience seem to be two contradictory concepts. However, knowledge, or background knowledge, can have an effect on the experience and, in some cases, lead to enhancement of the experience. And a lack of knowledge can be a barrier to the experience as such. Modern, abstract art can often be appreciated only with background knowledge so that you can give a work of art its place.

Due to the Internet, access to knowledge and information has expanded enormously in the last few years. The visitor to an event can obtain all possible background information prior to attending the event. A supplier should be well aware of the fact that visitors will come fully prepared, because they can obtain all the necessary information.

Expectations

The second factor that has an impact on a true experience concerns earlier experiences and the expectations arising from them. If an experience is stored in a mental frame of reference, it will become an experience. The memory of the experience is carried over to the next experience in the form of an expectation. An expectation, too, is often coloured by emotions; it is very much like an extension of the true experience. Fulfilling expectations is important, but surpassing them is better still. Naturally, expectations that are not fulfilled will be fatal to a positive experience.

Experiences do not have to be of a strictly personal nature for them to lead to particular expectations. The experiences of others can have a strong impact on an expectation. Digital media provide computer users with much scope to share experiences. In the light of these possibilities, people feel an increasing need to send their experiences and emotions into cyberspace; witness all social media like Twitter, the Foursquare online service, weblogs and discussion forums. Spontaneous virtual communities of people who share the same values and interests arise around events.

Many suppliers in the events sector increasingly regard these developments as an opportunity to gain a better understanding and knowledge about what really is important to people.

The focus of events should not merely be on the direct exposure phase (the moment when an event actually takes place), but indeed on the pre- and post-exposure phases as well, because it is there where the experience is extended in the form of an expectation and pleasurable anticipation; and when the event is over, there is the enjoyment of the memory and afterglow. This is well illustrated by the example of a Robbie Williams concert (Box 8.2).

Box 8.2

'Robbie Williams is going to give a concert!' This is the introduction to the story the fan is going to experience. This is the start of the pre-exposure phase of the experience. The moment when a fan has managed to obtain a ticket for that concert (the trigger within the story), the onset of pleasant suspense can be felt: the anticipation, counting the days, visiting websites to share those feelings with like-minded people. The arrival at the venue where the concert is given is the critical moment, the 'crisis': just a few more moments! Robbie enters the stage and starts his gig. This is the climax. When the concert is over, the post-exposure phase begins; the rundown of the storyline, with everything falling into place. The fan reads reviews, visits websites and buys a CD or DVD to experience the concert again, and invoke the emotion again.

For an individual, each experience is, as it were, a personal story that unfolds around the actual experience, and comprises the following components (see Fig. 8.3):

- the introduction
- the trigger moment
- growing suspense
- the crisis
- the climax
- the rundown.

A supplier must try to imagine the story of the experience in the hearts and minds of the visitors and feed this story in each of its phases. Of course, several climaxes is something not unheard of (see Chapter 9).

Motives

According to Neulinger, two things are of essential importance for the emergence of a leisure experience in an individual person (Beunders and Boers, 1997). First of all is the type of motivation. Intrinsic motivation is about the pleasure someone expects to have when kicking a ball, for example. In the case of extrinsic motivation, the reward is important: playing football to win. There is often a mix of the two.

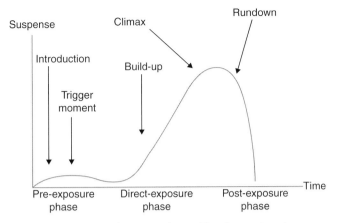

Fig. 8.3. Storytelling (source: Laurel, 1993, adapted by the authors).

What is also relevant is the degree of perceived freedom when an activity is performed: not every leisure activity is done voluntarily. The freedom to choose has an impact on the experience. There may be social obligations, for instance. For someone who does something because he is obliged to, the experience will be blocked in some way beforehand.

Moods

There is a difference between moods and emotions. Emotions are usually linked to an occurrence or object: moods are not. Generally, moods last longer than emotions. They are often the result of earlier emotions. Besides, they may make it easier for the emotions involved to arise, or indeed they may reinforce them. Therefore, moods have a great effect on how an experience is formed. The behaviour associated with a mood is aimed at ending an unpleasant mood and the continuation of a pleasant mood (Boom, 2006). A supplier can certainly exert an influence on moods.

Involvement

Moments of optimum involvement during an activity occur in a flow. A flow can also arise during events when a visitor feels completely immersed in an experience. This can be seen clearly in photographs of the visitors of Glastonbury Festival during one of the performances. However, involvement as a factor within the psychosocial framework is about the involvement that someone already feels, the way someone enters the experience. It may then be a matter of enduring involvement or one of situational involvement. In the case of situational involvement, someone is deeply involved in a particular activity for a very short time, but this involvement disappears when the activity is over. Think, for example, of booking a holiday. After everything has been organized and the trip has been made, there is no longer any involvement.

Enduring involvement does not have to coincide with a concrete activity or experience, but it certainly is often the result of one or more memorable, even transformative, experiences. Enduring involvement will not always be expressed in specific behaviour at a certain moment. Someone who is mad about sailing may be unable to do it for a while due to circumstances in his life. That does not mean, however, that the involvement has gone.

Research has shown that the higher the level of enduring involvement in an activity, the more likely it is that the person in question will get into a flow during the activity (Havitz and Mannell, 2005). Someone with a feeling of enduring involvement with the Rolling Stones, a true fan, is much more likely to get into a flow during one of their gigs than someone without it. From additional research, it has become clear that there is a reverse relationship as well: if someone undergoes an intense experience and gets into a flow, this will lead to stronger enduring involvement in relation to the activity.

Social context

The social context is of crucial importance to the experience. This applies first and foremost to the company with which someone undertakes an activity. The effect on the level of experience of a visit to an event together with colleagues can be totally different from that of a visit to the same event with the family. The impression formed of other visitors has an impact as well. What one person experiences as a jolly nice crowd, another may regard as irritatingly crowded.

The social context goes beyond the bounds of time of an event. As has been mentioned earlier, virtual communities have created new social contexts that have an effect on an experience, certainly also in the pre- and post-exposure phase. The role of staff is often regarded as part of the social context. This is a vital touchpoint, as will be demonstrated in Chapter 9.

Two factors of the psychosocial framework are not connected directly to a specific experience. As such, they can be said to be of a more transcending, more stable nature: that is, personality and values.

Personality

There are certain human traits that can have an effect on experience. Csikszentmihaly, the American-Hungarian psychologist, sees a relationship between creativity and getting into a flow, or being able to get into a flow. Open-minded people see something new and uncertain as a challenge that appeals to them (Nijs and Peters, 2002). A surprise will often be experienced as positive by this group. People with a closed mind, on the other hand, will find the uncertain and the unexpected stressful; this will have a negative effect on their experience.

Fantasy is something else that seems to be important to the ability to enter into an experience. Someone who, during an experience, does not stop thinking 'this is fake' or 'it will all be over soon' will have an experience that is less strong than that of someone who totally surrenders to it. In this sense, fantasy is not a distortion, but an enhancement of reality. 'Fantasy is liberating'.

At first sight, it may seem hard for a supplier to take people's personality into account: after all, a personality cannot be changed. But, a supplier can always make use of certain traits of the visitors of an event.

Values

It is becoming increasingly hard for companies, cities and organizations to distinguish themselves from their competitors on the basis of product attributes or quality. Therefore, the focus is shifting to values as a possibility to do so. Rokeach was one of the first to conduct a study of values (Boom and Weber, 2001). He distinguishes two types of values: terminal values as the desired end goals and instrumental values as a means of achieving those end goals (see Fig. 8.4).

The example of Festival Mundial demonstrates how values can come up in an event and how important they are.

Social harmony
- Peace
- Equality
- Freedom
- National security
- Salvation (eternal life)

Personal fulfilment
- Social recognition
- Comfortable life
- Pleasure
- Accomplishment

Love and affection
- Mature love (sexual and mature intimacy)
- Real friendship

Self-actualization
- Beauty (nature and art)
- Wisdom
- Inner harmony
- Self-respect
- Accomplishment
- Security
- Family care
- Salvation (eternal life)

Competence
- Ambitious
- Independent
- Creative
- Capable
- Logical (rational)

Personal contentment
- Happiness (being content)

Compassion
- Forgiving
- Helpful

- Cheerful
- Loving

Social attitude
- Polite
- Obedient
- Tidy (clean)

Integrity
- Responsible
- Honest
- Self-control

Fig. 8.4. Rokeach's value model (source: Boom and Weber, 2001).

Box 8.3   Festival Mundial

Festival Mundial is an international multicultural festival that has been organized in Tilburg (the Netherlands) for 20 years. In 2003, the festival was the subject of an extensive and thorough study of brand management (Schürmann, 2004). A distinction is made in the study between intrinsic attributes (features of the service itself) and extrinsic attributes (all remaining features added to the service) and within these categories a subdivision of non-distinctive attributes, distinctive intrinsic attributes, the brand and other extrinsic attributes (Riezebos, 2002).

Schürmann's study shows that the visitor of the closing festival is extremely satisfied with all facets of Festival Mundial. With respect to the non-distinctive intrinsic attributes – also called standard products – such as toilets, stages, signposting, the scores are very high. Distinctive intrinsic attributes that stand out are programming, location (the sun-drenched city park), the quality of infotainment, the range of food and drink available and the broad target group of Festival Mundial.

The respondents do not attach much value to the new logo. In contrast, however, the Festival Mundial word brand is extremely loaded. The experience of the brand invokes the following terminal values: security, equality, peace, happiness, pleasure and freedom.

The remaining extrinsic attributes are represented in the objectives of Festival Mundial. This is rendered into the message that the experience of the respondent comes first. A value fit has been found here between the concepts of objective and message from a different experience perspective. The values found in the answers of the respondents fall into the category of 'social harmony', according to the model of Rokeach. This means that the respondents attach much value to the terminal values of peace and equality. They are trying to contribute something substantial to an innovative, better society through active participation.

The scores of the distinguishing attributes are structurally higher. So, the conclusion can be that the visitor really comes for Festival Mundial with all its facets, and not only to get that so-called festival feeling. The visitors have a conscious experience of the Festival Mundial brand.

The absence of non-distinctive attributes causes dissatisfaction, while their presence is taken for granted. This is the explanation for the fact that the scores of non-distinctive attributes are structurally lower than those of the distinctive attributes. There should be nothing wrong with the non-distinctive intrinsic attributes of an event. Only then can the distinctive attributes be exploited to the full. (Source: Schürmann, 2004.)

Franzen elaborates on earlier research on values and distinguishes three types of values (Nijs and Peters, 2002).

1. *Functional values*: these are preferred qualities, attributes and achievements of the product itself. They are usually referred to as product benefits in day-to-day advertising practice.

2. *Symbolic values*: there are three subcategories:

2a *Expressive values*: these concern our relationship to others and how we want others to see us.

2b *Impressive values*: these are focused on our self-perception (feeling good about yourself, inner harmony, thrift, and so on).

2c *Terminal values*: these are the idealized pictures of life as we would ultimately prefer to live it. In fact, they are the highest ideals we aspire to.

3. *Social values*: these are the ideals that we cherish in relation to our direct environment and society as a whole (for example, peace on earth, conservation of nature and national freedom).

Figure 8.5 shows an example of this.

FROM STRATEGY TO CONCEPT

An event is a staged experience with the aim of attaining a particular goal. Starting from the experience and perception of the visitors and an analysis of the values of the visitor and the initiator of an event, we can take the following step: translating strategy into a concept (see Fig. 8.1 under 'Content').

WHAT'S IN A CONCEPT?

What do we mean by 'concept'? The word 'concept' is used frequently in the leisure sector, but not always unambiguously. Sometimes, it seems to be a meaningless, catch-all term: anything can be called a concept. Our definition of a concept is as follows.

> A concept (as the elaboration of an idea) is the active principle that creates coherence and gives direction to the realization of one or several goals.

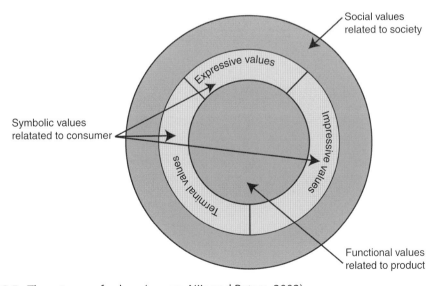

Fig. 8.5. Three types of values (source: Nijs and Peters, 2002).

EVENTS AS A STRATEGIC MARKETING TOOL

A concept does not disappear the moment when its realization in a product, or products, and place has been achieved. On the contrary, it ensures (permanent) coherence.

By active principle, we mean the way in which something essentially works, something it derives its right to exist from, in other words: What makes it tick?

The active principle within a concept can simply be there, like the cold North Sea extending a more or less cordial welcome to take a dip, but a concept does not emerge until this active principle is consciously exploited for the realization of a goal. To stay with the example: the New Year's Day Dip, with thousands of people taking a dive into the sea, is a concept in this sense.

A person, too, can grow into a concept. Jamie Oliver, for example, has an authentic active principle: a sincere, trendy boy who just happens to like cooking a great meal. The moment when this active principle is recognized and somebody has the idea of exploiting it consciously, Jamie Oliver can become a concept.

So, in the case of a concept, there is an underlying idea; the concept brings order to the various parts or building blocks, such as themes, products, personnel and communication.

The example below (Box 8.4) shows how a concept can be worked out starting from the objective to make opera accessible to the general public and build a bridge between opera and a young audience.

Box 8.4   Opera in the Bus

Once every 2 years, the Yo!Opera Festival rallies a large crowd by organizing an international youth opera festival in Utrecht, the Netherlands. The objectives are: building a bridge between opera and a broad/young audience, giving opera a place in the community and fulfilling a pioneering role in the development of repertoire and a new generation of (young) opera makers.

As it turned out, the concept of Opera in the Bus and the festival theme of Community Opera hit the bullseye and resulted in six splendid operas in moving buses, and each opera in its own way did something with the socio-historical context along specific bus routes. Of all the community projects that were also part of the festival, the opera apartment block was probably the highlight. Fifty-four households in all took a singer into their homes for *one* day. Members of the public could ring the bell and then the singer, standing in the doorway, sang his song or aria especially for those who had rung the bell. Six hundred amateur singers from 22 local choirs sang in a gigantic work for a choir from a text written by the mayor. Opera in the Bus took opera out of its ivory tower and into the streets. The Singing City, one of the parts of the project, with its river of choirs as its highlight, drew amateur singers and children from community centres and local meeting places to the theatre.

(Continued)

Box 8.4. Continued.

The noteworthy remarkable results are:

- The bus drivers' choir, specially formed for this festival, will continue to perform. The bus drivers are now writing their own lyrics.
- After the festival, several opera buses were invited to give performances elsewhere, both in the Netherlands and abroad.
- The river of choirs has been picked up by several other cities and festivals as a strong concept of a great performance with local choirs.

THE EXPERIENCE CONCEPT

We make a distinction between functional concepts and experience concepts. Functional concepts are aimed at functionality. Thus, the active principle of a transport cafeteria is the self-service principle. The physical environment, the staff, the activities: everything is aligned to the functions of 'fast' and 'easy'. A functional concept in the context of an event is, for instance, a meeting or a staff briefing; sharing a message simultaneously with everyone via live communication. Questions can be asked at once, participants can respond to each other, and so on.

The aim of the experience concept is realizing an experience on the part of the visitor. All choices, including those related to functional aspects, are in this case aligned to the concept of staging the planned event. An event aimed at realizing an experience is, of course, about an experience concept, so the functional concept does not have to be discussed here.

Criteria for a strong experience concept

A strong experience concept serves its purpose when the goal has been realized and the experience actually occurs. We provide five criteria for a strong experience concept. A strong concept:

- is meaningful, it contains a sort of inner truth. By basing the experience concept on values relevant to the target group, its authenticity can be felt. The point is that it is important to make a connection to what people feel.
- is distinctive and, ideally, unique. Today's consumers are spoiled: they have seen and experienced much. Uniqueness does not have to be a matter of something completely new; it can also arise from a surprising combination of existing elements.
- has endurance. A strong experience concept appeals to people over a longer period of time. It also leaves room, however, for regular innovation or extension without losing its power.
- has several layers. There is more than *one* possible interpretation, for instance, in the case of a concept for an event that is thrilling and interesting for more than one target group. In this sense, a concept has features of a fairy tale. A fairy tale, too, frequently has a core message within a story consisting of various layers. Therefore, storytelling is a key to strong experience concepts (see also Fig. 8.3).

- is well timed. A concept may be strong on paper, but if it is not realized at the right moment, it will lose its potential value. For this reason, it is vital to keep a close eye on trends and developments, not only from an analytical point of view, but also intuitively.

THE CREATIVE DEVELOPMENT OF AN EXPERIENCE CONCEPT FOR AN EVENT

We now know what a concept is, what a good concept is, and the conditions that have to be met to make a concept successful. But how do you arrive at a good concept in practice?

There is a key role for the creative development of an experience concept that connects supply and demand. Indeed, by linking the experience to values in an innovative way, a valuable experience will be created for the visitor to an event.

Creativity

Developing an experience concept by using purely analytical methods will not produce a result. Although knowledge and analysis are indispensable, creativity is the crucial ingredient for the process of developing a concept. Creativity has the following important aspects:

- Creativity is related to problem solving.
- Creativity is related to innovation; thinking of solutions that others have not yet thought of. This may be about not only coming up with completely new ideas but also the skilful combination of different areas of knowledge.
- Creativity is related to crossing boundaries; applying the knowledge and ideas of other subject areas will often result in a fresh look at the matter in hand.
- Creativity is not the result of activities that take place exclusively in the right half of the brain; it rather arises through the interaction between the rational, structural left half of the brain and the intuitive right half (Nijs and Peters, 2002).

The creative process always originates in the heart (see Fig. 8.6). If there is no heartbeat, there is no movement. It is vital to think from the heart, allow the heart to speak and act with heart and soul. From the heart, you go to the head, to the left half and the right half of the brain.

Left half of the brain: acquisition of knowledge

The left half of the brain is related to the phase of knowledge acquisition: making an analysis of the problem or idea. The point here is to challenge the problem itself, look at it from different angles and map out as many connections as possible: analyse the existing (internal and external) supply, potential networks, trends and developments and target groups.

Target groups can be analysed at the level of values. An existing experience can be analysed as well. Most studies of values and experience are *qualitative* ones that use methods such as depth

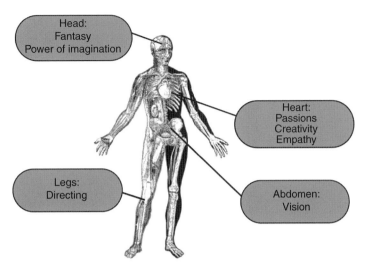

Fig. 8.6. The creative process.

interviews, group discussions, participatory observation and often (creative) techniques like laddering and visualization (mood boards, for example).

An analysis of values and experience is not enough on its own. Use as many sources as possible. Watch films, read stories, visit locations, look at the world around you and allow everything to inspire you.

Creativity comes into play as soon as switching between the left and right half of the brain occurs.

Right half of the brain: dreaming, experiencing, brooding, brainstorming

The phase of knowledge acquisition becomes a phase of musing over things. This is a chaotic phase during which hope, frustration and new insights alternate. Dreams are visualized and mutually communicated. A clear picture of the intended experience is of primary importance in this phase, and creative sessions are a vital tool. What are the emotions in question? What are the values that play a role and how can they be expressed? What are the images that match? What colours and scents? But, above all: what is the objective, what is the feeling with which a visitor leaves an event?

Developing an experience concept by means of creativity

One method for developing an experience concept is storytelling; you choose a story as the active principle within the concept. This makes it possible to put values and emotions into the experience from the inside out via this story. The story may be the story as the visitor will experience it; an experience often seems to have a storyline in the perception of the consumer. Expressing a concept in a one-liner is a way of narrating the story in its most essential form. This one-liner can also be used as a name or a form of communication.

Abdomen: creation of a vision and the experience concept

The abdominal phase (see Fig. 8.6) is about detachment and taking a look at every bit of knowledge and feeling that has arisen from the right half and the left half of the brain in the first phase. This can generate a clear, innovative and fitting vision. A vision is subjective by definition: it is a (personal) opinion or a bundle of opinions, a way of seeing or perceiving, an inner contemplation (Nijs and Peters, 2002). A vision can relate to three levels:

- the world
- humans in general (and the target group in particular)
- the 'product'.

Lego's corporate vision is phrased thus: 'We believe that play is the essential ingredient in a child's growth and development. It grows the human spirit. It encourages imagination, conceptual thinking and creation.' This is a vision of humans in general, and the child in particular. The link to the product is in the reference to play.

In line with a vision, a meaningful experience concept can arise that catches the essence of everything that someone knows and feels. This is about a *good feeling*: the concept must feel good, it must add up.

The Lego name says, in fact, what the concept is. Lego is derived from the Danish words 'leg godt', which mean play well. In Latin, Lego means 'I join, collect, gather'. What is clear from this vision of Lego is that dreaming up something for yourself and building something yourself is a good way to play.

Legs: staging the experience

An experience concept must 'land' somewhere sooner or later; it must make contact with the earth. The concept is translated into a concrete experience, but all the related products and means and channels of communication that go with it should ensue from the concept as well.

THE SETTING OF AN EVENT

In a good concept, attention is paid not merely to the content of an event but also to the form: the physical or virtual environment, or setting, in which the event takes place – atmosphere, decor and forms of communication. In this section, we will deal with the physical environment of an event (see the experience model in Fig. 8.1).

The physical environment has a great impact on an experience. Studies have shown that a location has to meet a number of basic conditions even before the question of a positive experience comes up. The Disney company is a classic example in this respect. In fact, Disney Parks have been designed completely in line with those basic conditions. A clean environment is a primary condition. The location of the park may be ever so nice, but dirty toilets or overflowing bins will destroy that beautiful picture at once.

Studies have shown that people are willing to take 21 steps on average to throw something in a rubbish bin. As a consequence, there is a rubbish bin every 20 steps in the Disney Parks.

Box 8.5

Empty Chubby Gus has been a familiar figure for decades in the Efteling, a Dutch theme park. The concept of this fairy-tale character has arisen from a reformulation of the question: 'How can we prevent litter lying around all over the place?' The question was changed into: 'How can we make a fun thing of the removal of litter?' (Nijs and Peters, 2002). Empty Chubby Gus is a talking litter bin, who shouts 'Litter here!' If a (young) visitor puts litter into his mouth, he will say: 'Thank you!'

The second basic condition concerns the location of available facilities. It is a given that sanitary facilities near the exit of a museum will shorten the time spent there, whereas providing a resting place and catering halfway will, in fact, prolong the stay (Nijs and Peters, 2002).

Recognizability is the third basic condition. Psychology tells us that people immediately look for points of reference to see how a location is laid out. When a visitor enters a big exhibition hall, he is often overwhelmed by a large number of signs with pictures and texts that try to tell him all sorts of things. This is very confusing. A similar confusion can occur at festival grounds. Several festivals help visitors to find their way by developing applications for smartphones, with the help of which visitors can consult the map and programming of the event interactively (for more about this aspect, see Chapter 9).

A place must hold surprises, but if roaming about means getting lost, the experience is disturbed at once (Hesselmans, 2005). Signposting is important. Basic information can also be cast in a meaningful form, for that matter. Use can be made of stilt walkers, for instance, or other characters at key points of the event location. It is their task to inform the visitor in a way that is felt as an experience.

THE EXPERIENCE TOOLS

The experience tools are the resources required for staging the event in such a way that the message touches the visitor (see Fig. 8.1). This section will subsequently discuss: thematizing, storytelling, the senses, play, co-creation and staff.

Thematizing

Thematizing is a frequently used tool in the events sector. Think, for example, of the theme, subject, of a congress. A theme as an experience tool is the external, recognizable explicit theme that is carried over into the decor, the details involved and communication.

Themes can be based on:

1. History or epochs, such as the Second World War, the Middle Ages or the Roman era, as a frame for thematic festivals.
2. Culture or (sub) cultures, such as (visual) arts, heritage, music, folklore, countries.
3. Fiction, such as books (*Harry Potter*), films (*SpongeBob*), fairy tales, legends or myths (Robin Hood).
4. Nature: jungle, beach, gardens, animals.
5. Technology, like trains in a railway museum.

This is a broad categorization. A combination of main themes is also possible. A railway museum, for example, can be based on history, heritage and technology.

Themes are aimed at a change in visitors' perception of reality; the point is to immerse them in another world. Ideally, space, time, matter and people (characters) are integrated into a coherent whole (Nijs and Peters, 2002).

According to Pine (presentation, International Business Forum, Imagineering Academy; Breda, 2003, unpublished), thematizing is the main ingredient for the creation of a memorable experience: an experience that leaves the visitor of an event with positive memories. As Pine says, it is essential for the theme to be loaded with as many suitable elements as possible, positive cues. Unsuitable elements, negative cues, should, of course, be avoided as much as possible.

Still, thematizing is not always a formula for success. A study of thematizing at leisure locations has shown that thematizing on its own is usually not enough for a memorable experience. Besides, it appears that the role of positive and negative cues depends strongly on the degree to which the visitor is involved in the theme. The lower the involvement, the less value someone attaches to suitable and unsuitable elements.

Storytelling

Storytelling is about narrating stories, which is as old as mankind. It is a perfect way of transferring values and norms (as in fairy tales), arousing emotions, involving people in an event and even bringing about a transformation. Stories can help people understand the world. People are in search of frameworks in order to give meaning to the world in which they live (Rijnja and van der Jagt, 2004). The point of stories lies not in the facts they mention, but in their meaning. Thanks to stories, you, as a listener or reader, can be miles away for a moment, be somewhere else in your thoughts, without losing your head (Gabriel, 2000). Stories activate pride, fantasy and desire (Rijnja and van der Jagt, 2004). These elements are linked closely to an experience.

A vital dimension of storytelling is authenticity, not in the sense of a 'true story' but in the sense of originality and credibility, involving real emotions and meaningful values. From a factual point of view, for example, *Lord of the Rings* is not very credible, but emotionally it is. In relation to thematizing, contextual authenticity in storytelling plays a role. A story will be better if located in its original environment. Thus, a story about Indians told in a teepee will probably evoke a stronger experience.

Layering is another essential dimension of storytelling. Powerful stories have several layers that can be interpreted at various levels. That is the very reason why children want to hear the same story time and again. They keep discovering new layers in a good story. The continual discovery of new elements in a familiar story is something that may also play an important role in the repetition of leisure activities.

Explicit storytelling means that a story is literally narrated by someone. The narrator can put emotions into the story and involve the audience in it by giving it a role, or through questions and answers.

Implicit storytelling means that a visual representation or object triggers a story in the visitor; he fills it with his own powers of imagination. An object may evoke a nostalgic memory from a personal or collective past. An old cardboard train ticket in a railway museum, for instance, may take visitors back to their own memories in their own personal story, to an experience from the past. An object can also be a metaphor to reduce a (true) story to comprehensible dimensions, like the suitcases with personal belongings in the memorial centre at Auschwitz (Poland) that stand for the personal and human tragedy of deportation.

With respect to the staging of the experience, it is of vital importance to start creating coherence between the experience tools such as storytelling and thematizing already at the concept level.

Stimulating the senses

Sensory perceptions cause emotions (Frijda, 1986), and emotions are the crucial factor for an experience. The stronger the stimulation of the senses, the more intense the experience (Pine and Gilmore, 1999). But, this is a relative matter. It is also possible for someone to have an intense experience while listening to music or looking at a painting.

In this section, we will discuss colours and scents in more detail. The example below (Box 8.6) shows how a big venue appeals to the senses by developing meeting moods.

Box 8.6

A convention and meeting centre has developed a unique concept on the basis of the knowledge that colours and other sensory stimulants have an impact on the mood and performance of people. This concept is called *meeting moods*. By using the answers to questions about the objectives and participants of a planned meeting, the client will receive a proposal for the best mood that best fits the meeting, the layout of the room, use of colours, catering, background music, and so on.

The potential target groups for an event are:

- colleagues
- employees

(Continued)

Box 8.6. Continued.

- board/committee
- relations
- students
- members/volunteers
- same-sector colleagues/specialists
- partygoers.

When dealing with an event for 'colleagues', for example, the next question will be: 'What is the objective of your event?' Subsequently, several objectives will be presented from which a choice can be made.

- We are going to speed things up with our colleagues. Power is what drives us!
- The important point for us is togetherness. Support, appreciation, but having a good time, too, are the things that are central to us.
- It concerns training sessions, a congress or brainstorming. We share knowledge or ideas.
- We are going to share successes and think of how to propagate them. Thrust out your breast, everybody will be proud!

Suppose that a choice has been made for training sessions, a congress or brainstorming. The final question is then: 'Which of the four fields typifies your organization best?'

1. We believe in long-term relationships on the basis of trust. We respect norms and traditions. We work within frameworks and regulation.
2. We like being inspired by trends. We are proud of who we are and what we do. Positive publicity is very important to us.
3. We decide on the basis of facts and key indicators. As a result of long experience, our name has become established. We accept our social responsibility.
4. We are among the leaders in our sector. The result is what counts. We are original, innovative and dynamic.

Suppose that option 3 fits your organization. The site then presents a film with impressions of a concept for an event. The meeting mood matching this example is 'inspiring'. The colour is blue. The room in which the meeting takes place has blue lighting. The catering is adapted to this: a water bar, a skewer with fruit, and so on. Scents, such as the lemon-like fragrance of flowers, of coffee beans and sweet pastries, are dominant. Subsequently, a mood board can be made that enables the client to prepare a made-to-measure meeting with one of the mood makers of the convention and meeting centre.
(Source: www.meetingmoods.nl, accessed January 2011, adapted by the authors.)

Colours

Colours greatly affect the mood of people, and moods, as said earlier, play a vital role in the creation of an experience. Colours can support the structure of a story (Hench, 2003). Colours activate people.

Hench describes the effects of different colours. Red, for example may suggest happiness and put people in a festive mood, but it may also indicate danger and call for alertness. Blue is usually associated with blue skies, with space and freedom. Brown suggests power, terra firma and deep roots. Green refers to nature, to green trees, abundance, peace and a healthy life. Dark places with cool colours may look threatening but when coloured lights or small pieces of glittering material are installed, they will become attractive and be imbued with a magic, romantic aura (Hench, 2003).

Scents

Experiments have shown that sight is the dominant sense, followed immediately by hearing. Processing scents takes place in the lymbic system of our brain. This area also contains the control mechanisms of emotions. A sense of smell is not always recognized as important, in spite of the fact that scents are related strongly to moods, experience and memories (Dekker, 2006).

Increasing use is made of scents at events; there are even aroma jockeys. This requires a subtle approach. If taste and scent clash violently (you smell cinnamon and taste beer), it can be so confusing that the experience is disturbing. Providing too many stimulants simultaneously is not advisable.

Scents can be utilized to divert attention from something that is relatively inconvenient before or during an event: queuing, for instance. Moreover, scents can be used to affect the experience during the pre- and post-exposure phase to increase anticipation or trigger memories.

Elements of play

Is there anyone who has never quarrelled with his best friends in the course of a game of *Risk* or *Settlers of Catan*? Is there anyone who has not felt that feeling of elation at scoring a goal in an insignificant practice match? Computer games, particularly online games, have gained enormous popularity the last few years. Besides, a parallel, perhaps paradoxical, development can be seen in the strong increase in the sales of board games over the last decade (Hover and Horsten, 2004).

A game is full of surprises, provides scope for creativity and enables the player to develop his cognitive and motor skills, and his emotional side. There are various kinds of games. Sometimes, it is disorganized and spontaneous. This is a setting in which pleasure and development are the primary factors. Computer games are different. They have been designed and organized in time and space. They are focused on the optimization of challenges and tactics (Verhagen, 2006).

Play and sports are closely linked. Though it sometimes seems as if freedom and pleasure are fading into the background in sports, especially in its professional arm, sports has been a popular leisure activity for its practitioners since ancient classical times, and during which emotions can run high.

Play is often associated with children. Yet, play is an important element of the leisure activities of adults as well. A game is the perfect way of involving people in an activity, both as spectators and as participants. When the spectator can actively influence a game, like in the *X Factor*, *Idols* and *The Voice*, the experience is reinforced.

Play has been utilized successfully for ages during (business) events. It disconnects people from their fixed patterns, carries them along into an experience and offers scope for interaction (the social context).

Co-creation

Co-creation means involving the customer in designing the experience that is most in accordance with the meaning that he personally wants to give his life (see also the section on co-creation in Chapter 2).

Consumers are now much better at getting access to information and, as a result, can make decisions that are well founded and better. The role of the consumer is changing. The individual consumer feels a growing need, in interaction with an organization, to create a value proposition that is meaningful for him personally (Prahalad and Ramaswamy, 2004).

It is the ultimate form of driven by demand. Co-creation is often presented as an innovative concept within the experience economy, but it is to a large extent based on the same principles as play. According to Verhagen (2006), the major similarities between play and co-creation are:

- the freedom of choice experienced
- intrinsic motivation
- the focus on interaction
- scope for creativity
- scope for self-development
- the fact that there is no pre-determined result.

It is obvious that co-creation, too, can be exploited as an experience tool. Co-creation between supplier and consumer has played a role in the event as an experience since time immemorial; an example is the battle between gladiators in ancient Rome, where the spectators were one of the parties that could decide the outcome. In the case of an event, the experience does not *really* occur until the spectator participates in it. An artist performing for an empty house is not an experience. The spectators who applaud, sing along or give expression to their involvement in other ways turn an event into an experience: there is interaction between supplier and consumer, and the experience becomes accessible to others. The way in which the fans of different countries dress up and present themselves during a world championship contributes to one's own total experience, but also to that of other people.

By involving a visitor of an event at the level of concept and product development, he becomes part of the co-creation process at an early stage. Digital media like the Internet open up many possibilities. This happens regularly in the context of events. Several big festivals enable consumers, via their websites, to vote for their favourite line-up.

A visitor who enters the co-creation process with the supplier at this level will undoubtedly have a strong personal experience: after all, he can express his creativity, and creativity is linked strongly to experience. Besides, he is involved strongly and personally before, during and, perhaps, after the process, and can share this with other people.

The flipside of co-creation is that a visitor who has been able to define his experience in advance knows exactly what he can expect: there is little room left for surprises, let alone that his expectations will be surpassed. In short, sometimes it is fun to prepare a meal yourself; at other times, it is exciting to have a surprise menu served to you at a restaurant.

The question whether co-creation is an interesting option for an individual consumer depends very much on the relevance of a specific activity to the person in question (to what extent does he *want* to be involved?). Besides, co-creation requires an effort, and not everyone will have the time and willingness to make that effort. It is a matter of balancing costs and benefits. The competencies of an individual play a part as well. There are people who simply lack the self-confidence, the ability to take the initiative or the creativity to take up the challenge. In this context, too, virtual communities can play the role of a safe 'family' in which individual people can get to work with co-creativity.

Optimum demand control in the form of co-creativity is certainly not the only way to guarantee a strong experience. A profound, meaningful experience can also occur in a supply controlled setting. It is then up to the supplier in the events sector to put himself in the shoes of the visitor, in his position, and whenever possible, arrive at a meaningful experience in consultation with each other (Box 8.7).

Box 8.7   Burning Man

A fine example of co-creation is Burning Man, an annual festival that has been organized in the USA since 1986. More than 48,000 participants travel to the remote Black Rock Desert in Nevada to be part of an experimental community for a week that challenges the participants to express themselves artistically in a huge settlement (Black Rock City) at the bottom of a dry lake.

The organization is carried out by a small group of regular staff and more than 2000 volunteers. Each year, there is a new theme to forge a bond between participants and to encourage them. The participants bring the theme to life in large installations in theme camps on the grounds. People take presents to give to others, and they

(Continued)

Box 8.7. Continued.

come with costumes, decorated cars, or whatever. Just being there is enough, too. There are no rules telling people how to behave and express themselves, except for rules that protect health, safety and the total experience of the event. Each individual can decide for himself how he wants to contribute and give to the community. Participants share food and drink, for instance. The event is concluded by the burning of the installations. A month after the event, no trace can be found of the city that for many has been the most important city in the country for a short while. Obviously, Burning Man is more than a temporary community. It is a desert city for the ultimate in self-expression and art. The impact of the Burning Man experience is so profound that a culture has formed around it in which people all over the world organize events to rekindle that magical feeling. (Source: www.burningman.com, accessed January 2011.)

Personnel

Personnel have a crucial role in shaping an experience, and this has nothing to do with acting out a role. It starts with obvious basic aspects such as kindness, accessibility and a readiness to help, aspects that in practice do not always turn out to be so obvious. As a contribution to the eventual experience, the vital competence required of staff is empathy, the ability to put oneself in the shoes of the visitor and try to surpass expectations.

The perfect example of the role of staff as bearers of the experience can be found in the Disney Parks. Each member of staff, from high to low, is a cast member. Being at work is being on stage, and everyone is part of the show. To many European ears, this sounds like something that is not our style. Still, lessons can be learned.

Every Disney shop has a budget that is available to an employee to use as he sees fit at a moment when he can create a special, magical event for a visitor. Not only does this enrich the experience of the visitor, but the cast member, too, will derive pleasure from this interaction. *Take five* means: however busy you are, take 5 s or 5 min each day to enjoy the personal interaction with the one visitor you create that magical moment for. Thus, experience cuts both ways. It also fills staff with new energy.

Storytelling is an essential component of the training of Disney's staff. The Disney Traditions programme consists, for a large part, of telling stories.

The staff engaged for events is often temporary staff, such as volunteers. In such a situation, there is relatively little scope for training programmes. But, it is here that storytelling comes in as an efficient and effective tool to help everyone involved get a feel for the right way to deal with an experience. A fascinating story about how enthralling a staff member was during an earlier event achieves more than a list of 20 instructions.

SUMMARY

The concept of an event should be aligned to the values of the target group. A conversion must be made into a perfectly staged experience. The tools required to do so are an analysis of supply and demand, the values of the target group and the experience model.

The experience model shows how an event will be experienced. In this, the psychosocial framework plays a vital role. There are three levels of experience: basic, memorable and transformative. The factors within the psychosocial framework are knowledge, expectations, motives, mood, involvement, social context, personality and values.

A concept, as the result of an idea, is the active principle that creates coherence and gives direction to the realization of one or more objectives. Clear criteria can be formulated for a strong experience concept, and creativity is indispensable to arrive at a concept that focuses not only on the content of an event but also on the form. Form refers to the setting of an event. The physical environment is part of it and should meet three basic conditions. Finally, the experience tools for an event are thematizing, storytelling, senses, play, co-creation and personnel.

chapter 9

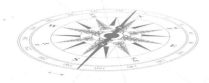

Touchpoints

Dorothé Gerritsen and Ronald van Olderen

In this chapter, we will focus on turning the experience concept into relevant touchpoints: the points of contact that occur during the three phases of pre-exposure, direct exposure and post-exposure. We will discuss two touchpoint models, one from the organization's perspective and the other from the visitor's perspective. The key question is how to create effective touchpoints so as to optimize the visitor or customer experience. In this process, other questions will be dealt with too: what precisely is a touchpoint and which points of contact are there between an organization and its clients or visitors? How can these points of contact be influenced? Which points of contact cannot be influenced? What are the consequences of managing the visitor experience of an organization?

LEARNING TARGETS

After studying this chapter, you will have learned:

- what touchpoints are
- what the difference is between a staged experience and a customer experience
- what the customer journey means
- how organizations can influence the customer journey of their visitors, in a positive and effective manner, by means of touchpoints.

Box 9.1   A warm welcome to cold Iceland

A magical, white moonlike landscape glittering in the sun, steaming geysers: never seen anything like it before. The unique experience starts straight away on arrival of a delegation of the Event Management specialization area: Ronald van Olderen, Esther de Beer, Moniek Hover and Dorothé Gerritsen. The 17th International Festivals and Events Association Europe Annual Conference in Reykjavik, Iceland, oozed Pure Energy! Reykjavik: a unique conference destination with the theme of Nurturing Creativity – expectations were high.

That's Reykjavik Pure Energy!

Reykjavik is a relatively small city with many suburbs, a lively festival and event scene and an artistic climate. Examples include the annual Arts Festival, featuring numerous cultural activities throughout the city, and the construction of a modern conference centre near the old harbour. The city is working hard on its image by means of its brand theme 'Pure Energy', on its infrastructure, efficient air routes with America and the European mainland, and there is talk of building the country's first railway line: in other words, a lot of potential. A European conference like this obviously generates good PR for Iceland in general and Reykjavik in particular. Add to this, postmodern people's need for unique experiences and the outcome is a highly interesting case.

From Arts Festival Reykjavik to audience development research

Every spring, artists like David Bowie and Led Zeppelin, also a series of photograph exhibitions and a giant marionette called the Little Giant transform the city into a hotbed of cultural activity. This setting, combined with the workshops on audience development, imagineering and managing creativity, ensured that the first conference day produced interesting insights for us.

The delicious Icelandic food made our Iceland experience complete. We learned and saw a lot of interesting things in terms of international cultural festivals in Europe, and in Iceland in particular.

The first day of the Iceland experience

Every day, we took part in some amazing and unique events, such as a dinner in the Power Plant, a brand new power station just outside Reykjavik. The delicious meal of lobster soup, salmon, lamb, along with plenty of wine, was a great way to conclude our first conference day. We walked back to the Hotel Plaza through the immaculate white wilderness.

Krum, krum, krum: Icelandic songs

The day started with a sing-along of rain songs and lullabies in the Arts Museum, led by Iceland's best-known conductor, which allowed us to focus our minds on the first speaker of the second day. Despite the unusual start to the day, the rest of it was fairly traditional.

(Continued)

Box 9.1. Continued.

Plenary sessions were followed by workshops, and then by a plenary panel discussion. We were reminded of what it is like to listen to one person for quite a long time. The topic of discussion was rather abstract, and bore little or no relation to our everyday professional activities. It was interesting, however, for the specialization area of creative industries and the international context, because of the primary focus on international cultural collaboration. The speaker was an expert in this area and approached the topic from an academic perspective.

BBC: Electric Proms

A completely different and especially practical story by Lorna Clark (BBC) underlined the enormous variety of speakers and topics presented at the conference. Straight from the heart, she told us how the concept and the actual event of the Electric Proms festival, a combination of classical and pop music, was developed, organized and communicated. Good examples and wonderful impressions of the festival by means of both image and sound. What was interesting, for instance, was the way the festival was announced on the various BBC channels: Lorna told us about eight different ways of how the BBC handled the announcement of the festival.

That same afternoon, Andrew Baron, one of Lorna's colleagues, delivered a workshop that concentrated on opening up festivals online. The lesson he taught us was mainly about managing word-of-mouth advertising through a highly targeted use of online social networks. An interesting example was the air guitar competition for listeners of BBC Radio 1 to promote Radio 1's Big Weekend. Listeners were asked to make films of themselves playing the air guitar along with their favourite band or artist, and to post these films on YouTube. In this way, and through the listeners' networks, the Big Weekend was promoted in a very informal way: a clever concept.

And this was only a selection of the facts and impressions that we gained. For more information, you are referred to www.ifeaeurope.com.

(Source: 17th IFEA Conference, Reykjavik, Iceland, 2008, adapted by the authors.)

WHAT ARE TOUCHPOINTS?

Touchpoints are interaction points between a company or organization and its clients or visitors. Several definitions of touchpoints can be found in the literature on marketing, branding and imagineering (creating experience worlds). Jenkinson formulated the following definition.

> A touchpoint refers to a point or moment of contact/communication between an organisation or brand and an individual consumer or stakeholder.

(www.mindz.com, January 2009)

It is a fairly new term within the events industry, and substantial efforts are currently being devoted to research into touchpoints. Events appeal to one or more of a visitor's senses in all three phases of pre-experience, direct experience and post-experience; what is there to see, smell, hear, feel and taste? Essentially, it is about the contact between, for instance, a brand, an organization and two or more interest groups.

Touchpoints affect perception, satisfaction and loyalty towards an organization.

> Brand touchpoints refer to every contact point of a brand with clients, prospects, and other stakeholders – before, during and after-sale. Touchpoint management should be understood as a multi-disciplinary strategic approach that leads to optimised performance in all market-oriented management areas.
>
> (www.accelerom.com, 2008)

Whether the touchpoints occur during the organization of a trade fair, a public event or a corporate event, the essence is that every moment of contact, every channel, every contact between visitor and organization is important and deserves careful consideration. After all, every contact has the potential to cause either a positive or a negative experience in the visitor, which has either a positive or a negative effect on the relationship or the experience of the event. Having to wait too long to be able to park one's car, for instance, may have a negative impact on the visitor experience. On the other hand, unexpected surprises may influence customers' opinions in a positive manner. To give an example, handing out umbrellas when it is raining can have a positive effect.

So, it seems that touchpoints occur in many different contexts: websites, registration systems, routing, entrance, facilities including toilets and cloakroom, temperature, product usage, networks, media, means of communication (newsletters, posters, flyers, programme booklets), virtual environments, personnel, artists, format and setting, entertainment, technology, DVDs, location, photographs, catering, audio-visual equipment, goody bags, fittings, decor. It is important to bear in mind that touchpoints go beyond communication. There are just some points of contact you do not have any influence on as an organizer!

Orchestrating touchpoints

As we have shown in the previous chapter, creating an effective event is something that depends on many factors. A good concept alone is not enough. Good planning and communication also are not enough, because events are experienced differently by different visitors, as a consequence of their psychosocial frameworks (see Chapter 8). As an event organizer, understanding psychosocial processes in visitors is not the only thing that matters; you need to go one step further and actually influence these processes. You can deliberately orchestrate important touchpoints in the three phases of exposure, so before, during and after an event. Whether you will achieve your intended objectives will depend partially on the way in which you manage your touchpoints. In this process, you need to be fully aware of the fact that the customer experience goes beyond the experience of the event itself. Engaging your target group is a strategic goal in all cases, and touchpoints play a crucial role in the customer experience (see also Chapter 10 on measuring effects).

FROM STAGED EXPERIENCES TO CUSTOMER EXPERIENCES

It is becoming increasingly difficult for businesses to set themselves apart from their competitors by means of products and services (see also Part I of this book). Consumers have access to unlimited information, and products are becoming increasingly alike. Competing successfully requires a different approach, with the perspective shifting from the supplier (organization) to the individual customer. After all, the value of the product or service is no longer the only thing that counts. What is at least equally important is the meaning the individual customer attaches to the product or service. Does the product or service adequately reflect the customer's values or respond to the customer's needs? In this respect, individual customer experiences are extremely important. As a result, event marketing is gaining in importance.

Figure 9.1 shows a continuum of value addition, which starts with the organization and ends with the client. If the focus of value addition lies entirely on the side of the organization, the customer will have a staged experience, orchestrated by the organization. The organization takes the value of the product or service as a guiding principle and builds a perfectly staged experience around it. The *Libelle* Zomerweek (a summer event for readers of *Libelle* – a Dutch women's magazine) is an interesting example in this respect (Box 9.2).

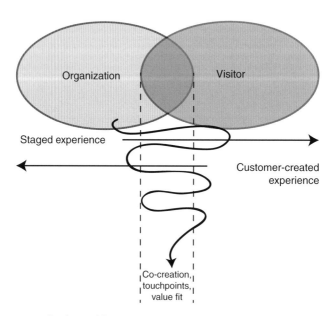

Fig. 9.1. Continuum of value addition.

Box 9.2

Libelle has been the most popular womens' magazine of the Netherlands for many years, and it is a strong multimedia brand. The magazine features articles on fashion, interior decorating, beauty, food and drink, tourism and human interest. The main brand extensions are Libelle.nl, the *Libelle* Zomerweek (Summer Week) and the *Libelle* specials. *Libelle* has a strong online community, with a focus on the everyday pleasures of life. A three-dimensional element of the brand is the *Libelle* Summer Week: the biggest outdoor event for women, attracting more than 75,000 visitors. The *Libelle* specials go more deeply into subjects that are important to women, such as interior decorating, life–work balance and travel. The core readers of *Libelle* are women aged between 30 and 55, most of whom are part of multiple-person households, usually families with children. *Libelle* readers represent the average Dutch woman, which is no surprise really, considering the magazine's huge circulation rate. They are contemporary women who put their family first. *Libelle* readers are slightly higher educated than the average Dutch woman, have a little more money to spend, have an active lifestyle, spend a lot of attention on their families and attach great importance to the future of their children. Furthermore, they prefer to undertake things like shopping together with friends or relatives rather than alone, and they are very much interested in make-up and fashion. On average, they have a more than average interest in home decoration and gardening. They also take pleasure in cooking meals (every day), preparing something special from time to time.

All these aspects are represented at the annual event *Libelle* Zomerweek. Not only the various *Libelle* topics but also the atmosphere and values that *Libelle* readers find important are reflected in the concept of the *Libelle* Zomerweek. The concept of the event is entirely consistent with the concept of the magazine; it is, in fact, a three-dimensional variant, which makes visitors feel at home. They experience something that matches their perception of the brand. It may be evident that the organizers of the *Libelle* Zomerweek orchestrate the entire visitor experience by means of programming and atmosphere. (Source: www.libellezomerweek.nl, accessed November 2009, adapted by the authors.)

The focus of value addition may also lie entirely on the side of the customer; in which case, we speak of customer-created experiences. Value and meaning are created by the customer himself, whereas the organization takes a supporting role. We will also give an example of this side of the continuum (Box 9.3).

Box 9.3

ING, a global financial institution, brings together directors and major shareholders at a dinner, just when some of them are planning to sell their businesses. ING creates an open atmosphere, centred around the personal situations of the guests and allowing them to

(Continued)

Box 9.3. Continued.

discuss these situations. In this setting, the guests admit that they are struggling with the idea of selling their businesses, with the sense of emptiness that will undoubtedly be the result of this, and with the question of how to do something useful with their lives again. ING plays a facilitating role in terms of helping its clients deal with this change in their lives. At this particular point, the clients do not derive any value from ING's financial services, but from the experience they undergo in this specific situation. ING will be rewarded with greater loyalty from these clients: the chance of any upcoming important financial transactions being awarded to ING will be increased substantially. (Source: Wiegerink and Peelen, 2010.)

Event marketing is about much more than consumer satisfaction. It is about consumer happiness and well-being, giving people a chance to reach their potential and bringing more meaning to their lives (see also Chapter 2).

The importance of physical contact

The process of value addition may be initiated by either the organization or the client. In reality, however, the boundaries are blurred: both parties engage in dialogue with each other and meet each other somewhere in the middle. In this process, there is still a great need for physical contact and non-verbal communication. Despite all the possibilities of Google, Facebook or LinkedIn, we continue to go to every networking party or dinner we can. Attitude and intonation – both difficult to infer from online activities – help you understand better the intentions of your conversation partner. A real conversation can also be steered in the right direction more easily, should any complications arise. What is more, when you see each other in person, you shake hands. This physical contact has a function. People have a fundamental need to belong, which is equally valid in business interactions.

The value fit

Without a value fit, the customer will have no interest or use in entering into a relationship with the organization, and the organization will not be able to generate any economic customer value. Value fit occurs when organizations and their customers share similar values. This means that the organization's involvement with the visitors of its event must be as great as possible, and that visitors must be given a more active role in the organization of the event (co-creation, see Chapter 8).

That is why event organizers are looking for answers to questions like: what is happening in the lives of our visitors at the moment? What touches them emotionally? Why does a visitor come to an event? What is important to the visitor prior to, during and after the event? Which values occur when, and how can we, as an organization, respond to this as adequately as possible?

The pre- and post-event stages are becoming increasingly important where it concerns the designing of the customer experience. The visitor comes into contact with the organization a long time before the event, but also afterwards, and this will determine in part how this person perceives, values and experiences his journey. The organizer of the event will deploy resources in every phase in order to give the visitor the experience he wants. This is obviously when the touchpoints come into the picture.

THE TOUCHPOINT MODEL

Based on the idea that a good concept based on values has the power to touch people's hearts, you can recognize and specify touchpoints. Remmers specified touchpoints for a theatre, as shown in Fig. 9.2, which could serve as input for a model for events.

The idea behind this model is that an organization, a theatre in this case, represents a number of values. The main question here involves the degree to which the theatre succeeds in communicating these values to its clients in all points of contact, in order to create an optimal visitor

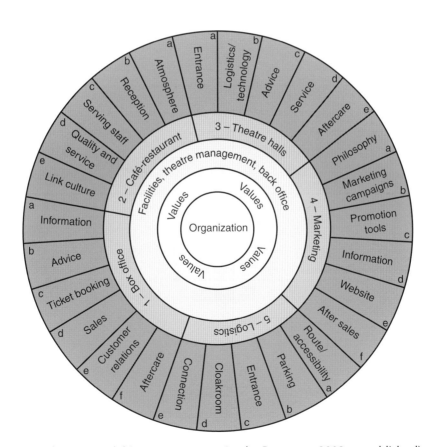

Fig. 9.2. Touchpoint model (source: presentation by Remmers, 2008, unpublished).

experience. The optimal visitor experience (customer experience) occurs when organization and visitors mostly share the same values: the value fit from the section above.

The organization's values are communicated to the visitors via the second layer in the model. The third layer consists of the back office: the theatre's management and the facilities. The fourth layer concerns the front office: those parts of the organization which are more visible and tangible to clients. These are the 'pillars' for the frameworks to which the specific touch-points can be attached (the outermost layer). Specific touchpoints to the visitor include parking space and entrance, and booking in advance options. In other words, how are the booking and parking systems organized, and how do visitors experience the various facilities.

With regard to events, we can make two models. Figure 9.3 shows the model from the perspective of the organization. This is Remmers' touchpoint model (Fig. 9.2), only without the touchpoints in the outer layer. The organization finds itself at the core, and in the subsequent layers from the inside to the outside: values, the three phases (before, during and after the event), back office, pillars (front office) and, finally, the actual touchpoints themselves.

The aim of the touchpoint model is to discover marketing and improvement opportunities for the organization. The various channels are identified, in order to optimize the visitor experience,

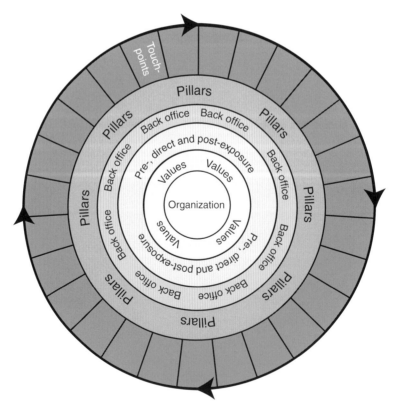

Fig. 9.3. Touchpoint model for events from the organization's perspective.

in which the visitor side is obviously the central focus. Let us take a look at, for instance, the touchpoint of websites. Someone who builds a website considers aspects like design and layout. In this process, the client is very important, because the site has to be user-friendly and the design can only be called a success when visitors actually regard the site as user-friendly.

VISITOR PERCEPTION OF TOUCHPOINTS

We have already emphasized that organizations need to get under the skin of their customers to find out what really matters to them in the customer experience. In terms of events, organizations need to address the question of what visitors consider important and how the desired experience drives the customer proposition. Which phases does the event visitor go through? In this respect, we are talking about the customer value chain or the aggregate (total) experience.

As we have already shown, the focus should be placed on the visitor's total experience. Suppose that someone has bought a ticket to a concert that is going to take place in a couple of months. Then something happens that forces this future visitor to choose another date to go to this concert. If this client (future visitor) is not adequately assisted by the organization or the ticketing agency in switching the dates – either via the website or by telephone – this will have a major impact on the visitor's experience prior to the event. If an organization takes the customer (and the customer's values) as a guiding principle, and thinks carefully through every interaction that the customer is going to have with the organization, it will be able to create and manage every touchpoint in every phase of the experience, so that the aggregate experience is supportive of the organization's promise to its clients. Even though there will always be aspects outside the organization's range of influence, this is still a solid guiding principle. Or, in other words, every touchpoint matters.

In Fig. 9.4 it is the visitor – along with his values and motives – that makes up the point of departure in which the three phases, before, during and after the event, are critical to the visitor's total experience. The third layer shows that the importance each individual visitor attaches to the touchpoints differs with each phase. Specific touchpoints can be placed in the outer layer, which has not yet been filled in.

TOUCHPOINTS FOR AN OPTIMAL VISITOR EXPERIENCE

Organizations can use the layers in both models to check whether the relevant touchpoints are applied in the right phase and in the right manner, so as to build the optimal visitor experience. Figure 9.5 shows that both perspectives need to be connected with each other. The visitor perspective is becoming increasingly important.

In a commercial setting, money will have to be made. So, it is very important to have an accurate understanding of which touchpoints have a high impact and which touchpoints have a low impact. Nevertheless, regardless of the type of objective, a touchpoint must always be applied effectively in order to arrive at an optimal visitor experience.

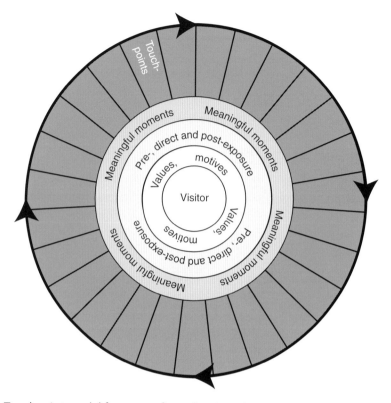

Fig. 9.4. Touchpoint model for events from the visitor's perspective.

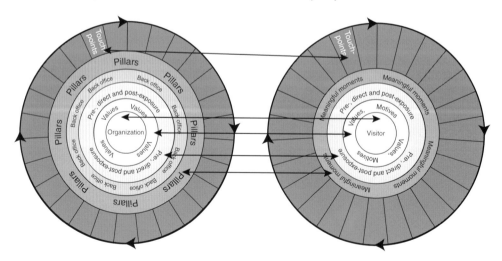

Fig. 9.5. Touchpoint value fit between organization and visitor.

When you are organizing an innovative event, for instance, you have to ask yourself the question of just how innovative you have to be in the choice of your touchpoints. Should you offer your visitors innovative catering services? Should you employ the latest hologram technology to add strength to your presentations? Should your room or hall be LED lit? Only when it is clear which aspects add value to the customer experience can well-considered decisions be made with regard to touchpoints – in terms of application and priorities – in which the cost aspect obviously plays a role, too, for the organization as well as the customer. The key question in this respect always concerns the extent to which the touchpoints will contribute to optimizing the visitor experience.

FROM EVENTS TO EXPERIENCES

Box 9.4

Expoproof is a company that organizes trade fairs. According to Expoproof's corporate vision, there are always three players involved: organizer, visitor and exhibitor. What you say about one player has a direct influence on the other two players. The visitor experience is the key success factor; the key question being: why does a visitor come to a particular trade fair?

There are several aspects that play a role in this respect, such as:

- overall quality of the trade fair
- the target group of the exhibitors
- atmosphere and presentation
- catering
- other visitors.

What Expoproof always tries to do is to facilitate networking for its visitors. Fellow professionals should be able to meet up and share ideas. The experience has to be very intense and at the same time relaxed: visitors should be able to find what they are looking for. Addressing a couple of issues at the same time, and organizing and facilitating these issues in an efficient manner, allows you to create the right visitor experience, causing the visitor to come back every year. The experience starts right from your first communication. The experience is also formed by the exhibitor's communication with the visitors. The experience starts upon the visitor's arrival at the trade fair. The moment of arrival and the moment of departure may have either a positive or a negative impact on the trade fair visitor (and organizer). If it is raining when the visitor arrives and he is unable to find a place to park his car, there is a real chance that he will decide to turn around and go home. And when entering the trade fair grounds, the way in which visitors are welcomed (with coffee or tea being served?) is obviously important, after which the actual trade fair experience begins. The moment of leaving the grounds is very important, too, because this will be the last thing the visitor remembers.
(Source: www.expoproof.com, accessed November 2009; van der Zwaag, 2009, adapted by the authors.)

The above example (Box 9.4) shows that the visitor experience is absolutely the most important thing to Expoproof. It also serves to show that selecting the right touchpoints is a strong tool for the organizer in creating a positive visitor experience.

Generally speaking, touchpoints may promote a positive visitor experience if they:

- are diversified
- create a memorable experience
- focus on values
- engage several senses
- inspire emotions
- are mutually consistent
- are chosen purposefully.

These aspects relating to the successful employment of touchpoints will be dealt with in the next subsections.

Satisfiers and dissatisfiers

Touchpoints can be categorized into satisfiers and dissatisfiers. Satisfiers are good touchpoints, surprising the visitor, or even exceeding the visitor's expectations. Dissatisfiers in themselves are good touchpoints, too. Nevertheless, they will not generate any greater appreciation for your organization. If these touchpoints are not positive experiences for the customer, they will be counterproductive. That is why dissatisfiers always represent important preconditions, on which – as it happens – organizations do not always have an influence. An example involving trade fairs, for instance, are catering services. If the price–quality ratio of the catering services is good, visitors will be extremely satisfied, but the organizer of the trade fair will not receive any extra appreciation for it. However, if the price–quality ratio is not good, visitors will mention this on the evaluation form and possibly also spread the word to other visitors, leading to a poorer assessment of the trade fair as a whole. The catering experience compromises the total visitor experience, although the catering services in themselves have nothing to do with the actual theme of the trade fair.

Magical moments

Satisfiers can be used as magical moments. Magical moments are the moments when customers experience a product or service that they had never imagined, that truly surprises them and that shows the organization's commitment to them. The customer experience cannot always be perfect, and it does not need to be so either. There will always be peaks and valleys (see also the section below on the pleasure–pain gap). The relationship between organizer and visitor is a commitment characterized by a certain degree of routine, but also (and this is where the opportunities can be found) by moments of excitement and relaxation!

A magical moment can be created in a very simple manner; for instance, by giving visitors a warm and hospitable welcome: something that organizations fail at regularly. Another example is that of an organizer texting messages to inform conference visitors about a full parking building, along with directions to another car park. On arrival, visitors are welcomed by hostesses: undeniably a satisfier that contributes towards optimizing the total experience.

Some touchpoints are difficult to influence, if they can be influenced at all. Take, for instance, the atmosphere of the location chosen by the client who commissioned the event. To the visitor, this may be a very important touchpoint, whereas the organizer does not have any influence on the visitor's needs or requirements regarding this item. In cases like these, suggesting a new location could be an option.

Peak-end rule

Experiences will be more memorable if the event has the certain structure of a story, complete with introduction and trigger moment. The story moves towards a climax and, in conclusion, it is brought to an end (see Fig. 8.3 in Chapter 8).

The announcement of an event in the pre-exposure phase can be seen as the introduction, or in other words, the beginning of the story. Then comes the tension building (including the use of sub-climaxes, if necessary), which will lead to the peak moment (climax). After that, the tension is brought down. The peak moment of the event must be chosen and timed carefully, and it has to ensure a positive ending. In actual practice, the peak moment is often too early, or the wrong peak moment is chosen. If the peak is too early, it will be difficult for visitors to hold on to the feelings that the peak experience evoked in them until the very end. A wrong peak may be entertainment that is incompatible with the visitor's way of life, as a result of which the visitor will obviously feel little connection. According to the peak-end rule, people judge their experiences by how they feel at the end, as shown in Fig. 9.6. The last memory of the experience is generally remembered, which influences the experience as a whole.

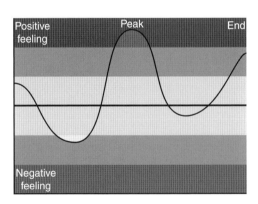

Fig. 9.6. Peak-end rule (source: presentation by Gast and Van Moorst, 2009; Kahneman, 2009, unpublished; adapted by the authors).

The post-exposure phase of events is often forgotten. What does the organization do to stay in touch with the visitors? Concert venue and nightclub, Club Vega, in Copenhagen (Denmark) conducted a survey of the post-exposure phase right after a concert, which led to a remarkable outcome. After the live performances in the concert hall, bright white lights were usually switched on rather abruptly. When this happened, the study showed, visitors felt like they were torn away from their experience, wanting to make a run for the nearest exit, which is in fact an entirely logical reaction. As a result of this finding, the lighting plan was adjusted, so that the lights went on gradually from faint to bright. Club Vega regularly carries out guest surveys, in a persistent attempt to optimize the visitor experience.

Pleasure–pain gap

The pleasure–pain gap plays an important role in the consumer experience process. The experience must not occur on the same level all the time; there must be peaks. That is why it is important for experiences to be heterogeneous. The distance between a positive pleasure touchpoint and a negative pain touchpoint should be as great as possible. The long queues at the ticket machine – refusing to accept anything but cash – of the brand-new car park after Rihanna's concert in the O2 World Arena in Berlin (Germany), when all people wanted was just to go home, is a typical example of a pain touchpoint. This incident made up an integral part of the evening's experience. Positive touchpoints, such as the quality of the music and the concert line-up, are then likely to be experienced as extra-positive, because everything that happens during the evening constitutes the aggregate experience of the individual concert visitor. The aggregate or total experience consists of positive and negative experiences, and everything in between. Due to the fact that negative experiences will always occur too, the positive ones are rated even more positively.

If maximum heterogeneity is achieved in an experience, the visitor will have the best possible experience. This experience may even exceed the peak moment. Obviously, any negative emotions evoked by the pain touchpoint must never exceed the critical limit. This is something of which the organization concerned must be absolutely aware. This gap is clearly depicted in Fig. 9.7. The figure also shows that the most important touchpoints – to the organization (e.g. from a branding perspective) as well as to the customer (customer value) – are applied primarily during the pleasure moments. These are displayed in light grey. It is therefore of crucial importance to identify and orchestrate these moments carefully, the magical moments.

The black touchpoints are not important, neither to the organization nor to the visitor. The small open circles are the satisfiers and/or dissatisfiers.

As we will see in the following example of a visit to the Geneva Motor Show, the visitor experience process (or the customer journey) consists of three phases:

- Pre-exposure phase:
  Gathering information about the event
  Registering for the event
  Travelling to the event
- Direct exposure phase:
  Arrival at the event
  Being at the event
  Visiting stands at the event
  Leaving the event

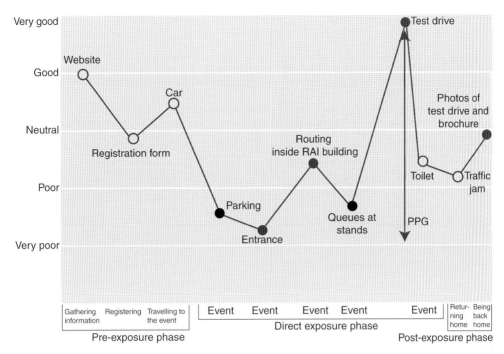

Fig. 9.7. Pleasure–pain gap, Geneva Motor Show (source: presentation by Gast and Van Moorst, 2009, based on Kahneman, 2009, unpublished, adapted by the authors).

- Post-exposure phase:
  Returning home
  Arrival at home

This customer journey shows that it is essential for exhibitors to allow interested visitors to actually experience their products, which means offering visitors the possibility to test-drive new cars. Test-driving a new car, which is not yet in production, certainly qualifies as a magical moment. Suppose that the visitor test-driving the new car gained a negative experience earlier at the event when he had to wait for what seemed like forever queuing for a certain exhibitor. And suppose he gets stuck in a 10-km traffic jam on the way home. The overall experience may still be concluded in a positive way, thanks to a photograph of the test ride and a brochure containing detailed information that is sent to his home address afterwards. So, as it turns out, heterogeneity makes for a more intense experience; without it, the experience would probably be rather bland.

Value-oriented objectives

The intensity of the visitor experience is achieved because of what the brand, product or service conveys or elicits. What is clearly connected with this is that the experience should be meaningful to the customer. If an organization is able to create an experience of this sort and convey the relevant values by means of an event, the organization has done well. In this respect, objectives are decisive to the nature and form of the event, and as such, to the experience too. If some 'dorky' engineering business wants to become exciting and innovative, the event to be organized will have to convey a different kind of image and lead to a different kind of experience than the ones commonly associated with the business.

It is difficult to focus purely on the experience. Intensive and effective experiences are developed through personalization. As we have seen already, the specific details of the experience depend on the type of company, the situation (which is perpetually changing) and the objectives. That is why objectives are increasingly formulated in a value-oriented manner.

Well-chosen touchpoints

Each individual is unique and has a different frame of reference, as we have shown already in Chapter 8. Since designing individual experiences would be too expensive, the process of creating the ideal experience often involves making certain choices. This involves looking for cheaper alternatives that are comparable experience-wise. Which touchpoints will have to be applied in which phase? What emotions do we want to evoke? How big is the target range? How many participants will there be? What is the duration of the event? Can the target group be accessed easily, and what costs does this involve? It goes without saying, for instance, that a clearly defined target group within a certain company can be accessed and engaged more easily than a vaguely identified target group.

THE CUSTOMER JOURNEY

The individual journey that a visitor makes (the customer journey) is an important point of departure to determine touchpoints for an event, as we have seen in the previous subsection on the Geneva Motor Show example.

The journey is packed with sensory perceptions and attendant emotions that determine how visitors are going to perceive the physical environment in all its aspects (touchpoints) and how they are going to respond to that; for example, the directional signage and reception area at an event like a trade fair. After all, there is a whole list of things you do not want to happen to your visitors when entering the complex: being sent in the wrong direction due to poor signage, then – after a long search – having to wait in line checking in their coats at the cloakroom and being served by uninterested hostesses. Situations like these will cause emotions like discontent, irritation, anger and disappointment, which will undoubtedly affect the experience of the rest of the event. If, on the other hand, visitors were directed to the car park by means of clear directional signs on the motorway, and after that, were given a warm welcome on entering, this would be a much better start.

Paying attention to the sequence of touchpoints is very important. Do the touchpoints make up a consistent whole and are they interconnected? Are they based on the concept that underlies the total chain of experiences?

Optimization of touchpoints

It has to be clear, for every touchpoint, which emotion exists in the visitor and which emotion is elicited. Only then will it be possible to determine whether the touchpoint applied is the right one or whether another touchpoint should be applied.

How can you make the customer's journey as comfortable and as easy as possible? We have already mentioned in Chapter 5 the use of applications for mobile phones so as to keep visitors updated on all performances, things worth knowing, news and a floor plan of the venue.

Table 9.1 presents a touchpoint form that organizations can use to analyse and improve the experience process, possibly by means of a mystery guest. The mystery guest goes through the entire process that the customer goes through and writes down his findings on a form designed especially for this purpose. Based on the outcome, an improvement plan can be set up.

ORGANIZATIONAL CONSEQUENCES OF ORCHESTRATING EXPERIENCES

In creating visitor experiences, the organizer must be able to empathize with the visitor – seeing what the customer sees, feeling what the customer feels – and, if necessary, optimize the process. It requires real skill and ingenuity to design the visitor experience in a real and virtual experience environment: the experience setting. This section will explore the consequences of touchpoints for internal and external processes, for the design process and for people. This includes a set of preconditions.

In Chapter 8, we emphasized that the solid foundation of an experience is made up of a vision, mission, values and the experience concept. This is demonstrated by, among other things, the Guest Experience Model in Fig. 9.8. Between the foundation and the visitor experience, there are three pillars: people, setting and process. Each of these three pillars contains touchpoints that affect both the virtual and the real visitor experience.

People

Whether it is the parking attendant, the security guard, the hostess or the stage performers, these people are all part of the *people* pillar. They have influence on the experience and are factors that organizations should take into account, constantly reassessing the desired behaviour of all people involved in the context of the customer's wishes and needs. It is also the organization's responsibility to train its staff to comply with these performance and conduct standards.

Setting

The *setting* is formed by the physical and virtual environment; for example, the natural environment of the amphitheatre of Verona in Italy during a classic opera like Aida, or the facilities of Bella Centre in Copenhagen. Decor, layout, communication and ambiance also

Table 9.1. Touchpoint form (source: Remmers, 2010, unpublished, adapted by the authors).

Touch-point	Issues	Current situation	Ideal situation	Item requiring improvement	Marketing opportunity	External impact	Internal impact	Priority	Go/No-go
1. Parking space	Safety Sufficient parking space Queue Signage Ease of parking	There is sufficient parking space at the venue, but the parking attendants do not let the traffic flow properly. Access to the car park is limited due to poor traffic flow	Give parking attendants better instructions, so that that they will be able to improve the traffic flow. Appoint a coordinator. Access gates with greater capacity	High	Low	High	Medium	High	Go

2. Physical environment	Hall entrance	The hall access doors only open partially (often only one door or even half of it). The position taken by the door attendant prohibits smooth visitor entrance. Control/ screening is unclear. This leads to discussions or even to some degree of aggressiveness	Open doors earlier. Instruct staff earlier. Appoint duty officer	High	Low	High	High	High	Go

(Continued)

Table 9.1. Continued.

Touch-point	Issues	Current situation	Ideal situation	Item requiring improvement	Marketing opportunity	External impact	Internal impact	Priority	Go/No-go
	Level of chair comfort	The atmosphere and technical aspects of the hall are in order. The chairs, however, are not comfortable for long sitting	Buy or rent other chairs	High	Low	High	Medium	High	Go
	Staff recognizability	Some staff members do not have a neat, well-groomed appearance	Uniform clothing for staff	High	Medium	High	Medium	High	Go

fall into the setting category. A website launched in the preliminary stage is an example of a touchpoint that makes an indirect contribution to the total setting of the event.

Process

The *process* contains all visitor–organization interaction required to facilitate the event, through personal interaction or otherwise. In other words, the process may involve the setting as well as the people.

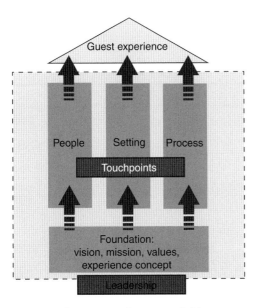

Fig. 9.8. Guest experience model (source: presentation by Van Wijngaarden, 2006).

The model by van Wijngaarden (see Fig. 9.8) concerns interaction at front office level. We believe that the process pillar also affects the back office procedures (see Fig. 9.9) of an event or organization. In this respect, one may think not only of booking systems and transport arrangements but also the volunteer workforce. The choice for certain touchpoints has consequences for the organization of the front and back office, the required information technology (IT) and the behaviour that the personnel will have to display.

Figure 9.9 is a brief schematic outline of the Geneva Motor Show example. The figure illustrates the visitor journey along the physical touchpoints, from direct front office contacts to back office, supporting processes and IT. We have left a few blank spaces in the figure.

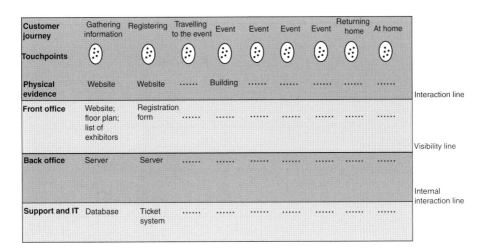

Fig. 9.9. From visitor journey to supporting processes (source: presentation by Gast and Van Moorst, 2009, unpublished, adapted by the authors).

SUMMARY

The individual event visitor, with his individual needs, is becoming increasingly important and should be the primary point of departure in planning and organizing events. The visitor embarks on a journey (the customer journey), calling in at touchpoints that are instrumental to an optimal visitor experience.

Touchpoints are points of contact; moments when a visitor or customer has contact with an organization or company. Touchpoints are becoming increasingly important in the events industry, and they are applied to control the points of contact, taking the customer's values and needs as the guiding principle (value addition and value fit).

Touchpoint models can be set up from the organization's perspective, as well as from the customer's perspective; however, the customer's perception of the touchpoints is always the guiding principle. Touchpoints should be diversified, inspire memorable experiences, evoke emotions, stimulate several senses, be value oriented, be mutually consistent and be well chosen.

Organizations can direct the visitor experience by means of the setting, the people and the process of interactions. Several touchpoint models have been developed for trade fairs and corporate events. See the appendices on the following pages.

Touchpoint Models for Trade Fairs and Corporate Events

Empirical data produced by research into trade fairs and corporate events served as the starting point in the development of two touchpoint models. Both models are based on the vision of professionals working for leading companies. Planning and organizing fairs and events is something that these people are involved in on a daily basis. They were asked to provide an as complete as possible description of touchpoints within their area of expertise. In addition, they identified priorities within each of the three phases of an event: the pre-exposure, direct exposure and post-exposure phase. The visitor's perspective of the visitor experience is a subject of current research and has not been incorporated in the two touchpoint models presented here.

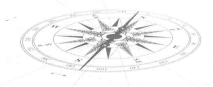

Touchpoint Model for Trade Fairs

As we have already seen earlier, there are generally three parties involved in trade fairs: the organizer, the exhibitor and the visitor. The touchpoint model (see Fig. 9.10) was developed on the basis of research among organizers of trade fairs. Their views of what touchpoints are, which touchpoints should be prioritized and in which particular phase, and which ones allow you to excel have all been taken into account. The following matters are crucial to a correct interpretation of the model:

- The details of a trade fair must always be considered carefully (e.g. programme, exhibitors).
- Co-creation is increasingly used to optimize experiences. In this process, the exhibitor's and the visitor's views are taken into account.
- The model contains only the most important touchpoints.
- It is still important to continue managing the various dissatisfiers.
- This model focuses on professional trade fair organizers. It is also possible to construct a model from the exhibitor's point of view.
- The organizer operates on the basis of the visitor's objectives: networking, familiarization, gathering information.

The core of the model is the trade fair organizer and his set of values. The trade fair will be successful if it satisfies or – preferably – exceeds the visitors' expectations. This is achieved through an accurate insight into the customer journey and by choosing the right touchpoints by means of questions such as: what do visitors find important? What do they hope to achieve by visiting the trade fair? What are the needs that lead them to visit the fair?

As is the case with any event, a trade fair can be classified into pre-, direct and post-exposure phase: the phases before, during and after the fair (the second layer from the core). The third layer represents, for each phase, the building blocks which the trade fair organizers think are the most important; the concrete touchpoints can be found in the outer layer. On the following pages, the pre-exposure phase of trade fairs will be set out in more detail.

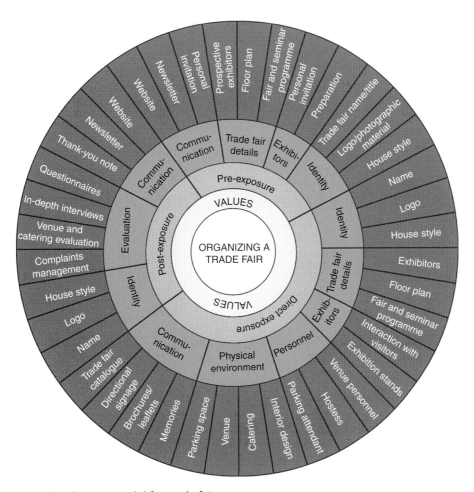

Fig. 9.10. Touchpoint model for trade fairs.

THE PRE-EXPOSURE PHASE OF TRADE FAIRS

Communication

Website

The website is often the first touchpoint. It takes mere seconds for visitors to form a first impression. Obviously, the website has to be up-to-date and contain relevant information: date, location, list of exhibitors, floor plan, seminar programme and a registration tool. When a potential visitor can find the information he is looking for easily, he will be more readily inclined to return to the site. Website designers have to take into account the various visitor objectives.

Newsletter/direct mail

Newsletter and direct mail campaigns involve information being sent by the trade fair organizer (via regular mail or e-mail) to potential visitors who have visited a trade fair before, or to people who have indicated a desire to be kept updated. In our current Internet age, direct mail is cheaper than other means of advertising, for instance paper-based mail. Direct mail should have a catchy subject title, as this will increase the probability of your mail being opened. It also has to contain valuable and useful information, but not an overload of information. During the period leading up to the trade fair, the information becomes more specific, and so more interesting. The first message, for instance, discloses that there will be a seminar programme, the second message provides a list of seminar speakers and the third one sets forth the various subjects. This will arouse curiosity in potential visitors. It is also possible for visitors to be informed about the trade fair programme, trends and developments, novelties and registration options.

Personal invitation

The next important touchpoint in the pre-exposure phase in the area of communication is the personal invitation. Since one-to-one communication is becoming increasingly important, potential trade fair visitors generally appreciate a personal invitation. It increases their feeling of involvement. Some trade fair organizers design and distribute these invitations themselves, in keeping with the overall 'look and feel' of the trade fair; other organizers leave the matter up to the exhibitors. The fact is that personal communication in the pre-exposure phase is very important to stimulate favourable expectations in trade fair visitors.

Trade fair details

Exhibitors

In the pre-exposure phase, prospective visitors examine both the subject area of the trade fair and the exhibitors that will be present. It is very important for the trade fair organizer to communicate the list of exhibitors well in time, because prospective visitors will use this list in their decision on whether or not to visit the trade fair. A good trade fair has a list of high-quality exhibitors. Co-creation with sector organizations, for instance, may be an important contributive factor in this respect. The exhibitors present will obviously determine the greater part of the expectations regarding the fair.

Floor plan

In the pre-exposure phase, many potential visitors often take a look at the floor plan to get an idea of what they will find where at the trade fair. The floor plan displays the names of the exhibitors and the locations of their exhibition stands, so as to enable the visitor to plan his route beforehand, preparing a personal stand-visiting schedule. This personal schedule will contribute to the expectations of the individual trade fair visitor.

Programme

Trade fair visitors want to meet exhibitors that are interesting to them, and this means that the trade fair programme is also very important. This programme consists of activities organized by the trade fair organizer. As the programme is distributed in the pre-exposure phase, visitors know what to expect at the trade fair.

Seminar programme

Not every trade fair has a seminar programme. If there are not going to be any seminars during a certain trade fair, it is important to communicate this early in the pre-exposure phase, so that visitors do not come to the fair with the expectation of attending a seminar. If seminars are held, it is obviously the speakers and subjects that will be important to the visitor's expectations. Seminars should comply with certain standards in terms of quality and subject matter, and they should be in keeping with the overall theme of the trade fair.

Exhibitors

Preparation by exhibitors

Exhibitors are an important part of the trade fair, and it is important that they prepare for the trade fair in the pre-exposure phase. As a trade fair organizer, you have no full control over this process, but you can exert some influence by offering standard exhibition stands, furniture and trade fair training. In addition, it is important for exhibitors to establish targets for themselves with regard to the trade fair; otherwise, they will be unable to measure any effects afterwards.

Personal invitation sent by exhibitors

Potential visitors will get a much greater sense of one-to-one communication if they receive a personal invitation from exhibitors, rather than from the trade fair organizer. Moreover, the exhibitor can attach information about any novelties he will be presenting at the trade fair.

Identity

Name/trade fair title

The name of the trade fair conjures up expectations, too. The name is mostly linked to the theme of the fair. The longer a trade fair has been in existence, the more its name will turn into a brand.

Logo

A logo is the symbol that gives the trade fair title its identity. It is the graphic representation of the fair title. As time goes by, a logo will also become part of the trade fair brand; it exudes the values and identity of the trade fair.

House style

The house style is used on the website, in brochures, direct mail and invitations. Use of colour, typeface and graphic design should be the same in all these touchpoints. As a result, the recognizability of the trade fair will be increased.

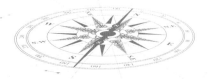

Touchpoint Model
for Corporate Events

The touchpoint model for corporate events (see Fig. 9.11) has been developed by means of expert interviews and case study analyses. Corporate events also generally involve three parties: the client/company, the visitor and the event management agency. A corporate event supports the strategic goals that have been determined by the company. For the purpose of a correct interpretation of the model, there are a few matters that require clarification first.

- The client determines the objectives, the message, the preconditions, the value and the budget.
- The choice and details of the touchpoints should be tailored to the company, the culture and the mindset of the company as well as the visitor: or in other words, the values. It will be the project manager, however, who gets to determine the creative details.
- If the client wishes, the event management agency can take charge of the creation and/ or execution of the event.
- The model shows the most important touchpoints. This does not mean that the touchpoints not mentioned are not important.
- The visitor experience is not an explicit part of this model.

The inner layer represents the organization/company and its values. The pre-exposure phase is used to provide information, encourage visits, arouse curiosity and build tension. The direct exposure phase is the event itself, and the post-exposure phase serves to sustain the experience. The third layer displays the pillars for the various touchpoints, and the outer layer contains the actual touchpoints. After the model, we will give you a more detailed explanation of the direct exposure phase of a corporate event.

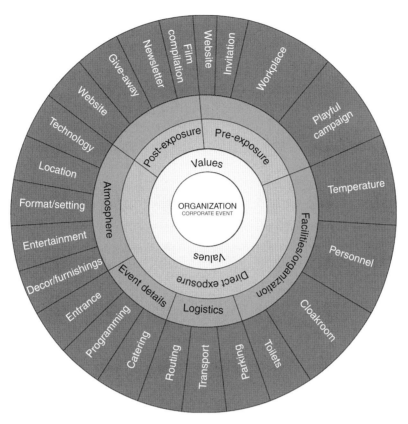

Fig. 9.11. Touchpoint model for corporate events.

DIRECT EXPOSURE PHASE OF A CORPORATE EVENT

Atmosphere

The atmosphere is critical to the visitor experience. The 'atmosphere' pillar consists of touchpoints in the form of experience optimization tools: location, decor, furnishings, technological aspects, format and setting, and entertainment.

Location

The location is often determined by the preconditions set by the client. Accessibility, immediate environment and professionalism are important aspects in choosing a location.

Decor

The interior design and the use of decoration are key determinants in the pillar called 'decor'. It should be in keeping with the concept and theme of the event. An eye for detail is important, as is creating a visually attractive and coherent atmosphere.

Technology

Technology can be classified into lighting, sound, visual aids and show elements.

LIGHTING.   Light is an important factor in atmosphere perception. With the right light effects, an ugly location can be transformed into a beautiful location. Light colours and intensity levels are tailored to the programme contents and the concept or theme. Light also determines the focus (either on the stage or the audience).

SOUND.   Everything must be clearly audible. In addition, sounds can be used to create excitement or enthusiasm, for instance.

VISUAL AIDS.   A picture is worth a thousand words. A certain combination of music and images may convey a feeling that needs no further explanation. Visuals may support a presentation. Live registration is also very functional. Speakers, performers and visitors themselves are displayed on big screens.

SHOW ELEMENTS.   The use of laser, fireworks or disco effects has an impact on the atmosphere. Moreover, show elements can be used to appeal to people's senses; for example, a fragrance machine or a snow canon.

Format/setting

The choice of a format/setting is an important atmosphere component. This involves, for instance, opting for a plenary setting or an informal setting with the speakers seated at tables. Or, you can have the speakers and the presenter sit on a stage. The focus may be on the stage, but also on the audience.

Entertainment

Entertainment may be provided at the entrance and may be related to the event or its various components.

Logistics

Logistics is an element that is noticed only when things go wrong. In other words, it is important to handle the logistics properly. Logistics in corporate events involve the touchpoints of routing, transport and parking facilities.

Routing

It is important that there is a clear visitor route. That is why efficient signage, which is checked on a regular basis, is essential. If visitors come by car, it is important that there is clear signage to direct them to the event venue. Additionally, it is important to give visitors directions from the location where they arrive to the location where the event takes place, possibly by hostesses. Bus and other public transport departure times must also be displayed clearly.

Transport

The mode of transport that visitors use to get to the event may be a car, coach, public transport or bicycle. The transport component can become an experience when it is given a little extra attention; for instance, playing a film or serving refreshments on the coach. If visitors come by car, a text messaging service may be an option; for instance, to announce a later start time for the plenary programme if many visitors are unable to arrive in time due to traffic congestion.

Parking

There must be sufficient parking space, obviously. Depending on the location, there will be parking attendants to show visitors a place to park.

Facilities/organization

To put it briefly: visitors simply expect the facilities and organizational infrastructure to be arranged adequately. If any aspect falls short of their expectations, this will be detrimental to the total experience. This component comprises the touchpoints of toilets, cloakroom, personnel and temperature.

Toilets

The toilets must be clean. Moreover, the toilets must be directly accessible from the entrance area.

Cloakroom

Cloakroom facilities must be organized efficiently. Visitors must not only be able to deposit their coats but also their laptops, for instance. The cloakroom must be directly accessible from the entrance area.

Personnel

High-quality personnel are important. All personnel who come into contact with visitors must be friendly and courteous; this particularly involves catering personnel and hostesses. All relevant information, in the form of a briefing session, must be provided to the personnel. If necessary, personnel clothing can be tailored to the theme of the event.

Temperature

In the case of outdoor activities, the temperature is a decisive factor. And in the case of indoor activities, there must be an adequate climate control system: in other words, not too warm and not too cold.

Event details

The way in which the details of the event are reflected in the various touchpoints is also crucial to the optimization of the experience. It involves the way in which the objectives and the message to be conveyed are integrated in the touchpoints of entrance, programming, programme contents and catering.

Entrance

It is important for visitors to feel welcome straight away. The entrance is an important factor in this respect. Interpersonal contact is one of the most effective ways to make visitors feel welcome. In addition, it has to be possible for visitors to register themselves, and drinks and snacks should be served. All activities in the entrance area must be service oriented.

Programming

There are plenary parts at every event, often either a plenary opening or a closing session. It is important to indicate when the plenary part begins. Festive events often have plenary closing sessions. In addition, the timing of the various activities is crucial, creating just the right balance between activity and rest.

Programme contents

The programme contents obviously differ with each event. As the contents should convey the message, this component is extremely important. The message can be communicated by artists, speakers, activities, and so on. Celebrities attract visitors.

Catering

Catering is important to the event as a whole. Drinks and snacks must be served to visitors on arrival at the entrance, as well as during the plenary activities. There are also events in which catering makes up the most important part of the event.

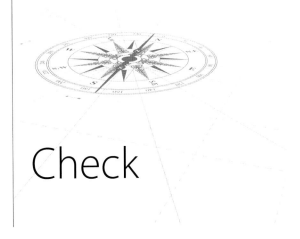

Part III

Check

In this part of the book, we discuss the 'check' phase of the strategic use of events, so the right-hand part of the EVENTS model.

In Chapter 10, we deal with effect measurement and evaluation. In the Appendices, examples of methods can be found that can be used to do this, together with examples from practice.

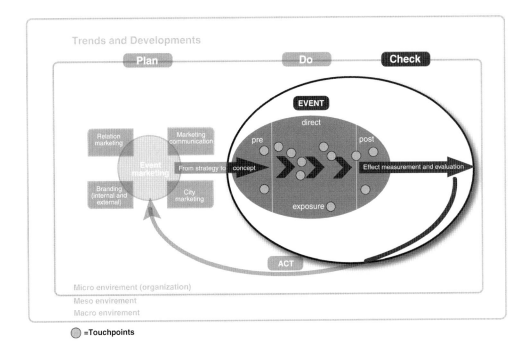

Effect Measurement and Evaluation

Dorothé Gerritsen and Ronald van Olderen

The central issues of this final chapter are effect measurement and evaluation. How do you study the impact of events? In the EVENTS model and in Chapter 1, the *Plan–Do–Check–Act* (PDCA) cycle was discussed briefly. Here, we will do that in more detail, because measuring effects and evaluation are only useful when the PDCA cycle is taken as a starting point. We will also describe effects and types of effects in relation to events. In this context, the key question is 'Who wants to know what, and why?' The formulation of proper objectives is crucial to measuring effects, as we will demonstrate. At the end of the chapter, we will describe how effect measurement and evaluation can be carried out.

LEARNING TARGETS

After studying this chapter, you will have learned:

- what is meant by effect measurement and evaluation
- what types of effects of events can be distinguished
- what you must take into account when measuring effects and evaluating
- how to build up a hierarchy of objectives
- the methods and techniques regarding effect measurement and evaluation
- how to design the measurement of effects on the basis of objectives
- how measuring effects and evaluation can be carried out.

Box 10.1   Capital of Culture: a money maker

If the cities of Brabant (the Netherlands) become the Capital of Culture, the euros will pour in, according to a study conducted by the University of Tilburg.

The tens of millions of euros invested by the province of Brabant and its five big cities in order to be crowned with the title of Capital of Culture of Europe 2018 will be recouped in spades. That is what Greg Richards says. He is the Professor of Leisure Science at Tilburg University who conducted research into the costs and benefits. To find out what they were, Richards listed the experiences of 25 cities that had previously been designated Capitals of Culture.

The professor comes to the conclusion that, as a result of more overnight stays, increased revenues of the catering industry and higher admission charges and the growth in business tourism, the benefits will be twice as high as the costs incurred. The front-runner is Liverpool, which was the Capital of Culture in 2008, and, according to the organization in that English port, made a profit of €800 million on an investment of €200 million. Lille and Glasgow also saw a big rise in their revenues. The Netherlands has been chosen, together with Malta, to deliver the Capital of Culture of Europe in 2018. This means that the city (or cities in the case of Brabant) will provide a year-long cultural programme for visitors from all over Europe.

To win that title, Brabant has already spent €4 million on preparation and cultural projects. A multiple of that amount, perhaps rising to €100 million, will be invested if a special jury designates Brabant as the Capital of Culture.

In addition to the cities in the province of Brabant (Breda, Tilburg, Den Bosch, Eindhoven and Helmond), four other Dutch cities are in the running: Maastricht, The Hague, Utrecht and Almere. (Source: Ullenbroeck, 2010.)

THE IMPORTANCE OF EFFECT MEASUREMENT AND EVALUATION

The benefits to cities that have previously been European Capital of Culture have proved to be many times higher than the costs incurred. That is clear from the newspaper article with which we opened this chapter (see Box 10.1). It mentions the effects of (cultural) events in those cities; more overnight stays, higher revenues for the catering industry and an increase in business tourism. It could also have mentioned another effect, a greater feeling of pride among the inhabitants of those cities. But how do you measure that? Effect measurements and evaluation take money, time and effort. However, effect measurements are becoming increasingly important, for the very reason that events are deployed more and more on the basis of strategic objectives. Clients want to know if, and to what extent, those objectives are attained. It is then crucial to be able to show what the contribution of the event has been.

Of course, to attain the objectives, more (communication) efforts are required than simply organizing events. Budgets are under pressure when the economy is doing less well. However, clients are usually still prepared to put money and time into events, if their efforts generate enough profits (return on investment). The organizer of an event is accountable for the results of an events policy. Accountability means that the contribution of an event to the strategic objectives is made clear to financiers and other interested parties on the basis of systematically collected data.

THE PLAN–DO–CHECK–ACT CYCLE

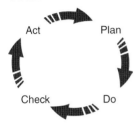

Fig. 10.1. PDCA cycle (source: Truscott, 2003).

Assuring the quality of an event and being able to show what an event contributes to the objectives requires a continual process of improvement and innovation modelled on the PDCA cycle (see Fig. 10.1), from which a company can learn by looking at the actions taken before, during and after an event. On the basis of the PDCA cycle, you can make interim adjustments, show the results afterwards and, with the help of a good evaluation, formulate new objectives for a new event.

The planning phase is meant to determine the course you take, set goals and formulate plans. The objectives may arise from a city marketing policy, for example, or a relationships marketing strategy (see Part I). You also identify the target group and interested parties (stakeholders), and how you want to reach your target group.

In the 'do' phase, you develop the concept and the design of the event, based on the objectives, target group and stakeholders (see Part II). This should include the execution of the event in the pre-, direct and post-exposure phases, together with the available people and resources.

In the 'check' phase, you monitor the implementation of the plans. Depending on what the client wants to know, you measure the effects, interim or post-event, on the target group and/or stakeholders. This enables you to measure whether an event has attained the set objectives.

In the 'act' phase, you analyse the collected data to be able to provide feedback to strategy making and new objectives.

EFFECTS

Effects are reactions to actions that are performed. If you deploy an event (an action = stimulus = experience), you can expect reactions. There are intended and unintended effects. The intended effects of an event ensue from the predetermined objectives. Unintended effects refer to consequences you could not have foreseen in advance. This may concern unintended negative effects such as bad weather or traffic jams, but also unintended positive effects like extensive media attention that you had not counted on.

We have already pointed out that it is impossible to determine beforehand whether an event will deliver the desired results. Sometimes, an event has no effect at all on an individual person, even if it has been organized perfectly. If, for example, a visitor has just heard that he has lost his job, this will have a great impact on how he experiences an event. Or the reverse: residents of the inner city appear not to be bothered at all by the enormous noise nuisance of a musical event close to where they live, whereas this could indeed have been expected to be a negative effect.

Types of effects

Various theories and models of the effects of events have been developed, and described in the recent literature. They emphasize the economic effects or economic importance of events. Hall (1992) has devised an effects matrix for public events in which other types of effects are included as well, together with the ways in which these effects show themselves. This provides an indication of how the effects can manifest themselves and be perceived in practice. Local and national governments, for instance, want to make their city or country better known, or portray a city as a sports city. These effects are related to tourism and the economy, and the ultimate goal is: developing new tourist facilities, organizing annually recurring events and stimulating repeat visits.

The matrix shown in Table 10.1 mentions both positive and negative effects: positive effects often have a negative counterpart. This matrix shows possible effects that can occur. Of course, this does not mean that the entire range of effects will occur. Which effects do occur depends on the size, theme and type of event. The matrix does not tell you anything about the impact of the effects. This differs from event to event. For all of those involved, it is, of course, essential that positive effects are worked out and communicated as well as possible and that negative effects are offset as much as possible.

Several of the effects mentioned can also occur when business events are organized. An example is the inconvenience to residents as a result of heavy traffic near the location of the event. There are other effects on a city as well, as illustrated by the recent Afghanistan summit talks in The Hague. Apart from the ability to organize those talks, security being of critical importance, the identity and the image of the city of The Hague were the decisive factors for the United Nations to choose it as the place to organize those top-level talks. The Hague, the city of the International Court of Law and the Peace Palace, conforms to the values of a crucial summit conference on a topical, political and international problem. International media attention for this conference contributed much to the image of The Hague as a city deeply involved in world politics.

The effects of public and business events

Measuring the effects of public events is slightly different from measuring them at business events. Business events are generally organized in closed spaces, and their principal goal is the

Table 10.1. Effects matrix for public events (source: Hall, 1992).

Effect	Manifestation	
	Positive	**Negative**
Economic	Increase in spending by visitors Increase in employment	Price increases Better alternative investments
Touristic/commercial	Awareness of potential as tourist destination Awareness of development potential	Bad reputation due to bad facilities, prices that are too high Competition with existing businesses
Physical (infrastructure)	Construction of new facilities Improvement of existing infrastructure	Damage to environment Destruction of heritage Too crowded with visitors
Sociocultural	Increase in participation in type of activity connected to event Strengthening regional tradition	Commercialization of traditions Adaptation of traditions to commercial requirements
Psychological	Improvement of civic spirit and sense of community Awareness of non-local views	Defensive reactions in host region Culture clashes Risk of enmity between visitors and residents
Political	International interest Improvement of planning skills	Increase in public spending Legitimation of existing ideology

achievement of an objective regarding a particular target group. As a consequence, the effects can be identified and controlled better. Besides, effect measurement is usually focused on the intended target group. As we have shown in Chapter 1, public events are often a vital platform for business events. There is an increasingly important role for objectives in relation to public events; for example, in the context of a city marketing policy. But, the various stakeholders of public events can also benefit from measuring the consequences of an event at the regional, urban or national level. What makes the measurement of effects a tough proposition is that stimuli external to an event must be excluded: how do you know that effects are from the event and not from other stimuli? We will discuss this in further detail in the section below that deals with methods and techniques.

Table 10.2 lists the different points of emphasis in a comparison of business events with public ones. It includes the consequences for measuring effects, but it is not an exhaustive list.

Table 10.2. Effect measurement of business and public events.

Corporate event	Public event
Invitees	Not exclusively for invitees Possible side events with no public admission
	Public admitted Admission tickets/no admission tickets
Usually business–economic goal, entertainment may be part of the programme	Entertainment of all sorts is usually the goal and the principal part
Direct communication possible to target groups	Less direct communication/mass communication
Consequence of effect measurement	Consequence of effect measurement
Effect measurement can be managed better	Harder to manage well
More control over event	Less control because of many activities in public space
Generally smaller scope	Often many people; crowd management is more complicated
Those who attend are known	Those who attend are diverse and unknown

EFFECT MEASUREMENT

Effect measurement comprises the collection of data for the analysis of an event to be able to: make adjustments before, during and after an event; account for everything; improve processes; and formulate new objectives. The question that arises in connection with effect measurement is, of course, whether you want to measure everything and whether you can. The answer is: no. A stakeholder who wants a record of the effects of an event must give a very clear indication of the goals of which the effects should be measured. In the context of the World Championship Football in Brazil, issues can be media attention and economic spin-offs for the local catering businesses, but also security or being proud of the country. When Samsung wants to organize festivities for all its employees because of its anniversary, the objectives will be quite different and, as a consequence, other effects have to be measured, such as thanking the employees and bolstering the image of Samsung as an employer in order to reinforce the feelings of loyalty and pride in its employees. What is required to measure the effects of an event is a clear focus and knowing what should be excluded.

Effects can occur in the short term, during and immediately after an event, for instance. Strategic objectives often require more time and will usually be attained in the longer run. For that reason, it is important not to restrict measurements to the periods during and immediately after an event. We will discuss this in more detail in the section below that deals with the hierarchy of objectives.

Who wants to know what, and why?

Each interested party wants to know what the effects of an event are from that party's own angle. The important question that should be asked before effect measurement and evaluation is: *who* wants to know *what*, and *why*? It is crucial to know from which angle measurements should be made. Do the city authorities want to know what the effects of an event are, or is it the sponsor who wants to know? The city of Pamplona (Spain), for example, wants to know what has been the impact of the Vuelta a España starting there. The Amstel (beer brand) sponsor wants to know what have been the benefits of organizing the Amstel Gold Race, a one-day, classic cycling race. For some, 'what' stands for hard cash, for others it is about feeling and name recognition. The organizer of the Amstel Gold Race, for instance, is curious to know about the impact of the event on the host community. Can you rely again on the necessary cooperation of those involved in that region? The interested party that carries out the effect measurement decides which effects have to be measured and who has to be measured.

WHY EFFECT MEASUREMENT AND EVALUATION?

Setting up effect measurements and an evaluation is done for a reason; otherwise, no money will be invested to find out whether objectives have been achieved. Ascertaining whether the investments involved in the organization of an event produce a good return is one reason. Another reason may concern accountability for the policy pursued. Interim measurements can be helpful to make adjustments if necessary, and/or to change plans.

Accountability

Regarding business and public events, effect measurement is used to account for the policy pursued and investments. Public events, for example, often take place in public spaces and make use of public resources. In view of retaining commitment and getting support, it is of great importance to city leaders to be able to show the positive effects of public events to the various stakeholders. Both quantitative and qualitative measuring methods are used. Appendices 3, 4 and 5 provide examples of effect measurement and evaluation with regard to big public sports events and demonstrate the vital role of accountability.

Return on investment

Budgets are under pressure and organizations want to know whether the policy that has been pursued produces any returns on investment (ROIs). How much is budgeted for, what is the return and does this meet the predetermined objectives? Having a good feeling about an event is no longer enough. It is very clear: an event must make money, or be cost neutral at the very least. Appendix 1 deals specifically with the ROI model which has been developed from the meetings industry. Appendix 2 discusses a model for return on communication.

Making adjustments

Measuring the interim results of an event and those after an event is very useful. It is a tangible form of self-reflection, turning opinions into facts. A negative result should be a reason for finding out how things can be done better next time. The result can be used not only to dot the i's and cross the t's regarding a supplier, for example, but also to inform customers about improvements that are being made. The results are used to assure quality and to improve it continuously. Measurements are not only useful for making adjustments but also they can serve as input for the next time. Carrying out measurements is, then, a starting point and not something of a conclusion. After all, results are useless if nothing is done with them: take, for example, the PDCA cycle in this connection.

Looking back

Effect measurement and evaluation ensure structure in the design of an event. It is a way of thinking and structuring. Thinking about measurement forces an organization to consider consciously the 'what' and the 'why'. This not only applies to the objective, important as that may be, but also in deciding which indicators will be the basis of measuring the objective. By reviewing an objective during the course of planning an event, it can be improved. The point here is a detailed description of an event.

OBJECTIVES OF EFFECT MEASUREMENT: THE 'WHAT' QUESTION

We have already pointed out that it is important to know from what perspective an effect measurement is carried out: who wants to know something? The next question is: what should be measured?

Providing an answer to the 'what' question appears to be easier than it is in practice. It seems like an open door, something very obvious. However, it turns out that it is often not easy for clients to indicate exactly what an event is supposed to achieve and what exactly the effects are that should be measured. Take, for instance, the Geneva Motor Show, which is a leading trade fair for the car sector in the Netherlands. Nearly all brand dealers present themselves with novelties and actions to their colleagues, the trade press and the consumer. But how can you tell whether this trade fair is successful when there is the same number of visitors as 2 years earlier? Or is a client only satisfied when the number of visitors is relatively higher? Or do you want to attract target groups that have been ignored up to now? Or are you not satisfied until all brands have submitted *x* quotations? In other words: what are the goals, strategic or otherwise, that the Geneva Motor Show wants to attain? What do the various parties involved want to accomplish? So, the 'what' question can be used to determine what the effects are that should be measured and whether or not an event is successful.

The hierarchy of objectives

Objectives can be set at various levels, and therefore we can speak of a hierarchy of objectives. The strategic effect objectives are at the top of the hierarchy, the operational effect objectives are in the middle and the attainment objectives are at the bottom.

Strategic effect objectives

Strategic effect objectives are formulated on the basis of corporate objectives and the marketing and communication objectives derived from them. They are based on the long-term vision and mission of an organization and indicate what is the contribution of event marketing to attaining those objectives. What was the effect on the target group or stakeholders? It is, in fact, about measuring the effects of an event on the brand, the relations, the staff of the organization, the visitors to a city, and so on. The ultimate effect is the effect on money: has an event contributed to an ROI?

Earlier in the book, you have seen that events can be utilized for many different reasons; for example, to reinforce customer relations, increase loyalty, or swell the feeling of pride of the residents of a city where a public event takes place. An event may also be intended to promote brand loyalty, increase sales and consolidate business relationships. All these examples relate to objectives that ensue from the strategic goals of the enterprise in question. The effects will generally become manifest only in the course of time. The impact of an event on the commitment and loyalty of a relation will not be noticeable at once. In this context, the importance of the pre- and post-exposure phases should not be forgotten. Working on customer relations and loyalty are objectives that cannot be realized in the short run: it takes time and requires more than merely an event marketing strategy. Besides, other factors may be involved, factors that cannot, or can hardly, be influenced, like developments in the market.

To be able to measure effects, it is necessary to record information continuously and keep it up-to-date in an information system, define concrete behaviour and, if necessary, compare measurements to see if there are any changes.

At the beginning of Chapter 4, we presented SNS REAAL as an example of a company that applied a clear relationship marketing strategy. We return briefly to this example here to indicate what is strategic in the objective. SNS REAAL is a retail bank and insurer that wants to position itself differently in relation to intermediaries as a result of changing developments in the market: as a partner in business. This is linked to an important development, that of consumers increasingly bypassing intermediaries when buying insurance and banking products.

It has become harder and harder for intermediaries to sell their products. Besides, it turned out that the intermediaries knew nothing, or very little, about the marketing support that SNS REAAL offered them. By using event marketing, SNS REAAL not only ensured that its positioning as a partner in business got through to the intermediaries, but also that they were now actually making use of the new ideas in the field of marketing and the marketing support provided to them by SNS REAAL staff. This has eventually boosted the sales of the banking and insurance products of SNS REAAL.

Operational effect objectives

Operational effect objectives refer to the process of an event. Among other things, they concern the degree of satisfaction and appreciation on the part of visitors and other stakeholders. The satisfaction approach is based on the assumption that satisfaction is a cognitive, calculating process: afterwards, the visitor reasons, mainly rationally, what he thought of an event and whether it came up to his expectations.

Effects occur before, during and after an event. Measuring those effects in the short and medium term involves processing information, attitude and behaviour. As a rule, the focus is on the organizational aspect, the logistics, the facilities, customer satisfaction and appreciation. In other words, the operational part of an event is measured, often by means of questionnaires, feedback from the client, interviews and observation.

Measuring how an experience actually feels is a more problematic matter. It is rather hard to measure emotions. One method that is used in practice is interviewing the consumer during the experience. Another option is an interview before the experience, observation during the experience and an interview after the experience. The section below on methods and techniques provides information on other methods to measure emotions.

A perfectly organized event is the basis for attaining objectives in the longer run. If the visitors highly appreciate an event and are satisfied with it, it will be much more likely that the strategic effect objectives will be attained. For example, if customers or staff feel appreciated and identify with a brand or company, the likely effects can be seen in lower absenteeism, greater commitment to the company, a higher turnover, and so on.

The graph in Fig. 10.2 shows the relationship between customer satisfaction and customer loyalty. The graph sets off the degree of satisfaction and retention (keeping customers and customer loyalty) against each other. The degree of loyalty increases substantially as the degree of satisfaction increases (from 4 to 5).

The likelihood of satisfaction leading to loyal customers is high, but in practice things may work out differently, as the example of the Soundwave festival in Australia will demonstrate. Soundwave is an annual music festival held in major cities around Australia. The festival originated in Perth, Western Australia, and began travelling to the other Australian capital cities in 2007. It features a number of international and Australian music acts, from various genres including rock, metal and punk (http://soundwavefestival.com/). A visitor to Soundwave may be very satisfied about the programme in a particular year because it includes a performance of his favourite band, but this does not mean that he feels connected to the brand and the values of the Soundwave festival. Or the reverse: a regular visitor to Soundwave is not satisfied about the line-up of the programme in that same year, but he still attends because he is a regular, loyal visitor and has felt a connection with the Soundwave brand for years.

Attainment objectives

Attainment objectives are objectives aimed at the quality and quantity of the target group to be reached at an event. Which part of the target group comes into contact with an event and in which way? Attainment objectives involve potential reach and effective reach: there is a target group and of the people in that target group, a certain percentage attends an event. The potential reach comprises the entire target group for which an event is organized. The effective reach refers to that part of the target group that actually attends the event. So, this is about quantitative data on reach. The question whether the visitors to an event are actually the people targeted by the supplier is a qualitative matter.

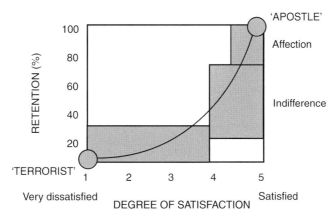

Fig. 10.2. Impact of customer satisfaction on customer loyalty (source: van Tilborgh, 2008).

Box 10.2

IMEX is a trade fair for professionals in the event industry, where suppliers and firms offering innovative concepts present themselves. At this fair, Messe Frankfurt pulls out all the stops each year at a big stand where visitors receive a warm welcome. The objective Messe Frankfurt wants to achieve by taking part in the trade fair is making contact with 60 serious prospects out of 11,000 visitors. This is a clear indication of the quantity of the target group to be reached. Not everyone of those 11,000 people fits the target group of Messe Frankfurt: visitors include staff of agencies that organize

(Continued)

Box 10.2. Continued.

events, marketing communication professionals, managing directors or owners, but not all of them have the power of decision, nor are they all in search of a big location for an event like that of Messe Frankfurt. In contrast, qualitative reach means focusing on those of the 11,000 visitors who have concrete plans for an event between now and one year's time and who make their decision on the location of the event in the centre of Germany.

The preparations for participation in the trade fair on the part of Messe Frankfurt are aimed both at the quantity and the quality of the visitor target group, and include registration of the visitors' details. The team manning the stand of Messe Frankfurt succeeds in making about 40 good contacts. The effective reach is 40 serious potential clients. All sorts of details about those persons have been collected, including name and address, function, budget, interests, and so on.

What are good objectives?

An objective should:

- be embedded in the strategy of the organization/supplier of the event
- have measurable units (= performance indicators)
- be logical, transparent and lucid
- be formulated in terms of SMART (specific, measurable, acceptable, realistic, time bound).

A good objective is formulated from the perspective of a company or organization and comes from the heart of that organization. Based on its mission and vision, an organization decides in what areas it wants to be successful: or, what are the critical success factors? The list is headed by the financial–economic success factors. Then there are critical success factors derived from them in the fields of, among other things, marketing, personnel, quality and processes. Indicators are linked to critical success factors, which are then made measurable by setting a performance level or standard. Thus, an objective emerges in which the performance indicators are interwoven. Performance indicators are variables on the basis of which an organization can be analysed and results can be measured. They are, in fact, objectives formulated in terms of SMART.

SMART stands for:

S = Specific: what exactly should be accomplished where
M = Measurable: link to statistical performance indicators
A = Acceptable: with some ambition
R = Realistic: formulated in such a way that the objectives are attainable
T = Time bound: linked to a certain moment in time or a deadline.

Formulating a good objective is essential as a starting point for the concept and design of an event, but also as the basis for proper effect measurement. The interpretation of an objective should be unambiguous. An unambiguous interpretation is harder to arrive at when measuring psychological effects such as loyalty or commitment. Concepts are often interpreted in different ways; therefore, they should be defined clearly in advance, so that they mean the same thing to all parties concerned.

There are two important reasons for formulating proper objectives for an event, as we said above.

1. It puts you in a better position to work out a concept and design for an event that fits the target group and the stakeholders.

2. It is easier for you to demonstrate to what extent an event has contributed to attaining the objectives because you can measure the effects better.

Figure 10.3 shows the relationship between formulating objectives and setting up effect measurement and evaluation.

Here is an example to clarify the SMART principle in relation to a critical success factor. Reaal Verzekeringen, part of SNS REAAL, wants to inform its intermediaries of a crucial change in its product portfolio. The vital relations of Reaal Verzekeringen are (in)dependent partners of the company. They are part of the distribution chain that sells Reaal's products to the consumer.

For Reaal Verzekeringen, the critical success factor is 'professional and well-informed sales people/intermediaries'. The performance indicator in this example is 'knowledge', and knowledge is an indicator that can be measured. The SMART objective in this example is: after the new product portfolio event for the intermediaries/sales people of Reaal Verzekeringen, 95% of them are fully informed of the extension of the product portfolio, have all the necessary information and are able to advise (potential) policyholders.

By formulating proper objectives that contain measurable units and are embedded in the strategy of an organization, those objectives are formulated along SMART lines and their effects can be measured. Critical success factors and objectives can be formulated at several levels.

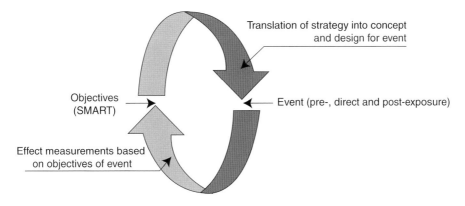

Fig. 10.3. Relationship between objectives and effect measurement.

Similarly, you can go through the PDCA cycle (see Fig. 10.4) at several levels. At the highest level, we find the strategic effect objectives as discussed in the preceding section. The operational effect objectives can be found one step down, and the attainment objectives are at the bottom. Figure 10.5 shows the hierarchy of objectives in diagram form.

Qualitative objectives are often formulated within event marketing. An effect measurement must then convert the feelings and emotions evoked during an event into data that show that those feelings and emotions have brought about a different attitude, and sometimes even different behaviour, in people. Naturally, an effect measurement also shows whether the financial objectives have been achieved, or achieved to a substantial extent.

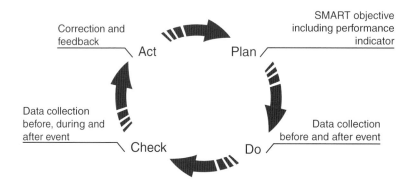

Fig. 10.4. PDCA cycle including SMART objective (source: Truscott, 2003, adapted by the authors).

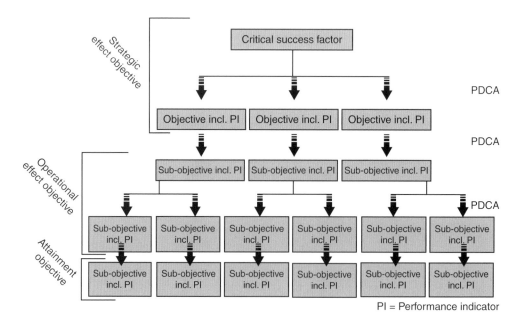

Fig. 10.5. Hierarchy of objectives.

METHODS AND TECHNIQUES: THE 'HOW' QUESTION

The quality of an effect measurement depends on the way in which the measurement, or the collection of data, is organized. So, the focus is on the 'how' question. There should be a pre-determined plan for evaluating an event.

Drawing up a plan for effect measurement and evaluation

For the purpose of effect measurement, the objective must be worked out in indicators and measuring tools. Each situation is different, and each event has different starting points and objectives. Moreover, each visitor perceives and experiences an event in his own way. So, each event requires a unique approach focused on a specific situation. Four steps can be helpful:

Step 1. Knowing what you want to measure.
Step 2. Selecting indicators.
Step 3. Making measuring tools operational.
Step 4. Collecting data.

Knowing what you want to measure

Effect measurement starts with the client. What does the client want to be meaured? Is it the satisfaction of participants right after the event? Is it satisfaction on the part of the staff? Is it a change in behaviour? Is it numbers of visitors? Is it emotions during the event? Is it an increase in turnover or staff loyalty? Plenty of questions, which all have an impact on the initial phase of a measurement and determine the nature of the measurement. Does the measurement refer to the attainment level only or to the operational effect objective, or does it include both? As a rule, the measurement of strategic effect objectives takes a longer period of time. So, the client specifies the questions to be answered, and this determines the selection of indicators and measuring methods.

Selecting indicators

The selection of indicators depends on what you want to know, as we saw before. For measuring an experience in the short run (operational effect objectives and attainment objectives), possible indicators are:

- the layout of the space available
- the atmosphere
- the number of visitors
- the quality of catering
- security.

This concerns basic experience. Measuring an experience in the longer run (strategic effect objectives) requires indicators that are related to the behaviour and conduct of the target group or stakeholder with regard to a company or organization. This is, then, about a memorable or transformative experience. Possible indicators in this case are:

- commitment
- loyalty
- trust
- social behaviour.

Making measuring tools operational

Indicators have little practical meaning without the operationalization of a measuring tool. The specific application of a measuring tool determines its development. Is it an international, national or regional event that has to be assessed? What is the available budget? What is the number of respondents? Is the measurement feasible? On the basis of the answers to questions like these, a choice of method is made: surveys, interviews, observation, 360 degree feedback, emotional measurement, an experience report, or a number of other methods. A combination of measuring tools is possible as well, of course.

Collecting data

When the measuring tools have been selected and operationalized, it is time for Step 4: collecting the data on the basis of which the analyses are made. For example, when the commitment of employees is the objective of an event, a survey of these employees can be conducted besides assessment interviews and observations during the performance of their tasks, to find out to what degree the employees show different behaviour. This is input for measuring the employees' commitment to the organization.

Baseline, first and second measurement

It is crucial to establish the baseline, the starting point of the measurement. This cannot always be done properly. In that case, a first effect measurement can serve as the baseline for the second measurement.

In the case of the European Swimming Championships (see Appendix 3), the first effect measurement of 3 years before served as the baseline for subsequent measurements. Ideally, each measurement starts with a baseline measurement or an analysis of the initial situation. Thus, it can be shown whether and to what extent an event has had an impact on the expected effects, such as stronger loyalty, a stronger brand preference, or stronger ties to a city.

The first measurement is done during or shortly after an event. It is intended to measure how an event has benefited a visitor. At this point, feedback should be provided to the objective, or objectives.

The second measurement is done at a later time on the basis of questions like: to what degree does the experience leave a lasting impression? Has the event actually changed the visitor? So, the point here is measuring whether and to what extent the experience during and after the event has brought about a change in attitude, or even in behaviour, in the visitor. To make it possible for measurements to be compared, identical performance indicators should be used.

Box 10.3

In discussions with several important internal key people, the brand Diesel has formulated a new mission for the coming years. A part of that mission is a greater display of social responsibility. Top management would like to see that all employees are aware of this part of the new mission, in particular, assume a positive attitude towards that mission and conform to it in their conduct. They also want employees to come up with initiatives and ideas themselves regarding a greater contribution to society on the part of Diesel. This is, in fact, about an objective at the transformative level. A transformation does not occur just like that. It takes time and an intensive campaign, with a staff event as its highlight.

The initial situation is analysed: the employees know nothing, or hardly anything, about the new mission, are still not aware of the desire to create more social commitment among the employees and still do not act in accordance with the new mission. The campaign starts with a number of (communication) activities, and there is a follow-up after the staff event.

The first measurement takes place shortly after the event and measures whether and to what extent the employees know about the new mission and what the event has contributed (the memorable experience). About 6 months later, another, second measurement is done to find out to what extent the employees actually think differently and conduct themselves differently, in line with the new mission. Has there been a transformation?

QUANTITATIVE AND QUALITATIVE RESEARCH

Assessing events involves doing properly prepared research. A combination of qualitative and quantitative methods is often the best approach to substantiating the effect of an event. For example, a researcher who wants to have a complete picture of how a programme was appreciated by the public would like to have a representative picture of the opinion of the entire audience. In practice, most measurements are quantitative, due to accountability requirements and the need to show ROI. To conduct in-depth research into the values and experience of an event, it is necessary to have extensive interviews with the respondents (visitors or groups of stakeholders) to find out why an event has had certain effects on an individual and why other effects had no impact at all. This is what qualitative research is about.

Quantitative measurement

If you want to know how large groups of visitors have experienced an event and what has been its impact, your first step obviously involves quantitative research. In most cases, you will then take a random sample requiring the respondents to fill out a questionnaire. If you want to measure strategic effect objectives, you will have to take several measurements: this is referred to as monitoring. Besides, the effects will then only be visible in the longer term, which makes it necessary to undertake a measurement some time after the event as well, as we discussed earlier.

Surveys

Research based on surveys means that data are collected with respect to a large number of research units through systematic interviews or observation. Surveys are applied to several types of effect measurement, and, as a rule, a random sample is taken from the research population and chance determines who will be part of the sample. If this is not possible, a select sample will be taken.

A questionnaire must be drawn up in such a way that it can comprise several types of questions and scaling methods: open-ended and closed-ended questions; the Guttman or Osgood scale; and Likert's scale method.

Closed-ended questions come with possible answers, whereas a respondent has to produce an answer himself in the case of open-ended questions. The Guttman scale provides respondents with a statement in combination with 'yes' and 'no' options. Likert's scale method is an ordinal ranking scale.

The respondent can indicate to what extent he agrees with the statement, often on a five- or seven-point scale ranging from 'strongly disagree' to 'strongly agree'. The Osgood scale (semantic differential) is an ordinal scale enabling respondents to indicate on a five- or seven-point scale to what extent they think that certain qualifications correspond to the subject in question. This is a method that is used frequently to test attitudes to products.

A questionnaire is more than the sum of a large number of questions. It is vital that the questions that belong together are indeed grouped together. Questions should also be asked in a proper sequence and cause no irritation on the part of the respondent. In this respect, the tunnelling technique may be useful: start with the more general questions and continue with more specific (hard/personal) ones.

This description of research into effects is a general one and only describes frequently applied methods. When conducting proper research, it is, of course, advisable to consult the available literature.

Qualitative measurement

There are several methods that can be used to measure whether the objectives of events have been attained. Interviews, observations and laddering are methods frequently used in qualitative research. Qualitative research is intended to find out what the underlying thoughts, values or motives are of the respondents, usually when objectives have been formulated that are related to feelings such as pride, commitment and preference. Getting a complete picture that is representative of the entire group is not the primary aim in the first place. Apart from that, qualitative research is also quite useful in the concept development phase of an event, as we said in Chapter 8. The information from quantitative research can be tested in the context of qualitative research.

In-depth interview

Qualitative research can be done by using in-depth interviews. They are meant to track down unconscious thoughts. A list of topics is used in conducting in-depth interviews. This list has a fixed structure: introduction, research subject, questions and conclusion. Questions may be different from respondent to respondent, and they may be not only open-ended questions (in relation to so-called probing questions) but also statements on which the respondent gives his opinion.

Laddering

Laddering, or meaning structure analysis, is a research technique that can, for instance, be used in the course of an in-depth interview. This technique is based on the *means-end chain theory* (Reynolds and Gutman, 1988), which starts from the premise that consumers buy products and services to achieve important goals in their lives; this refers to values that people find important. This was illustrated in Chapter 6 by the example of the Black Cross event.

The laddering technique comprises three phases: finding out what are the essential attributes, the interviewing process and analysis.

During the first phase, the attributes of a product or service essential to the consumer are tracked down to become the items of research. This can be done by asking spontaneously for essential attributes, and also by using a sorting task. The most essential attributes, with a maximum of four, are the input for the second phase: the interview phase. The interview phase is intended to reveal the meaning stucture: the meaning that a consumer attaches to the essential attributes. With each question, the interviewer probes deeper and deeper into the answer of the respondent. The starting point is quite explicit (concrete attributes). Subsequently, the interview shifts to the more abstract terminal values that are important to a consumer by way of abstract attributes, functional consequences, psychosocial consequences and instrumental values. What is derived from this are meaning structures called 'ladders'. When there are 20 respondents and four ladders per respondent, 80 meaning structures will have been drawn up at the end of the interview period to be used for later analysis.

In the analysis phase, the researcher transfers each individual ladder to a value map, in which the most frequently mentioned attributes, consequences and values, and the relationships between them, are displayed graphically.

This process of analysis is fairly complicated and takes much time. To be able to make a value map, code lists have to be made first on the basis of the answers of the respondents. Then, each individual ladder is codified. The result is input for a matrix that displays how often the attributes, consequences and values are mutually connected. With the help of this matrix, a value map can be drawn up so that it is clear at a glance what the meaning is that consumers attach to a product or service.

The value map can serve as input for strategies regarding communication, segmentation or positioning. In advertisements, for example, the most important psychological consequences or terminal values can be accentuated. But, the value map can also be used for feedback on the objectives of an event.

Please note that conducting an in-depth interview with 'why' questions does not mean that you apply laddering. There is no laddering until you really uncover meaning structures and transfer them to a value map. Laddering is so popular because this technique enables you to transform qualitative interviews into a neat and clear value map that you can put to use immediately.

Observation

By observation, we mean the systematic study of the particular behaviours of a person. This includes only those aspects of behaviour that are relevant to the research. As a researcher, you should take this into account during your preparations. If you intend to make use of observation during an event, you will have to plan beforehand who you are going to observe and when. You also have to decide on the basis of which aspects you want make your observations.

Other methods

We have already described the most frequently used and helpful methods with regard to the effect measurement and evaluation of events. There are still quite a number of other methods, of which we mention a few here:

- experiment, with or without control groups
- camera registration of emotional expression
- having visitors keep a diary or journal
- feedback without hypotheses or tested questionnaires.

In addition, there are various advanced methods to measure emotions that are applied in the advertising and communication sectors. The PrEmo test is one of them. This is a tool that allows a respondent to give expression to his emotions with the help of animations on seeing and hearing certain forms of communication such as logos, advertisements, packaging and products. Thus, it is possible to register the emotions evoked in the respondent by the logo belonging to an event. Yet another method is the IRP technique: measuring appreciation by registering physical changes; for instance, in eye reflexes and blood circulation in the skin.

SUMMARY

Effect measurement is becoming increasingly important for the very reason that events are exploited more and more on the basis of strategic objectives. In this context, the PDCA cycle is a vital tool. Hall (1992) devised an effect matrix for public events that, besides the economic effects, measured touristic/commercial, physical, sociocultural, psychological and political effects.

Possible reasons for an effect measurement are: determining whether the investment has been profitable (ROI) and accountability for the policy pursued. Moreover, interim effect measurements are useful when adjustments have to be made.

Several objectives can be distinguished regarding effect measurement (hierarchy of objectives): strategic effect objectives, operational effect objectives and attainment objectives (the 'what' question). A proper objective is logical, clear, transparent and formulated in terms of SMART. Methods and techniques used in effect measurement are related to the 'how' question: it must be decided which indicators and measuring tools are relevant to the objective. The baseline of the measurement should be established in advance.

Effect measurement can be both quantitative and qualitative. A combination of qualitative and quantitative methods, with the emphasis on qualitative methods, often works best. Examples of qualitative methods to measure effects are the in-depth interview, laddering (with the value map as its graphic result) and observation.

Effect Measurement
and Evaluation

There is not yet an extensive body of literature on the effect measurement and evaluation of events. Most practitioners/people involved in day-to-day practice increasingly appreciate the importance of measurements, and this is something that cannot be separated from the formulation of proper objectives. There is no ready-made model of effect measurement and evaluation, as we have already pointed out in this chapter. Each event is unique, and therefore it is necessary to construct a made-to-measure evaluation model on each occasion. Existing methods can then be a source of inspiration. That is why we describe cases and examples of models for effect measurement and evaluation in these appendices. They can be useful in designing a model of effect measurement and evaluation for your own event.

Appendix 1 discusses the ROI model that has come from the meetings industry. The model for return on communication devised by Wünsch takes the approach of communication studies and is the subject of Appendix 2. Appendices 3, 4 and 5 provide examples of effect measurement and evaluation at big public sports events. Appendix 3 is an impact study of the European Swimming Championships at an indoor location. In contrast, Appendix 4 deals with an outdoor event: the 2009 World Championships Cyclo-Cross. In the fifth and final appendix, we present a study of the effects of the 2008 Amstel Gold Race on the host community.

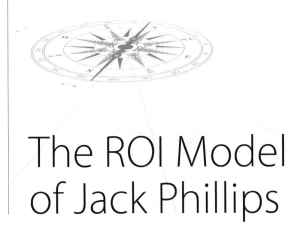

Appendix 1

The ROI Model
of Jack Phillips

BACKGROUND OF THE ROI MODEL

An event should make money or demonstrably reduce the expenditure of a company. That is the idea behind the ROI model devised by Phillips *et al.* (2007). ROI stands for return on investment. Elling Hamso, founder of the European Event ROI Institute, advocates the introduction of this model in the meetings and events industries. It must bring about a change in behaviour among organizers and clients in the sense that they continually ask themselves: why do we organize a meeting or an event? Within the sector of business events, courses are provided at the moment to put this model into practice.

The development of the ROI model for the events sector has everything to do with the profession-alization of this sector and developments in the 1990s that saw a rise in the need for recognition of the profession of organizing. A project within an organization called Meeting Professionals International (MPI) was part of those developments and it provided professionals in the meetings sector with training to teach them how to demonstrate the value of events to customers and employees. The logic behind it was that if top management understood the values of an event or conference in the light of organizational and business objectives, they would be more willing to fund meetings. Besides, the event organizer would become more of a 'strategic team member'. This approach has proved itself so far. Times have changed, and today it is essential in business and industry to account for goals, expenditure and values, using proven methodologies. This holds good for events as well.

AN ANALYSIS TOOL

The ROI model devised by Phillips has become more sophisticated over the past 20 years, also with respect to the events sector. As we showed in Chapter 10, it is becoming more and more important to demonstrate what an event has achieved and also to pay attention during the decision process to the expected returns prior to an event. In the light of these developments, it is only logical that systematic methodologies are also introduced in the events sector to enable it to prove that an event is a professional tool of increasing strategic importance. This means that professional analysis tools are required.

TARGET GROUP

The clients are the most important target group for the output of the calculations, the report in fact. The data collected to make those calculations concerns data on the visitors to an event.

WHAT IS THE ROI MODEL ABOUT?

The ROI model comprises several steps: planning, data collection, data analysis and reporting. These four steps are displayed in Fig. 10.6.

Planning

The goal of an evaluation should be clear from the beginning, because this largely determines the scope, the tools to be used and the data to be collected. This step is about the formulation of the needs of the target group and the objectives of the organization. This may involve several

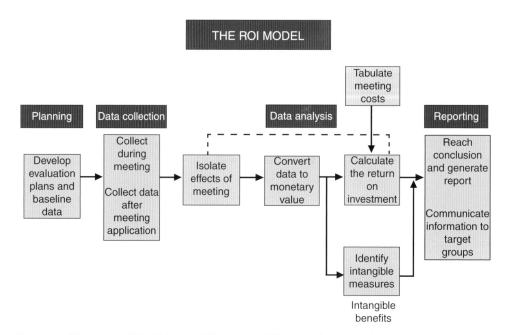

Fig. 10.6. The steps of the ROI model (source: Phillips *et al.*, 2007, adapted by the authors).

levels, as we said earlier in our discussion of the hierarchy of objectives in Chapter 10. The model presents a ranking order of objectives ranging from preference needs via learning needs, performance needs, business needs to pay-off needs. These objectives are used to define the levels of measurement and the last one mentioned, pay-off needs, makes it possible to measure ROI.

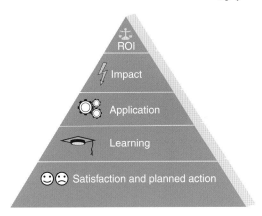

Fig. 10.7. ROI pyramid (source: www. roiinstitute.net, accessed January 2011).

The other objectives refer to *impact*, *application*, *learning* and *reaction*, respectively.

Hamso's method (see Fig. 10.7) involves a pyramid, or a *chain of impact*. What does this mean? The bottom section of the pyramid is linked to *satisfaction and planned action*, also referred to as preference needs, so this is about measuring participants' satisfaction: with catering and hospitality, for example. It concerns preconditions (satisfiers) that have to be met first to get any response at all from the visitors and participants of an event. In relation to this, it is the wishes of those who attend an event that are decisive with respect to structure, location, time required, and so on.

The second level from the bottom of the pyramid is about *learning*: has the event achieved its aims as far as the visitors are concerned? For example, after an event, the visitor should have a better idea of new policy intentions, or make new contacts, or make use of a new system. In other words: learning goals have been formulated for the target group of an event. And in this vision, each event has an over-arching learning goal. In the case of so-called network events, relationship learning can be measured; this should be clearly defined to make a later assessment possible.

Application, the third level, is about the result of what has been learned. How do employees who have attended an event, for instance, deal with what they have learned? After a visit to a stand at a trade fair, will those visitors really start using that energy-saving product? The rule of measuring predetermined goals applies here as well.

The fourth level is related to the *impact* of an event: what is the meaning of an event to an individual? What does that which has been learned and its practical application produce in hard cash? Hamso emphasizes that, at this level, it is important to determine the period over which the effects of an event must occur.

The final level at the top of the pyramid (*ROI*) concerns the financial result. Once the financial result is known, the ROI percentage can be calculated. Thus, ROI can be calculated by the following simple sum: divide profit by costs and multiply by 100. To be able to draw the conclusion that a particular ROI percentage is indeed the one originally aimed at, the objectives must have been formulated in clear and concrete terms.

The first two levels of the ROI pyramid are always there and, as a consequence, can be measured. The levels above level 2 can really only be measured in the case of large-scale events or a series of events as part of a campaign.

The ROI model as a planning tool

At first sight, the ROI model appears to be a tool for measuring the results of an event afterwards. But, it also intended as a planning tool. The idea behind this is that properly thinking through in advance which objectives should be measured later at various levels is very useful to the design of an event. This means that the model can make an event better and more effective from the start.

An online tool is now available that enables the organizers of events to measure the impact of events without much of a problem.

Data collection

Both hard data (such as sales, costs and time) and soft data (such as customer satisfaction and brand awareness) are collected with the help of questionnaires and interviews, among other things. So, this is data collection as referred to in Fig. 10.6. The trick is in selecting the most effective method for the event in question, one that is feasible within the constraints of time and budget. There are various items that must be measured:

- input and indicators
- responses and perceived value
- learning
- application and implementation.

These items will be explained further below.

Measuring input and indicators

When measuring input and indicators, you can take into consideration the total number of participants in an event, the number of days and hours, cost per participant, and so on. As an event organizer, you should, of course, know how much money it takes to organize an event, taking into account that there are various types of events. This can be included in the analysis. Another obvious indicator would be the visitors of an event. Data on the target group, for example, require an answer to the question of what percentage of the total target group has participated in the event. Naturally, the target group can be divided into further segments and then analysed. Visitors can also be monitored to see how much time they spend on an activity, which can be done per segment as well. Another kind of analysis, one that is made less often, is an analysis of the reasons for organizing an event. The list of indicators may also include the extent to which technology and the Internet are used, efficiency and the degree of outsourcing.

Measuring responses and perceived value

Measuring responses and perceived value is the start of the first operational phase of the ROI model. This involves the actual collection of data during and at the end of an event. So, here the focus is on responses and perceived appreciation. This is about feedback, of course. Feedback from the public is crucial to gaining an insight into the way in which an event has been experienced. Customer satisfaction is the central point here. Though many event organizers measure the success of an event only on the basis of data on the reactions of visitors, the ROI method shows that this is merely *one* item of the entire data collection. Success is determined not only by the participants, as an interested party, but also by speakers and facilitators. There are also sponsors, of course, who are not directly involved in an event but who do have an interest. And the client, as the one who pays for an event, should not be forgotten either. The client has asked for an event, has initiated it, supports it, approves budgets, taps sources and is very much dependent on the success or failure of an event.

Collecting data is, in practice, often about aesthetic issues (*non-content*), but the focus should be on *content*. Examples of non-content data are location, transport and catering. Examples of content data are new information, the quantity and quality of new contacts and the quality of speakers.

Measuring learning

Especially when an event revolves around learning, knowing the number of participants who say they have learned something is of great importance. In this model, learning is an essential success factor.

If no learning goals are linked to a meeting or event, it is merely about entertainment. Many measurements of events are still done from the entertainment perspective, and questions are asked whether there was a nice atmosphere and a good experience. But, of course, this does not tell you anything about learning. Especially in light of the last two decades, during which organizations have slowly been transformed into learning organizations in order to be able to survive in competing *global markets*, and also in light of economic changes, learning should be at the top of the agenda, also with respect to meetings and events. Continually finding new ways to serve customers is what this is all about. Organizations have to become more innovative and anticipate technological developments with a view to more efficiency, restructuring and reorganization processes. Therefore, meetings and events are becoming increasingly important as *learning tools*, as platforms for teams and larger groups where individual people can cooperate and create new knowledge. In this context, networking will continue to grow in importance, both within and outside organizations.

How do you measure learning? You can, for instance, devise a quiz or test, though participants sometimes see this a something of a threat. Questionnaires, with a combination of questions on *non-content* and *content*, are often useful in this case, too.

Measuring application and implementation

Some events are intended to spur people into action, but quite often this is not achieved. For example, participants do not use afterwards what they have learned at a congress. Without a successful implementation (i.e. after the event), no changes will occur at the next level of the ROI pyramid, the level of impact. Especially when participants are expected to take action after an event and tackle things differently (behavioural objectives), it is necessary to measure application and implementation. This is valuable, not only because it provides data on the success of an event, but also on the factors that have contributed to this success: information that can be used for future events. Factors such as a stimulating environment, an inspiring speaker, workshops that seamlessly match the level of the participants, to mention a few. Measurements at this level are carried out with a view to the long term and concern the question to what extent the participants apply at a later time, in the context of work or leisure (the post-experience phase), the knowledge and skills they have gained during an event. The measurement can be done by the use of questionnaires, observations, interviews and focus groups.

Data analysis

Isolating effects

This step, *data analysis* in Fig. 10.6, specifically *Isolate effects of meeting*, deals with specific techniques for measuring the impact of an event. Take, for instance, an analysis of a group of persons that has attended an event and a group that has not (control group). If, after an event, a significant improvement can be found in *business performance* on the part of the participants, the issue becomes one of demonstrating the relationship with the event in question.

Whenever the performance of an organization does not come up to expectations, or there seems to be a chance of improvement, the feeling that there should be a meeting or event will often spring up. If business needs are the driving force, these business needs and the objectives linked to them are the most important subjects of evaluation, during or after an event. Think back to hard and soft data, as described earlier. An example: a team of employees in a department does not cooperate adequately and, as a result, productivity is too low. Obviously, the business objective is clear: productivity must be raised. An event is used as a tool to realize this goal. Consequently, this productivity goal is then the crucial indicator to be measured after the event. The event is utilized as a strategic tool and it is essential to measure whether this goal has indeed been attained.

When an event is organized at a company for the reason given above, an analysis of the event should make it clear whether productivity has increased, quality improved, cost savings or work satisfaction achieved in relation to a predetermined objective. Already, available data collected within an organization, business unit or department can also be used for analysis. Customer relationship management (CRM) systems and databases for the systematic collection of data are tools that come to mind in this respect. They can be used for evaluation, or questionnaires can be used again, but whatever method is used, the question should always involve the link between the objective and the contribution that the event has made to attaining this objective, according to the participants.

Control groups, trend line analysis and estimates

To demonstrate that changes have actually been effected by an event, use can be made of control groups, trend line analysis and estimates.

CONTROL GROUPS. As a researcher, you compare the group of people who have participated in the event (the experimental or pilot group) with the control group (the group for comparison) that has not participated. Conditions should be the same as much as possible, to exclude other influences. Such research is hard to conduct in practice.

TREND LINE ANALYSIS. The performance of an employee may be the basis of trend line analysis. We return to the example of labour productivity. Productivity is recorded by a company over the course of a year and plotted on a timeline. After the event, actual performance is compared to what it was before the event on the timeline. If there is a clear upward or downward deviation in the line, you can reasonably assume that the event is a primary cause of this deviation. It is not an exact method, but trend analysis presents a plausible picture of the (probable) impact of a meeting.

ESTIMATES. Estimates can contribute to measuring the impact of an event, but this is not really a precise method of analysis and should at least meet a number of criteria. A primary condition is the use of the most credible source; in the case of events, this may be not only a participant but also the organizer or the media. These parties can often provide good estimates of the impact of an event. They know the market.

An example: when you ask exhibitors at a trade fair about the quality of visitors to their stands, it will give you a fairly reasonable picture of the visitors to the trade fair in question. On the basis of, for example, follow-up appointments, interest shown and business cards handed out, an exhibitor is quite capable of indicating whether the objectives of the trade fair have been attained, as far as he is concerned.

Translating data into financial results

To calculate ROI, the data collected have to be translated into economic values and compared to the cost incurred for an event. In Fig. 10.6, this is referred to as *Convert data to monetary value*. According to the model, this can be done in several ways, such as using experts, databases and estimates. To return to the example of a company with a stand at a trade fair, the obvious question is whether the company can tell how many follow-up appointments actually result in a quotation, and eventually in a sales order. Naturally, the company itself sets the economic value of the order, or orders.

Identifying less tangible effects

In addition to economic value, there are less tangible effects after an event. The ROI model attempts to convert the value of both tangible and less tangible data into financial results. Sometimes, this is not possible, which does not mean that an event has been less valuable.

The economic value will often become visible only over the course of a longer period of time. This is also referred to as an indirect effect.

Direct and indirect costs

This concerns all the costs incurred, direct and indirect, for organizing a meeting or event. This is referred to in Fig. 10.6 as *Tabulate meeting costs*.

Calculating ROI

ROI is calculated by dividing the revenues of an event by the costs incurred: the *cost–benefit ratio* (CBR). This is *Calculate the return on investment* in Fig. 10.6.

$$\text{BCR} = \frac{\text{Meeting benefits}}{\text{Meeting costs}}$$

$$\text{ROI}\,(\%) = \frac{\text{Net meeting benefits}}{\text{Meeting costs}} \times 100$$

This is the basic formula that is also used for other investments.

REPORTING

The reporting step is a crucial one, because conclusions are drawn on the basis of all the data from the preceding steps (*Reporting* in Fig. 10.6). An account is rendered to various parties who have an interest in the effects and impact of an event, and the organizer, too, can profit from it the next time. Reporting may also lead to the implementation of quality improvement to obtain a higher return on the objectives formulated. The Love & Marriage trade fair, for example, carries out continual quantitative and qualitative research into the needs or wishes of visitors and reports the results to its exhibitors. They are then in a better position to align their own objectives to (potential) visitors and get more out of their participation in the trade fair.

A CRITICAL NOTE

Calculating ROI is certainly not suitable to all events. This also acknowledged by the developers of the ROI model and by the European Event ROI Institute. Besides, not every event lends itself to a measurement at five levels. It is, for instance, useful to calculate the ROI with regard to approximately 5% of all congresses organized. All other events must be measured at level 1 of the pyramid (*Satisfaction and planned action*): 30–40% can be measured up to and including level 3.

Within the framework of the ROI model, all sorts of data are collected and quantified. However, on closer inspection, it turns out that estimates are still used in several steps of the model. This makes the outcome less reliable and precise than you would expect at first sight. Moreover, various data collection methods are mentioned of which it is not very clear how they should be integrated.

The Wünsch Model: Return on Communication

BACKGROUND OF THE MODEL

This model has ensued from the increasing importance of experience, and thus events as well, and it has the world-famous idea of *The Experience Economy* of Pine and Gilmore (1999) as its starting point. Wünsch (2008) finds that events generally generate many intangible effects. In spite of this, he went in search of a model to make those effects measurable and tangible. This gave rise to several questions: how can events be classified exactly? How can they be made mutually comparable? What can be learned from other events? But also: how should events be evaluated? What exactly should be evaluated? What is the intention? Are there any existing models? What models should be developed? Is it hard data that are required, such as number of visitors, sales and turnover figures, or soft data, such as image, reputation and recognition?

In general, management is interested in return on investment (ROI): the board, client or organizer wants to know what are the concrete returns of the investments in an event; something that is always hard to find out in the case of events. This is also a major concern in marketing communication and advertising; expenditure is studied critically and weighed, including the expenditure on events. Return on communication is based on return on objectives (ROO) and has been developed in the domain of process and project management. The basic idea is that if the objectives at the start of the project, or event, are clear and quantifiable, interim adjustments can be made, and that on the conclusion of the project there will be a clear picture of the costs and results.

FOCUS OF THE MODEL

Various perspectives with respect to the organization of events can also be seen in this model. The focus of the Wünsch model is on the communication objectives. These should be clear and measurable. The model can be used to show clients and financiers what the ROI will be.

AN EXPLANATION OF THE MODEL

The starting point of this model is the assumption that an event is a mode of communication. An event should be positioned somewhere between mass communication media like TV and radio and interpersonal or face-to-face communication. An event is really a special form of group communication. It is a platform that is suitable for one-on-one communication, but it can also reach out to bigger groups. It can be a social network of *close or less close relationships*. What such a social network should generate during and after an event is called the return on communication (ROC). An assessment of the result of that communication can then be made on condition that clear communication objectives are coupled to an event; this makes the ROC the chief determinant of the success of an event. Three perspectives are involved in the ROC (see Fig. 10.8).

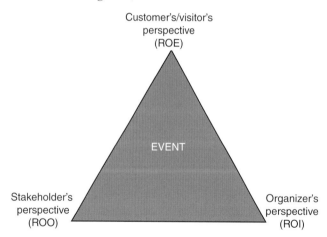

Fig. 10.8. Three perspectives of return of communication (source: Wünsch, 2008).

We will explain Fig. 10.8 on the basis of the Festival Mundial. Mundial Productions BV is the organizer who tries to organize this festival in Tilburg (the Netherlands) as efficiently as possible and within budget. The various stakeholders, such as the city of Tilburg and several firms, are concerned with idealistic objectives, for instance, fostering tolerance in a multicultural society. Naturally, this objective is shared by the organizer himself. The visitor will have a positive experience due to the programming and the unique set-up of the programme.

The ROC comprises:

- the return on objectives (ROO = the extent to which goals have been achieved)
- the individual return on event (ROE = the degree to which individuals have been influenced)
- the return on investment (ROI = the extent to which resources have been used efficiently).

The corresponding formula is as follows:

$$ROC = (ROO \times z1) + (ROO \times z2) + (ROO \times z3)$$

In the formula, z stands for the value assigned by stakeholders (government, public, guests, management, citizens, employees) to a specific event. The plus sign can also be replaced by a multiplication sign to assign a value to the dependence of the individual factors.

The ROC is determined by various perspectives, as shown below:

ROC = involvement, satisfaction	total perspective
ROE = experience/intensity (density)	participant in event
ROO = effectiveness/reach	stakeholder
ROI = efficiency/usefulness	client

At the start of each event, it should be decided from which perspective the ROC will be considered. In other words: if it is the intention to measure whether an event has been organized efficiently on the basis of predetermined objectives and resources, the focus should be on the perspective of the sponsor of the event (ROI). If an answer is required to the question whether an event has been effective and what reach it has had, measurements should be made on the basis of the goals of the relevant stakeholders (ROO). If the primary question is in what degree a visitor to an event has really been affected, the perspective of the participant (ROE) is the correct choice. The total effect of an event as a communication tool can be learned by measuring satisfaction and involvement, taking all three perspectives into consideration (ROC).

A CRITICAL NOTE

The Wünsch model has not been fully developed and not a lot of experience has been gained with it in practice. The range of ideas is interesting, but requires further development. The model is less suitable to the evaluation of events that have objectives other than communication objectives. (Source: Wünsch, 2008, adapted by the authors.)

Appendix 3

Economic Impact Study – European Swimming Championships, Eindhoven 2008

A STUDY OF THE ECONOMIC IMPACT OF THE EUROPEAN SWIMMING CHAMPIONSHIPS IN THE CITY OF EINDHOVEN

KEY FACTS

Type of event: 11-day international indoor sports event.
Study commissioned by: City of Eindhoven.

IN GENERAL

The European Swimming Championships 2008 was held from Thursday, 13 March until Monday, 24 March at the Tongelreep National Swimming Centre in Eindhoven (the Netherlands). The European Swimming Championships is a very large biannual international sports event that each time is organized in a different European city, and only once before in the Netherlands: that honour went to Utrecht in 1966. During the 29th championships, the programme comprised of three swimming disciplines: swimming (long distance; 50-m pool), synchronized swimming and diving. As many as 878 swimmers from 42 different countries participated in the event, which was attended by more than 31,480 people. Approximately another 130 million people all over the world watched the event on television, altogether about 400 h of TV coverage. In addition to contesting for gold, silver and bronze medals at the 2008 European Championships, many competitors used the meeting to earn starting permits for the 2008 Olympic Games, which made the event all the more interesting for the spectators. Besides, quite a number of side events were organized around the championships to involve the old and the young actively in the event. For instance, the 'EKNZB house' was set up, where thematic discussions and congresses were held for members of the swimming association, and training sessions for young competitors were organized, focused on the disciplines of swimming, synchronized swimming and diving. During the European Championships Swimming Festival, children from groups 7 and 8 of Eindhoven's primary schools were introduced to the sport of swimming, and a mini championship was organized for student swimmers. And finally, the entire city was festooned with banners and posters, in keeping with the atmosphere of the event.

WHO WANTS TO KNOW WHAT, AND WHY?

The European Swimming Championships were a very important event for Eindhoven in the context of Sports 2008. For that reason, the Sports Committee of the Department of Social Development of the city of Eindhoven wanted an elaborate evaluation of the event on the basis of questions like: how will Eindhoven be put on the map from both a national and international perspective, and what will be the impact on the city's image? What is the economic impact of this event on the city? How have those who live near the venue of this event experienced it? So, quite a few questions, which were submitted to various parties in the form of three studies. The results of these studies have been described in an extensive evaluation report (van Schendel, 2008) that can be used by the city authorities to account for the policy pursued to win the nomination of the city of Eindhoven for this big event.

Here, we focus on the economic impact of the event on the city of Eindhoven. Relevant questions in this context are:

- How much money was spent on various aspects of the European Swimming Championships?
- What are the differences in spending when comparing those within the COROP area of Zuidoost-Brabant, those outside that area and those abroad? A COROP area is part of a regional division of the Netherlands for the purposes of statistical analysis. There are 40 COROP areas.
- What part of the money spent is additional, and what is the economic impact of those sums?

CONTRACTOR

The NHTV International University of Applied Sciences has many years of experience in the field of research into (sports) events and is often asked to undertake an economic impact study for organizers, sponsors and government. As a result of the identical systematic working method, it is possible to compare various studies with each other.

COROP AREA AND INPUT–OUTPUT MODEL

The subjects of research of the event are the visitors, the athletes and their coaches, the press and the organization. It is specifically their spending behaviour that is the subject of study. For the purposes of this research, use is made of the input–output model that applies to the COROP area that includes Eindhoven: Zuidoost-Brabant in this case. The Central Office of Statistics has data of the input–output model, specified for each COROP area. The model consists of a system of multipliers that indicate to what extent the national income changes when autonomous spending changes. It also describes the economic structure of a region. On the basis of the defined input (spending), the model calculates the output. This output is the potential economic production in the area as a result of the event. In other words: if the event had not taken place, there would have been no production.

Ultimately, the economic impact applies to the additional amount of spending. In the context of this study, additional means that only those respondents from outside the COROP area are included in the calculations of who would not have come to Eindhoven if the European Swimming Championships had not been held there. This means that the spendings of the inhabitants of the region, the percentage of visitors who would still have been in Eindhoven if the event had not taken place (substitution effect) and the subsidy from the government are not regarded as additional spending. These spendings would have been realized in the region anyway (see Fig. 10.9).

RESEARCH METHOD

First, on the basis of interviews with the organization concerned, the average expenditure and the numbers of participating teams, companies and reporters have been established.

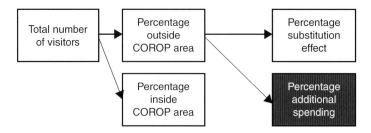

Fig. 10.9. Additional spending (source: van Schendel, 2008).

Subsequently, quantitative research was conducted through exit polls among the event visitors. Every fifth visitor leaving was surveyed, spread across several days of the event. Sold-out races were calculated in and more polls were conducted during the last few days than at the start.

On the basis of the number of visitors (31,480) and the size of the sample (389), the findings, with 95% certainty and a confidence interval of 5%, are generally binding. This means that the findings can be 5% higher or lower, with a certainty of 95%.

The questions for this study are based on the objective of the client and on the required input for the model: visitor profile plus residing inside or outside the COROP area, spending profile (number of overnight stays, travel within the area, food and drink, merchandise), while allowing for the substitution effect. The substitution effect indicates whether a person from outside the COROP area would have been present if the event had not taken place.

CONCLUSIONS ON ECONOMIC IMPACT

Of the people surveyed who came from outside the COROP area (57.6% of the total), 89.2% would not have come to the region if the European Swimming Championships had not taken place. So, this concerns additional spending (see Table 10.3). This means that the participants, the press and the organization are largely responsible for the additional spending on this event. From the study, it is clear that visitors from the Netherlands rarely booked a hotel and, as a result, spent little on overnight stays. Spending on food, drink, merchandising and travel (in and around Eindhoven) was not very high.

Average spending per person was linked to the number of visitors (31,480), the number of participants/coaches (1298) and the number of reporters (400), and subdivided on the basis of the type of expenditure.

Table 10.3. Additional spending.

	Average (€)	Spending (€)
1. Overnight stays	75.54	3,241,560
2. Food and drink	12.70	504,063
3. Merchandising	4.73	163,775
4. Travel (in and around Eindhoven)	3.61	72,603
Subtotal		3,982,001
Of which 89.2% additional		3,551,943
5. Organization		2,940,000
Additional spending		6,491.943

The additional spending of €6,491,943 was then worked out in the input–output model. As a result of money circulating in a particular business sector, production in other sectors is increased. If the catering industry achieves a big turnover, for instance, there is work for the suppliers of meat, fish, vegetables and fruit as well. These mutual economic relationships are incorporated in the input–output model (Table 10.4).

The expenditure of the various target groups has subsequently been divided over the various business sectors and this completes the model. The potential production as a result of the sports event was €7,469,948.76, as can be seen in Table 10.4.

The conclusions were:

Table 10.4. Input–output model.

	Input per business sector (€)	**Output per business sector (€)**
1. Agriculture, forestry, fishery	0.00	50,309.56
2. Mineral extraction	0.00	2,648.62
3. Industry, energy and water companies	0.00	89,625.19
4. Construction	0.00	17,993.83
5. Commerce	146,087.00	193,845.75
6. Catering	3,341,095.00	3,785,494.38
7. Transport, storage and communication	64,761.00	81,206.68
8. Financial institutions	0.00	62,950.64
9. Lettings, business services	2,940,000.00	3,068,098.72
10. Government, defence, social services and sub-education		50,977.72
11. Health and welfare	0.00	47,694.39
12. Environmental services, culture, services	0.00	19,103.28
13. Imports	0.00	0.00
Total	6,491,943.00	7,469,948.76

- the event generated a considerable economic boost
- it was the press, the participants and the organization that were mainly responsible for the economic input
- the event caused little trouble because it did not take place in the city centre and lasted only 11 days.

A CRITICAL NOTE

It is very hard to be complete in a study of the impact of an event. There are always external factors that can hardly be controlled. Companies or sponsors, for example, can develop activities in the context of the European Swimming Championships of which the organization or researcher has no knowledge. As a consequence, the related expenditure is not included in the input–output model.

In this case, exit polls were conducted with each fifth person leaving the event. But, not every visitor was willing or able to cooperate, so sometimes it was the sixth or seventh person leaving, which was a risk with regard to the reliability of the research.

Finally, it is always hard to pin down additional spending. With respect to this study, a conscious choice has been made for the COROP area and the substitution effect. (Source: de Kort and van Schendel, 2008, adapted by the authors.)

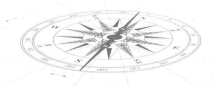

Economic Impact Study – World Cyclo-Cross Championships 2009

A STUDY OF THE ECONOMIC IMPACT OF THE WORLD CYCLO-CROSS CHAMPIONSHIPS IN HOOGERHEIDE IN 2009

KEY FACTS

Type of event: 2-day international outdoor sports event.
Study commisioned by: municipality of Woensdrecht, the Netherlands.

IN GENERAL

Various cycle races and world championships are organized under the aegis of the UCI – the Union Cycliste Internationale, or the International Cycling Association. Thus, it happened that Hoogerheide, which is a part of the municipality of Woensdrecht, was awarded the organization of the World Championships Cyclo-Cross in 2009. The championship races on 31 January and 1 February 2009 were organized by the Grote Prijs Adrie van der Poel Foundation in collaboration with the KNWU, the Dutch cycling association. On Saturday, 31 January, the championships for juniors and promising cyclists took place, and on Sunday, 1 February, it was the turn of the ladies, the top cyclists and young talented cyclists.

WHO WANTS TO KNOW WHAT, AND WHY?

The Grote Prijs Adrie van der Poel course has featured in the programme of the UCI World Cup Cyclo-Cross for years, and the cyclo-cross is one of the prominent events in the municipality of Woensdrecht. Prior to being awarded the organization of the championships, the municipal authorities underwrote part of the organizational costs and granted a permit for this event after the approval of the municipal council. It matters very much for the authorities to be able, afterwards, to render account for the policy pursued and to show the tangible results of this 2-day event. Has Woensdrecht been put on the map? It is also thought that the findings can be an inspiration for future policy. In addition to an impact study, a study was conducted among residents and entrepreneurs to find out about their experiences. The outcomes have been described in an evaluation report. The key questions were almost identical to those asked with regard to the European Swimming Championships:

- How much does the World Championship Cyclo-Cross contribute to the region in financial terms?
- What are the differences in spending between people from inside and outside the COROP area of Zuidwest-Brabant?
- What part of the spending is additional?

COROP AREA AND INPUT–OUTPUT MODEL

The target group of this study comprised all visitors to the World Championships Cyclo-Cross, with the exception of VIPs, cyclists and accredited persons. So, there is a difference compared to the target group of the European Swimming Championships where, in contrast, the participants were part of the research population. The COROP area is delineated by the postal codes of 4600 to 4799, and the results of the surveys were used as input for the input–output model for this region.

RESEARCH METHOD

Desk research and interviews with the organization and the city officials of Woensdrecht provided an insight into the various items of the budget. On both days, visitors were surveyed on leaving the track at four different exits. Every fifth person leaving was surveyed. On Saturday, 131 surveys were conducted, and 249 on Sunday. On the basis of the estimated number of visitors (48,900), a figure obtained during an interview with the Communication Department of the city, and the size of the sample, 380 valid surveys, it can be stated with a certainty of 95% that the results could have been 5% higher or lower.

The survey questions were almost identical to those asked in the study of the European Swimming Championships, based on Likert scales and response categories.

CONCLUSIONS ON ECONOMIC IMPACT

Of those surveyed, 65% came from outside the COROP area. Within this group, 85% visited the region primarily because of the event; this meant that 85% of the visitors spent additional money. Research shows that spending on travel (in and around Zuidwest-Brabant) and food and drinks was substantially higher than during the European Swimming Championships.

The figures for additional spending are presented in Table 10.5, subdivided into types of spending. Total additional spending has been calculated by linking the total number of visitors of 48,900 and average spending.

The additional spending of approximately €2.8 million is regarded as input in the input–output model. The results can be found in Table 10.6.

The potential production in the region as a result of the event was approximately €3.3 million. The conclusions were:

- As a result of the event, an additional amount of more than €2.8 million was spent in the region.
- In comparison to the European Swimming Championships, there were more visitors. These visitors spent their money differently: on food, drinks and overnight stays in the region. Mind you, this concerned a 2-day outdoor event.
- The event had a positive effect on the image of the region, as well as international interest in and recognition of the region. This became clear from an experience study that was done at the same time.

Table 10.5. Additional spending.

	Average (€)	Spending (€)
1. Overnight stays	53.51	917,856
2. Food and drink	28.66	907,223
3. Merchandising	4.19	132,544
4. Travel (in and around north-west Brabant)	11.86	375,436
Subtotal		2,333,059
Of which 85% additional		1,983,100
5. Organization		850,500
Additional spending		2,833,600

Table 10.6. Input–output model.

	Input per business sector (€)	Output per business sector (€)
1. Agriculture, forestry, fishery	0.00	20,354.00
2. Mineral extraction	0.00	6,673.00
3. Industry, energy and water companies	0.00	42,360.00
4. Construction	0.00	8,093.00
5. Commerce	102,609.00	138,552.00
6. Catering	1,533,023.00	1,769,820.00
7. Transport, storage and communication	308,968.00	334,944.00
8. Financial institutions	39,000.00	55,460.00
9. Lettings, business services	850,000.00	891,149.00
10. Government, defence, social services and sub-education		23,463.00
11. Health and welfare	0.00	24,489.00
12. Environmental services, culture, services	0.00	9,073.00
13. Imports	0.00	0.00
Total	2,833,600.00	3,324,430.00

A CRITICAL NOTE

It is very hard to be complete in a study of the impact of an event. There are always external factors that can hardly be controlled. Companies or sponsors, for example, can develop activities in the context of the World Championships Cyclo-Cross of which the organization or researcher has no knowledge. As a consequence, the related expenditure is not included in the input–output model.

Exit polls were conducted with each fifth person leaving the event. But, not every visitor was willing or able to cooperate, so sometimes it was the sixth or seventh person leaving who was surveyed, which was a risk with regard to the reliability of the research.

Another matter is that it is always hard to pin down exactly what is the additional spending. With respect to this study, a conscious choice was made for the COROP area and the substitution effect.

Finally, the calculations are based on estimates of the number of visitors to the event. These numbers are obtained from external parties; the exact number is not known. The fact is that, at the moment, there is no uniform measuring tool to measure visitor numbers at public events, although there are those who claim that exact measurement is possible. (Source: van Schendel, 2009a, adapted by the authors.)

Amstel Gold Race 2008

A STUDY OF THE HOST COMMUNITY'S PERCEPTION OF THE EFFECTS OF LARGE-SCALE SPORTS EVENTS

KEY FACTS

Type of event: 2-day cycling event.
Reasearch commissioned by: the Amstel Gold Race organization.

AMSTEL GOLD RACE

The Amstel Gold Race is the biggest cycling event of the Netherlands and it has been an annual event held in the vicinity of Valkenburg since 1966. The past few years, this cycling event has comprised of two different races in one weekend:

- The official UCI Pro Tour Classic Amstel Gold Race with professional racers. The 43rd Amstel Gold Race took place on Sunday, 20 April 2008.
- The non-professional version of this cycling classic, in which amateurs and recreational cyclists can participate. The 7th rally of this particular race took place on Saturday, 19 April 2008.

The Amstel Gold Race is the pride of Dutch cycling. The event features on the UCI Pro Tour calendar and the professional cyclists who participate can earn points for the UCI Pro Tour rankings, which used to be the World Cup rankings. In the history of this event, the winners have included many international top cyclists, among them Eddy Merckx and Bernard Hinault, multiple winners of the Tour de France, but also prominent Dutch cyclists such as Jan Raas,

Michael Boogerd and Erik Dekker. A warm and friendly atmosphere is created in pubs and restaurants in the various cities along the course.

The non-professional version of the Amstel Gold Race is completed the day before the official race and follows the same course as the professionals. This event draws a maximum of 10,000 racers to the south of Limburg each year. There are four different courses of 50, 100, 150 and 200 km, respectively. The participants will have the opportunity to climb famous hills such as Keutenberg, Gulpenerberg and, of course, Cauberg, just as the professionals will do the next day. Once they have finished their race on Cauberg, they will be welcomed as true heroes by friends and family who have come to Valkenburg for this special occasion. A considerable number of participants then stay on in the area for another day with their friends and family to watch the professionals race.

WHO WANTS TO KNOW WHAT, AND WHY?

The organizer of the Amstel Gold Race wanted to carry out research among the local population and other parties in the region to find out how the inhabitants and businesses had experienced the event.

- The organizer wants information about the commitment of the inhabitants of the region the race course passes through and about the extent of their commitment.
- The province grants the permit and needs the input from various cities and villages affected by the Amstel Gold Race in the south of Limburg, because the course passes through several of them.
- The organizer wants to prevent the cities and villages from lodging objections to the race.
- The organizer does not receive any subsidy from the government.
- The organizer wants to have a good idea of the population's support for the event.
- The organizer wants to measure public opinion and present the results to the various interested parties.

The findings of the study can be found in an extensive evaluation report (Willemsen, 2008, and van Schendel, 2009a, edited by the authors) and can be used by the organizer to back up new applications for permits and discussions with sponsors.

FOCUS OF THE STUDY: A PERCEPTION STUDY

The leading question was how the host community had experienced the event and which effects were felt. In this context, the host community was defined as:

> The inhabitants and entrepreneurs of a city, or cities, where a large-scale event, sports or otherwise, takes place, and where the tangible effects can be felt. In this case, it affects the

municipalities of Beek, Eijsden, Gulpen-Wittem, Nuth, Maastricht, Margraten, Meerssen, Simpelveld, Stein, Vaals, Valkenburg on the Geul and Voerendaal.

(Willemsen, 2008, and van Schendel, 2009a, adapted by the authors)

Besides the economic effects, there are other effects of events that can be of great value: for example, promotional and social effects. These effects are much less tangible and depend largely on personal experiences, or perception. National and/or regional governments apparently find it hard to make good decisions purely on the basis of economic effects where it concerns the granting a permit for an event, or whether or not it should be subsidized, because those economic effects are not always convincing in practice. The host community plays a vital part in the exploitation of events, something to which a city marketing policy rarely pays sufficient attention. Sometimes, residents and companies feel hardly any involvement in the development and profiling of a city or region, which may incur the risk of a string of legal objections that can delay an event taking place. When there is little or no involvement, it is more likely that residents and companies experience an event as a nuisance. Yet, the moment when the host community feels involved in an event, it can have a very positive impact on the image of a city or region. In that case, the effects of an event are experienced as positive ones and, as a consequence, it meets with approval.

The perception study was intended to provide answers to the following questions:

- Which effects are perceived by the host community?
- How are these effects experienced?
- How can effects be influenced by the perception building blocks?

THEORETICAL FRAMEWORK

This case is based on earlier theoretical studies regarding models of experience and perception, the effects of events and defining the concept of host community and large-scale events. The theoretical model will not be discussed here.

On the basis of the theory, research has been carried out in the host community of the Amstel Gold Race by presenting it with statements to find out which effects occur (Phase I), how they are perceived (Phase II) and how they are experienced (Phase III) (see Fig. 10.10). The effects mentioned in Hall's effects matrix (see Table 10.1) were taken as starting points (economic, tourist/commercial, physical, psychological and political).

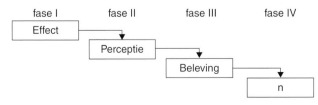

This means that we now have an evaluation model for how the host community experiences the perceived effects of a large-scale sports event. It provides the organizer with an insight into

Fig. 10.10. Evaluation model.

the question of which parties within the host community are positive or negative about hosting the Amstel Gold Race.

In Phase IV, *n* stands for the percentage of respondents who have a certain experience when an effect is perceived. The percentages can be used to check whether the predetermined objectives have been attained. It is also possible to compare the results to similar ones of other events. Bear in mind that this concerns a description that does not provide explanations for the cause and effect relationship of an experience.

RESEARCH METHOD

Prior to the Amstel Gold Race, interviews were conducted among the host community. For the sake of representativeness, the respondents were selected on the basis of gender and age, using figures for national distribution. These interviews generated certain statements regarding the event. Later, on the first and second day after the Amstel Gold Race, this was followed by the quantitative part of the study among entrepreneurs and residents of the various municipalities along the course of the race. In consultation with the client, the addresses and streets for the sample were selected and data collected. On the basis of a sample of 350 respondents out of a total population of 380,000 within the various municipalities, the findings, with a certainty of 95% and a reliability of 5%, are generally binding.

The 52 questions and statements of the survey are based on the research model and qualitative research, and there were four central issues:

1. The personal characteristics of the respondent.
2. The perception and experience of the effects of the Amstel Gold Race.
3. The personal experience.
4. The possible personal impact of this experience.

Possible answers related to subjects 2, 3 and 4 were given using a Likert scale (agree strongly, agree, neutral, disagree, strongly disagree).

CONCLUSIONS OF THE PERCEPTION STUDY

Relevant characteristics of the sample population

The study shows that 75% of the host community likes sports and more than 50% also likes the Amstel Gold Race and/or cycling. However, approximately 50% does not feel personally committed to or involved with this event, and this also holds good for approximately 70% in their work situation. It appears that within the host community, more men than women are sports enthusiasts. Men also feel more involvement with the Amstel Gold Race in their work situation. Entrepreneurs feel involved more often than residents.

Perception and experience of effects

The host community has not perceived effects regarding the Amstel Gold Race that are either clearly positive or negative. Only 19.9% of the host community has a clear or very clear perception of the effects. Nevertheless, the experience of the effects is largely positive for 32.8% and neutral for the rest. Moreover, it turns out that the host community finds the effects experienced as positive (86.9%), important, and the effects experienced as negative (85.5%), acceptable.

The tourist/commercial and sociocultural effects have been perceived most clearly by the host community and at the same time experienced as most positive. There is no clear perception of the psychological, political, economic and physical effects, and they are experienced as moderately positive. Finally, in comparison with the residents, entrepreneurs have more frequently experienced the economic effects as positive.

Perception of the Amstel Gold Race and related effects

The vast majority (93.6%) of the host community has experienced the Amstel Gold Race at a basic level. This comes down to a fleeting experience, with little that is worth remembering and leaving no lasting impression. Only 6.4% described the experience as memorable, which means that for them it was certainly worth remembering and left a fairly lasting impression.

The conclusion can be that the experience of the host community is by and large a positive one. Approximately 30% of those surveyed agrees, or strongly agrees, with five positively formulated 'experience statements', whereas more than 90% disagrees, or strongly disagrees, with five negative statements. Besides, they are proud of the fact that the Amstel Gold Race is organized in the region, and approve of attracting major sports events to the region. A last finding is that especially attending or actively following the event via the media, with the accompanying feelings of pleasure and positive surprise, can lead to a positive experience.

Possible influence on the experience of the effects of the Amstel Gold Race

It turns out that the experience of the effects of large-scale sports events on the host community cannot be or hardly be influenced by the use of experience building blocks (see Chapter 8). Indeed, only 13% of those surveyed say that their personal experience can be influenced; this concerns young people (under 40) more often than older people (over 40). An additional conclusion is that the experience of those young people can be influenced mainly through the experience building blocks of identity, physical environment, products and staff.

The final conclusions are:

- it is hard to influence the experience of effects
- attention should be paid to the sociocultural and physical effects to enhance their perception
- the commitment to and involvement in sports events should be stimulated to achieve a more positive experience

- experience building blocks should be used to influence the experience of young people (under 40)
- generally speaking, the host community is very proud of an event like the Amstel Gold Race.

By comparing the results of similar cases, it is possible to draw conclusions. For example, a comparison can be made between the World Championships Cyclo-Cross and the Amstel Gold Race. During the World Championships Cyclo-Cross in Hoogerheide, 12% of the residents found the event irritating, a percentage that is considerably lower than that for the Amstel Gold Race. One of the main reasons for this finding was that the course of the cyclo-cross race was partly on public roads and, as a result, parts of the roads were blocked for a few days. On the basis of those figures, the course of the World Championships Cyclo-Cross in future races has been changed so that there is less inconvenience for the local population. This is an example of the way in which the knowledge of negative effects can be used to compensate for them or to minimize them.

A CRITICAL NOTE

The questionnaires for the respondents were felt to be long and difficult. In spite of the fact that they were dealt with orally (very labour-intensive) so that questions could be explained at once, it proved to be fairly hard to keep the attention of the respondents.

It remains a problem to find out what exactly are the causes of different outcomes, because so many factors are involved; factors such as scale size, the number of visitors, media attention, type of sport, and so on. This is a labour-intensive type of research. (Source: Willemsen, 2008, and van Schendel, 2009a, adapted by the authors.)

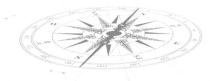

Bibliography

Alberts, P. and Buitendijk, N. (1995) *Relatiemarketing; hoe het echt werkt*. Jubels Cobypoint, Amsterdam.

Ashworth, G.J., Pellenbarg, P. and Voogd, H. (2004) *Place Marketing; Marketing in the Planning and Management of Places*. Routledge, London.

Baarda, D.B. and de Goede, M.P.M. (2006) *Basisboek Methoden en Technieken; handleiding voor het opzetten en uitvoeren van kwantitatief onderzoek*. Wolters-Noordhoff, Groningen, the Netherlands.

Ballantyne, D., Christopher, M. and Payne, A. (2002) *Relationship Marketing; Creating Stakeholder Value*. Butterworth-Heinemann, Oxford, UK.

Barendse-Schijvens, S. (2009) *Van Medewerkers naar Medemerkers*. Kluwer, Deventer, the Netherlands.

Berci, F., Mommaas, H. and van Synghel, K. (2002) *City Branding; Image Building & Building Images*. NAi Publishers, Rotterdam, the Netherlands.

Beunders, N. and Boers, H. (1997) *De andere kant van de vrije tijd*. Toerboek, Leiden, the Netherlands.

Biel, A.L. (1999) *Exploring Brand Magic. How to Use Advertising to Build Strong Brands*. Sage Publications, Thousand Oaks, London, New Delhi.

Boom, E. and Weber, A. (2001) *Consumentengedrag: beslissen, gedrag en marketingstrategie*. Wolters-Noordhoff, Groninge, the Netherlands.

Boom, M. (2006) *Op weg met geur: geurbeleving in de vrije tijd*. NHTV internationaal hoger onderwijs Breda, Breda, the Netherlands.

Borg, M.B. ter (2003) *Zineconomie*. Scriptum, Schiedam, the Netherlands.

Bos, N. (2009) *Van Evenement naar belevenement; een onderzoek naar de touchpoints in de bedrijfsevenementenbranche*. NHTV internationaal hoger onderwijs Breda, Breda, the Netherlands [unpublished].

Boswijk, A. and Peelen, E. (2008) *Een nieuwe kijk op de experience economy; betekenisvolle belevenissen*. Pearson Prentice Hall, Amsterdam.

Boswijk, A., Thijssen, T. and Peelen, E. (2005) *Een nieuwe kijk op de experience economy; betekenisvolle belevenissen*. Pearson Prentice Hall, Amsterdam.

Boswijk, A., Thijssen, T. and Peelen, E. (2007) *The Experience Economy: A New Perspective*. Pearson Education Benelux, Amsterdam.

Boswijk, A., Peelen, E. and Olthof, S. (2012) *Economy of Experiences*. European Centre for the Experience Economy, Bilthoven, the Netherlands.

Buizert, A. (2004) *Customer Relationship Management; ook tijdens de organisatie van een bedrijfsevenement*. NHTV internationaal hoger onderwijs Breda, Breda, the Netherlands.

Buuren, K. van (2009) *Keihard op de kaart met behulp van publieksevenementen; afstudeeronderzoek naar citymarketing en de rol van publieksevenementen*. NHTV internationaal hoger onderwijs Breda, Breda, the Netherlands.

Buuren, R. van (2006) *Beleef je eigen verhaal; onderzoek naar impliciete en expliciete storytelling in oorlogsmusea*. NHTV internationaal hoger onderwijs Breda, Breda, the Netherlands.

Buursink, J. (1991) *Steden in de markt: het elan van citymarketing*. Coutinho, Muiderberg, the Netherlands.

Chernatony, L. de and McDonald, M.H.B. (1992) *Creating Powerful Brands; The Strategic Route to Success in Consumer, Industrial and Service Markets*. Butterworth-Heinemann, Oxford, UK.

Cordewener, E. and Scholts, A. (2004) *Meer dan een feestje; hoe een evenement bijdraagt aan de marketingstrategie*. Wageningen, the Netherlands [unpublished].

Curry, J. (1991) *Customer Marketing; een praktisch antwoord op de vraag: 'In welke business zitten we eigenlijk?'*. Management Press bv, Amsterdam, Brussels.

Dekker, E.L. (2006) *Belevingsonderzoek naar geur als belevenisinstrument; ik ruik je wel maar ik zie je niet*. NHTV internationaal hoger onderwijs Breda, Breda, the Netherlands.

Dekkers, M. (2005) *Co-creatie*. NHTV internationaal hoger onderwijs Breda, Breda, the Netherlands.

Delnooz, P. (2000) *Onderzoekspraktijken*. Boom, Amsterdam.

Denekamp, M. (2005) *The 4 Steps to Heaven; hoe moet eventmarketing zijn voor een optimale merkbeleving?* NHTV internationaal hoger onderwijs Breda, Breda, the Netherlands.

Diener, E. and Biswas-Diener, R. (2008) *Happiness; Unlocking the Mysteries of Psychological Wealth*. Blackwell Publishing, Malden, Massachusetts.

Dijkema, S. (2008) *Celebrate Our Specialness or Our Ideas*. NHTV internationaal hoger onderwijs Breda, Breda, the Netherlands [unpublished].

Dijksterhuis, E. (2008) *Slimme steden*. Uitgeverij Business Contact, Amsterdam.

Disney Institute (2003) *Be Our Guest; Perfecting the Art of Customer Service*. Disney Editions, New York.

Dreimüller, A.P. (2002) *Het ondernemersplan en de balanced scorecard; over richting en verrichting*. Academic Service, Den Haag, the Netherlands.

Farquhar, P.H. (1989) Managing brand equity. *Journal of Advertising Research* 30(4), 7–12.

Fatingan, A., Pancham, A., Niamat, Z. and Govers, R. (2009) Evenementen, media en de invloed op place image. *Vrijetijdsstudies* 27(3), 35–45.

Floor, J.M.G. and Raaij, W.F. van (2006) *Marketingcommunicatiestrategie*. Stenfert Kroese, Amsterdam.

Florida, R. (2002) *The Rise of the Creative Class*. Basic Books, New York.

Franzen, G. (2006) *The SWOCC Book of Brand Management Models*. Stichting wetenschappelijk onderzoek commerciële communicatie, Amsterdam.

Franzen, G. and Berg, M. van den (2002) *Strategisch management van merken*. Kluwer, Deventer, the Netherlands.

Franzen, G. and Bouwman, M. (1999) *De mentale wereld van merken; een merkassociatief systeem*. Samsom, Deventer, the Netherlands.

Franzen, G. and Holzhauer, F. (1987) *Het merk*. Kluwer, Deventer, the Netherlands.

Franzen, M.P. (1996) *Het merk op weg naar de 21e eeuw*. SWOCC, Amsterdam.

Frijda, N.H. (1986) *The Emotion; Studies in Emotion and Social Interaction*. Cambridge University Press, New York.

Frijda, N.H. (2005) *De emoties; een overzicht van onderzoek en theorie.* Uitgeverij Bert Bakker, Amsterdam.

Gabriel, Y. (2000) *Storytelling in Organizations; Facts, Fictions and Fantasies.* Oxford University Press, Oxford, UK.

Gehrels, C. (2003) *Kiezen voor Amsterdam; merk, concept en organisatie van de citymarketing.* NHTV internationaal hoger onderwijs Breda, Breda, the Netherlands.

Getz, D. (2009) Policy for sustainable and responsible festivals and events; institutionalization of a new paradigm. *Journal of Policy Research in Tourism, Leisure and Events* 1(1), 61–78.

Gilmore, J.H. and Pine, B.J. II (2007) *Authenticity; What Consumers Really Want.* Harvard Business School Press, Boston, Massachusetts.

Gilmore, J.H. and Pine, B.J. II (2008) *Authenticiteit; wat consumenten echt willen.* Academic Service, Den Haag, the Netherlands.

Gool, W. van and Wijngaarden, P. van (2005) Beleving op niveau: vrije tijd, van vermaak tot transformatie. *Clou* 2(16), 16–18.

Groenendijk, J.N.A., Hazekamp, G.A.Th. and Mastenbroek, J. (2000) *Public relations: beleid, organisatie en uitvoering.* Samsom, Alphen aan den Rijn, the Netherlands.

Hall, C.M. (1992) *Hallmark Tourist Events, Impacts, Management and Planning.* Belhaven, London.

Hart, H.W.C. van (1998) Van massamarketing naar one-to-one marketing en relatiemarketing. *Bedrijfskunde* 70(3), 24–29.

Havitz, M.E. and Mannell, R.C. (2005) Enduring involvement, situational involvement and flow in leisure and non-leisure activities. *Journal of Leisure Research* 37(2), 152–177.

Hench, J. (2003) *Designing Disney; Imagineering and the Art of the Show.* Disney Editions, New York.

Herlé, M. (1999) *Te kijk staan.* Samsom, Alphen aan den Rijn, the Netherlands.

Herlé, M. and Rustema, C. (2005) *Corporate Communication Worldwide.* Wolters-Noordhoff, Groningen/Houten, the Netherlands.

Hesselmans, K.H.N. (2005) *Thematisering als belevenisinstrument; onderzoek naar succes- en faalfactoren van thematisering in de attractieparkensector.* NHTV internationaal hoger onderwijs Breda, Breda, the Netherlands.

Hoogendoorn, B., Vos, M. and Crijns, E. (2008) *Schitterend organiseren.* Sdu, Den Haag, the Netherlands.

Hospers, G. (2009) *Citymarketing in perspectief.* IVIO-Wereldschool bv, Lelystad, the Netherlands.

Hover, M. and Horsten, P. (2004) *Handleiding cursus imagineering.* NHTV internationaal hoger onderwijs Breda, Breda, the Netherlands [unpublished].

Hover, M. and Kops, C. (2004) *What's in a Concept?* NHTV internationaal hoger onderwijs Breda, Breda, the Netherlands [unpublished].

Hover, M. and Mierlo, J. van (2006) *Imagine your Event; Imagineering for the Event Industry.* Event Management Expertise Centre, NHTV internationaal hoger onderwijs Breda, Breda, the Netherlands.

Ind, N. (2007) *Living the Brand; How to Transform Every Member of Your Organization into a Brand Champion.* Kogan Page, London.

Kapferer, J.N. (1992) *Strategic Brand Management; New Approaches to End Evaluating Brand Equity.* Kogan Page, London.

Keller, K.L. (1993) Conceptualizing, measuring, and managing customer-based brand equity. *Journal of Marketing* 57(1), 1–22.

Kempen, S.G.G. van (2005) *Evenementen, de oplossing van relatiemarketing.* NHTV internationaal hoger onderwijs Breda, Breda, the Netherlands.

Kneepkens, S.J.R. (2005) *Eventmarketing; geen real goods maar feel goods*. NHTV internationaal hoger onderwijs Breda, Breda, the Netherlands.

Kort, P. de and Schendel, A. van (2008) *Eindhoven Swimming; evaluatie EK Zwemmen 2008*. Bureau BiO gemeente Eindhoven en NHTV internationaal hoger onderwijs Breda, Eindhoven en Breda, the Netherlands.

Kotler, P., Haider, D.H. and Rein, I. (1993) *Marketing Places; Attracting Investment, Industry and Tourism to Cities, States and Nations*. Free Press, New York.

Kralingen, R. (1999) *Superbrands; merken en markten van morgen*. Samsom, Deventer, the Netherlands.

Kuiper, G. (ed.) (2008) *Basisboek Eventmanagement; van concept naar realisatie*. Coutinho, Bussum, the Netherlands.

Lafferty, X. and Chalip, L. (2006) Effects of hosting a sport event on destination brand; a test of co branding and match-up models. *Sport Management Review* 9, 49–78.

Landry, C. (2006) *The Art of City Making*. Earthscan, London.

Landuyt, I. and Ummels, T. (2008) *CityMakers; Marketing the City*. BV De nieuwe aanpak, Nederhemert, the Netherlands.

Lane, K. (1993) Conceptualizing, measuring and managing customer based brand equity. *Journal of Marketing* 57(1), 1–22.

Laurel, B. (1993) *Computers as Theatre*. Addison-Wesley Publishing Company, Reading, Massachusetts.

Levitt, T. (1980) Marketing success through differentiation – of anything. *Harvard Business Review* 58(1), 83–91.

Liebregts, S. (2007) *Medewerkers worden MedeMerkers*. NHTV internationaal hoger onderwijs Breda, Breda, the Netherlands.

Lier, H., Heijboom, R, and Waijers, A. (2009) *Van experience naar challenge economy*. Noordhoff Uitgevers, Groningen, the Netherlands.

Mark, M. and Pearson, C.S. (2001) *The Hero and the Outlaw; Building Extraordinary Brands Through the Power of Archetypes*. McGraw-Hill, New York.

Meeng, J. (2009) *Onderzoek naar de evaluatie van eventwerking in de health care industrie*. Nyenrode Business Universiteit, Breukelen, the Netherlands.

MeerWaarde Onderzoeksadvies (2000) *Evaluatie EK 2000; kosten en baten*. Samsom, Alphen aan den Rijn, the Netherlands.

Michels, W.J. (2006) *Communicatie handboek*. Wolters-Noordhoff, Groningen, the Netherlands.

Michels, W.J. (2009) *Essentie van communicatie; boeien, binden, verrassen, verleiden*. Noordhoff Uitgevers, Groningen/Houten, the Netherlands.

Mierlo, J. van and Ummels, T. (2009) Glazen Huis in Breda sprekend voorbeeld, Rol evenementen steeds belangrijker bij marketing stad. *UNCOVER People* 3, 49–52.

Morsch, P. (2009) *3800 knuffels…Hadden ze nut?; een onderzoek naar de invloed van participatie van merken aan evenementen, en de invloed hiervan op het merkimago*. NHTV internationaal hoger onderwijs Breda, Breda, the Netherlands.

NIDAP (2008) *Bedrijfsevenementenonderzoek*. NIDAP, Amsterdam.

Nijs, D. and Peters, F. (2002) *Imagineering; het creëren van beleveniswerelden*. Uitgeverij Boom, Amsterdam, the Netherlands.

Noordman, Th.B.J. (2004) *Cultuur in de Citymarketing*. Elsevier Overheid, Den Haag, the Netherlands.

Notten, P.W.F. van, Rotmans, J., Asselt, M.B.A. van and Rothman, D.S. (2003) An updated scenario typology: an attempt at syntheses. *Futures* 35, 423–443.

Oldenboom, E. (1999) *Brood & Spelen; de economische en maatschappelijke waardering van grote sporteven-ementen*. MeerWaarde, Amsterdam.

Ooijen, M. van (2009) *De juiste weg van doelstelling naar concept; put yourself into everything you create*. NHTV internationaal hoger onderwijs Breda, Breda, the Netherlands.

Pappot, S. (2008) *Merkwaardig*. NHTV internationaal hoger onderwijs Breda, Breda, the Netherlands.

Peelen, E. (2009) *Customer Relationship Management*. Pearson Education, Amsterdam.

Phillips, J.J., Myhill, M. and McDonough, J.B. (2007) *Proving the Value of Meeting and Events*. ROI Institute/MPI, Birmingham, Alabama/Dallas, Texas.

Piët, S. (2003) *De emotiemarkt; de toekomst van de beleveniseconomie*. Pearson Education Benelux, Amsterdam.

Pine, J. II and Gilmore, J.H. (1999) *The Experience Economy; Work is Theatre and Every Business a Stage*. Harvard Business School Press, Boston, Massachusetts.

Pine, J. II and Gilmore, J.H. (2000) *De beleveniseconomie; werk is theater en elke onderneming creëert zijn eigen podium*. Academic Service, Den Haag, the Netherlands.

Prahalad, C.K. and Ramaswamy, V. (2004) *The Future of Competition; Co-creating Unique Value with Customers*. Harvard Business School Publishing, Boston, Massachusetts.

Projectgroep IDEA (2007) *Event rendement Meter; een onderzoek naar het meetbaar maken van (psycholo-gische) effecten van bedrijfsevenementen*. NHTV internationaal hoger onderwijs Breda, Breda, the Netherlands [unpublished].

Projectgroep Nyenrode (2009) *Onderzoek naar de rol van eventmarketing*. NHTV internationaal hoger onderwijs Breda en IDEAleerstoel Eventmarketing en -communicatie aan de Nyenrode Business Universiteit, Breda en Breukelen, the Netherlands [unpublished].

Project Rotterdam Festivals (2008) *Scenariostudie Rotterdam Festivals*. NHTV internationaal hoger onderwijs Breda, Breda, the Netherlands [unpublished].

Rennen, W. (2007) *CityEvents: Place Selling in a Media Age*. University Press, Amsterdam.

Reynolds, T.J. and Gutman, J. (1984) Laddering: extending the repertory grid methodology to con-struct attribute–consequence–value hierarchies. In: Pitts, R.E. Jr and Woodside, A.G. (eds) *Personal Values and Consumers Psychology*. Lexington Books, Lexington, Kentucky, pp. 155–167.

Reynolds, T.J. and Gutman, J. (1988) Laddering theory, method, analysis and interpretation. *Journal of Advertising Research* 28(1), 11–31.

Richards, G. and Palmer, R. (2010) *Eventful Cities*. Butterworth-Heinemann, Oxford, UK.

Riel, C.B.M. van (1996) *Identiteit en imago*. Academic Service, Schoonhoven, the Netherlands.

Riezebos, H.J. (1995) *Unravelling Brand Value: Theory and Empirical Research About the Value of Brands to Consumers*. Erasmus Universiteit, Rotterdam, the Netherlands.

Riezebos, R. (2002) *Merkenmanagement*. Wolters-Noordhoff, Groningen, the Netherlands.

Rijkenberg, J. (2005) *Concepting; het managen van conceptmerken in het communicatie-georiënteerde tijd-perk*. BZZToH bv, Den Haag, the Netherlands.

Rijnja, G. and Jagt, R. van der (2004) *Storytelling: de kracht van verhalen in communicatie*. Kluwer, Alphen aan den Rijn, the Netherlands.

Rippen, J. and Bos, M. (2008) *Events en beleven*. Boom, Amsterdam.

Rooij, P. de (2008) Loyaliteitsstrategieën voor theaters. *Vrijetijdstudies* 26(4), 19–28.

Rooijackers, M. (2007a) Beleving? Geluk! *Leisure Trends* 1(4), 24–26.

Rooijackers, M. (2007b) Consumeren met betekenis? Toekomstscenario's voor de vrijetijdseconomie in 2020. *MMNieuws* 9(9/10), 5–6.

Rooijackers, M. (2008) Verlangen naar authenticiteit? *MMNieuws* 10(4/5), 22–23.

Rooijackers, M. (2009) Gaan voor geluk? *Uncover People* 3, 30–31.

Rotterdam Festivals Culture Plan 2009–2012 (2008) *Deeper into the City, Further in the World*. Rotterdam Festivals, Rotterdam, the Netherlands.

Rotterdam Festivals Culture Plan 2009–2012 (2008) *Audience Development. Towards a Large and Diverse Cultural Audience in Rotterdam*. Rotterdam Festivals, Rotterdam, the Netherlands.

Ruler, B. van (1998) *Strategisch management van communicatie; introductie van het communicatiekruispunt*. Samsom, Deventer, the Netherlands.

Schendel, A. van (2008) *Rapportage economische effectmeting EK zwemmen 2008*. Event Management Expertise Centre NHTV internationaal hoger onderwijs Breda, Breda, the Netherlands.

Schendel, A. van (2009a) *Belevingsonderzoek WK veldrijden*. Event Management Expertise Centre NHTV internationaal hoger onderwijs Breda, Breda, the Netherlands.

Schendel, A. van (2009b) Effecten van grootschalige sportevenementen beleefd; case: sportevenementen met elkaar vergeleken. *Vrijetijdstudies* 27(4), 29–41.

Schijns, J.M.C. (2000) *Relatiemarketing; stapsgewijs naar customer loyalty*. Samsom, Alphen aan den Rijn, the Netherlands.

Schmitt, B. (2004) *Customer Experience Management*. Wiley & Sons, Hoboken, New Jersey.

Schreuder, G. and Gosman, B. (1997) *Relatieversterkende evenementen*. Samsom bedrijfsinformatie, Alphen aan den Rijn, the Netherlands.

Schulz von Thun, F. (1982) *Hoe bedoelt u?; een psychologische analyse van menselijke communicatie*. Wolters-Noordhoff, Groningen, the Netherlands.

Schürmann, E.J. (2004) Een praktijkcase bij Mundial Productions; merkmanagement in de evenementenbranche. *MMNieuws* 6(4/5), 11–13, 27.

Seligman, M. (2002) *Authentic Happiness; Using the New Positive Psychology to Realize Your Potential for Lasting Fulfillment*. Free Press, New York.

Smith, S. and Wheeler, J. (2002) *Managing the Customer Experience; Turning Customers into Advocates*. Financial Times Prentice Hall, London.

Sterk, R. and Kuppenveld, E. van (2007) *Organisaties en hun bedrijfscommunicatie; relatiegericht aangepakt*. Wolters-Noordhoff, Groningen/Houten, the Netherlands.

Stern, M. (2003) *Het evenement als sales instrument*. Kluwer, Alphen aan den Rijn, the Netherlands.

Stopel, E. (2005) *Branding with a Bass*. NHTV internationaal hoger onderwijs Breda, Breda, the Netherlands [unpublished].

Storm, C.M. (1987) Competitie en competentie; van vier P's naar drie R's. *Harvard Holland Review* 12, 7–17.

Storm, C.M. (1992) Complicaties in communicatie; breng uw brouwerij tot leven. *Harvard Holland Review* 31, 17–28.

Tilborgh, N. van (2008) *Event rendement Meter; van gevoel naar feiten*. NHTV internationaal hoger onderwijs Breda, Breda, the Netherlands [unpublished].

Truscott, W. (2003) *Six Sigma; Continual Improvement for Business, A Practical Guide*. Butterworth-Heinemann, Oxford. UK.

Ullenbroeck, P. (2010) Culturele hoofdstad goudmijn; onderzoek opbrengsten ambitieus project overstijgen ruimschoots de kosten. *BN De Stem* (22 juni 2010), pp. 1–3.

Verhaar, J. (2009) *Projectmanagement 1; een professionele aanpak van evenementen*. Uitgeverij Boom, Amsterdam.

Verhage, B.J. (2009) *Grondslagen van de marketing*. Noordhoff, Groningen, the Netherlands.

Verhagen, D. (2006) *Co creatie wordt groot!* NHTV internationaal hoger onderwijs Breda, Breda, the Netherlands.

Verhoeven, P. (2006) *Meten of gemeten worden; hoe kunnen (zachte) doelstellingen van een bedrijfsevenement het beste gemeten worden?* NHTV internationaal hoger onderwijs Breda, Breda, the Netherlands [unpublished].

Vyncke, P. (2002) Lifestyle segmentation: from attitudes, interests and opinions, to values, aesthetic styles, life visions and media preferences. *European Journal of Communication* 17, 445–464.

Wiegerink, K. and Peelen, E. (2010) *Eventmarketing*. Pearson Education Benelux, Amsterdam.

Wijngaarden, P. van (2006) *Guest Experience Model* [unpublished].

Willemsen, H. (2008) *Beleving van sport; onderzoek naar de beleving van de effecten van grootschalige sportevenementen door de host community*. NHTV internationaal hoger onderwijs Breda, Breda, the Netherlands.

Wünsch, U. (2008) *Facets of Contemporary Event Management; Theory and Practice for Event Success*. Bad Honnef, Bonn, Germany.

Zande, T. van der (2007) *De toegevoegde waarde van live communicatie*. NHTV internationaal hoger onderwijs Breda, Breda, the Netherlands.

Zwaag, I. van der (2009) *Van bereiken naar beRAKEN; een onderzoek naar touchpoints in de vakbeursbranche*. NHTV internationaal hoger onderwijs Breda, Breda, the Netherlands.

Zwol, C. van (2010) Film + prosecco + meezingen; met jouw mensen iets beleven, daar draait het om in de bios. *NRC next* (1 April 2010), p. 14.

PROFESSIONAL JOURNALS

Adformatie
Experience magazine
Expovisielive
Feestelijk zakendoen
High Profile Events
Marketingtribune
Quality in Meetings
Tijdschrift voor Marketing

WEBSITES

All websites accessed in January 2011, unless stated differently.

www.2interact.nl
www.accelerom.com
www.ah.nl
www.ahoy.nl

www.belastingdienst.nl
www.Bloemencorsozundert.nl
www.bogra.nl
www.boomfestival.org
www.burningman.com
www.calanza.com
www.cappeu.org
www.castlebar4dayswalks.com
www.centerparcs.nl
www.cgr.nl
www.clcvecta.nl
www.cliniclowns.nl
www.cliniclownsinternational.org
www.cosmit.it
www.cruyff-foundation.org
www.db-online.nl
www.dirkkuytfoundation.nl
www.effectmeting.nl
www.efpia.eu
www.estrelladamm.com
www.evenement2005.nl
www.event10.nl
www.expoproof.com
www.expoproof.nl
www.expovisie.nl
www.fz.nl
www.gouden-giraffe.nl
www.grand-am.com
www.heineken.nl
www.heinekenthecity.nl
www.hema.nl
www.high-profile.nl
www.hypsos.com
www.ifeaeurope.com
www.ifea.com
www.imex-frankfurt.com
www.ippanetwork.org
www.itbberlin.com
www.jdvhotels.com
www.libellezomerweek.nl
www.maisonvandenboer.com
www.marketingonline.nl
www.marketingtribune.nl
www.meetingmoods.nl

www.miele.de
www.miele.nl
www.mindz.com
www.modekwartier.nl
www.nidap.nl
www.nojazzfest.com
www.nu.nl
www.patheinternational.com
www.redbull.com
www.rockinriolisboa.sapo.pt
www.roiinstitute.net
www.rolandgarros.com
www.rotterdamfestivals.nl
www.salon-auto.ch
www.sensation.com
www.snsbank.nl
www.stichtingvlinders.nl
www.sziget.hu
www.ted.org
www.tennisdailynews.net
www.trendslator.nl
www.visma.nl
www.volvooceanrace.com
www.wikipedia.org
www.wimbledon.com
www.worlddatabaseofhappiness.eur.nl
www.yo-opera.nl
www.yourevent.nl

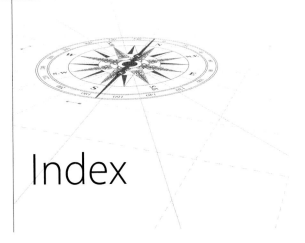

Index